Linux® Patch Management

Linux® Patch Management

Keeping Linux® Systems Up To Date

Michael Jang

PRENTICE HALL

Upper Saddle River, NJ • Boston • Indianapolis • San Francisco
New York • Toronto • Montreal • London • Munich • Paris • Madrid
Capetown • Sydney • Tokyo • Singapore • Mexico City

Many of the designations used by manufacturers and sellers to distinguish their products are claimed as trademarks. Where those designations appear in this book, and the publisher was aware of a trademark claim, the designations have been printed with initial capital letters or in all capitals.

The author and publisher have taken care in the preparation of this book, but make no expressed or implied warranty of any kind and assume no responsibility for errors or omissions. No liability is assumed for incidental or consequential damages in connection with or arising out of the use of the information or programs contained herein.

The publisher offers excellent discounts on this book when ordered in quantity for bulk purchases or special sales, which may include electronic versions and/or custom covers and content particular to your business, training goals, marketing focus, and branding interests. For more information, please contact:

> U. S. Corporate and Government Sales
> (800) 382-3419
> corpsales@pearsontechgroup.com

For sales outside the U. S., please contact:

> International Sales
> international@pearsoned.com

This Book Is Safari Enabled
The Safari® Enabled icon on the cover of your favorite technology book means the book is available through Safari Bookshelf. When you buy this book, you get free access to the online edition for 45 days. Safari Bookshelf is an electronic reference library that lets you easily search thousands of technical books, find code samples, download chapters, and access technical information whenever and wherever you need it.

To gain 45-day Safari Enabled access to this book:
- Go to http://www.awprofessional.com/safarienabled
- Complete the brief registration form
- Enter the coupon code NIFZ-9PSE-SFJV-ZXEA-6J1S

If you have difficulty registering on Safari Bookshelf or accessing the online edition, please e-mail customer-service@safaribooksonline.com.

Visit us on the Web: www.phptr.com

Library of Congress Cataloging-in-Publication Data

Jang, Michael
  Linux Patch Management : keeping Linux systems up to date / Michael Jang.
      p. cm.
  Includes index.
  ISBN 0-13-236675-4
  1. Linux. 2. Operating systems (Computers) 3. Computer security. 4. Software maintenance. I. Title.
  QA76.76.O63J368 2006
  005.4'32—dc22
                          2005028070

ISBN 0-13-236675-4
Text printed in the United States on recycled paper at R. R. Donnelley in Crawfordsville, Indiana.
First printing, January 2006

My dear Nancy, I miss you. I wish you were still here on this earth with us. This world is less without you. I do my best to carry your spirit with me. I will always love you.

My dear Donna, thank you for finding me. Thank you for marrying me. I love you with all my heart. I will love you forever.

"Where you lead, I will follow." I thank your dearly departed Randy and my dearly departed Nancy for helping us find each other.

To the young widowed of the world, we will always grieve for our dearly departed mates. However, we can find happiness again.

Contents

About the Author

Michael Jang holds RHCE, SAIR Linux Certified Professional, CompTIA Linux+ Professional, and MCP certifications, and has written books on four Linux certifications. A full-time writer specializing in networks and operating systems, his most recent book is *Mastering Red Hat Enterprise Linux 3* (Sybex, 2004).

Preface

Welcome to *Linux Patch Management*! This is the book that can guide you through managing patches and updates on one Linux computer or networks of Linux computers.

WHAT THIS BOOK IS ABOUT

It's important to keep Linux computers up to date. Linux developers are constantly updating key services to enhance security, add features you need, fix bugs that hinder your productivity and the productivity of your users, and help your systems to work more efficiently. These updates are known as patches. Most Linux distributions make gigabytes of patches available over the Internet. These updates cannot help you unless you know how to manage patches for the different Linux systems on your network.

This book assumes you have some sort of high-speed Internet connection that can help you download these patches. You may need to download hundreds of megabytes of patches, and that is not realistic on a 56Kbps telephone modem. If you have to download hundreds of megabytes on all the Linux computers in your office, you might overload all but the fastest business-quality high-speed connections.

In this book, I describe how you can manage patches on Red Hat/Fedora, SUSE, and Debian Linux systems. While Red Hat and SUSE have developed specialized update tools for their distributions, it's also possible to use community tools, such as apt and yum, on many Linux distributions.

To this end, you can use this book as a guide to managing patches on the noted distributions. In addition, you can use apt and yum on a number of other Linux systems. As a Linux administrator, you can use this book to learn to manage the hundreds of megabytes, or even gigabytes, of patches on a wide variety of Linux systems.

After you learn to manage patches on individual Linux systems, you can extend those skills to managing a group of Linux computers on a network. If you have a sufficient number of Linux systems, you may even want to build your own patch management repositories.

Patches on one or two Linux computers may work well with a standard high-speed Internet connection. If you have a substantial number of Linux computers, you might download the patches from each of these computers over the Internet. To keep these downloads from overloading your Internet connection, you can pay a premium for an even higher-speed connection.

Alternatively, you can use the techniques described in this book to configure a local patch management repository. This can help you avoid buying a faster high-speed Internet connection. *Thus, a patch management repository can help you save a lot of money*. In addition, you can update a group of computers more quickly when you download patches from a local repository.

Red Hat supports patch management on a group of Red Hat Enterprise Linux (RHEL) computers through the Red Hat Network. SUSE supports patch management on a group of SUSE Enterprise Linux Server and Workstation computers with YaST Online Update and Zenworks Linux Management. You can use these tools to manage patches on individual systems or on networks of these distributions. Red Hat and SUSE provide these tools to help you manage patches. If you have a large number of systems, these tools can help you keep the loads on your Internet connection to a minimum and speed up the updates you need.

But this book is not limited to Red Hat and SUSE Linux. It also can help you keep the loads on your Internet connection to a minimum when managing other distributions, including Debian and Fedora Linux. It also uses the tools designed by Conectiva (now Mandriva) for RPM-based distributions. The skills you learn can help you manage patches on allied distributions, including Yellowdog, Ubuntu, Progeny, Lycoris, and the "rebuild" distributions that use the source code released for Red Hat Enterprise Linux.

WHAT YOU NEED TO KNOW BEFORE READING THIS BOOK

This book assumes you have some experience with Linux. While it does not require that you have a network of Linux computers, you can take full advantage of the techniques described in this book only if you have such a network.

Some of the tools described in this book require a subscription. For example, access to the Red Hat Network Proxy Server requires a specialized subscription to the Red Hat Network. Access to SUSE Linux Enterprise Server updates requires subscription access to the YaST Online Update Server. Access to Novell's Zenworks Linux Management also requires a subscription. If you want to try out these tools, navigate to the associated Web sites. Trial subscriptions may still be available. And read this book!

Some of the tools described in this book are freely available. They are already included with many Linux distributions. Some have been customized by third parties for popular distributions, such as Red Hat Enterprise Linux. They are designed and maintained by the Linux community and are available courtesy of the GNU General Public License (http://www.gnu.org/copyleft/gpl.html).

WHO YOU ARE, AND WHY AND HOW YOU SHOULD READ THIS BOOK

This book is designed for experienced and budding Linux administrators. Patch management is a critical Linux administration skill. This book can help you manage patches on individual Linux systems and can help you manage patches on networks of Linux computers.

With these skills, you can keep your Linux systems up to date with the latest security, feature, and bug updates. You can keep a network of Linux systems up to date in this way with a minimum load on your Internet connection.

If your experience is limited to one or two Linux computers, this book can help you think beyond them to network management and what you will need to do in the workforce for a large group of Linux systems.

You can use this book to evaluate the patch-management features associated with several different distributions. The more patch management tools you know, the more you can do to maintain different Linux distributions on your network. For a general overview of patch management clients, read Chapter 1, "Patch Management Systems."

If you're evaluating patch management using the Red Hat Network and the associated Proxy Server, read Chapter 2, "Consolidating Patches on a Red Hat/Fedora Network." If you're evaluating patch management using the YaST Online Update Server or Zenworks Linux Management, read Chapter 3, "SUSE's Update Systems and rsync Mirrors." You'll also find information on how you can use rsync to mirror repositories from most all Linux distributions.

If you're evaluating patch management on Debian Linux systems, read Chapter 4, "Making apt Work for You." As Knoppix and Ubuntu are built on Debian, the same tools can help you manage systems associated with those distributions, as well. You'll learn how to create a Debian repository on your own network.

If you prefer the apt patch management commands associated with Debian Linux, you can also use them on many RPM-based distributions. If that is what you want, read Chapter 5, "Configuring apt for RPM Distributions." That chapter will show you how to create an apt-based repository for a RPM-based distribution on your own network.

If you prefer the affinity of yum for RPM-based distributions, read Chapters 6 and 7. Chapter 6, "Configuring a yum Client," details how you can use yum to keep your systems up to date. Chapter 7, "Setting Up a yum Repository," details how you can create yum repositories on your own network.

HOW THIS BOOK IS LAID OUT

Here is a brief summary of all the chapters:

☞ Chapter 1 provides a basic overview of how you can manage patches on an individual Linux system. Techniques that we describe cover RHEL, SUSE Linux (formerly known as SUSE Linux Professional), SUSE Linux Enterprise Server, Debian Linux, Fedora Linux, and some of the rebuilds of RHEL. This chapter also previews some of the tools you can use to create a patch management repository on your own network.

☞ Chapter 2 starts by providing a model of how you can create a repository for Fedora Linux. It continues with a focus on the Red Hat Network, specifically the associated Proxy Server, which can help you cache updates. It also adds more detail on how you can manage patches on systems with RHEL rebuild distributions.

☞ Chapter 3 is focused on the patch management tools created by SUSE and Novell for their Linux systems. It also describes how you can use rsync to mirror update servers for all Linux distributions. You can point YaST Online Update to a variety of local or network sources, such as a local patch management server, which you can copy from the mirror of your choice. Finally, we describe how Zenworks Linux Management can be installed on SUSE Linux Enterprise Server or even RHEL to administer patches on a variety of SUSE and RHEL clients.

☞ Chapter 4 guides you through the fundamentals of the apt commands, along with their capabilities. By the time you complete this chapter, you'll know how to use various apt commands, the aptitude utility, and the GUI Synaptic Package Manager to manage your system. Finally, this chapter guides you through different tools available for downloading and synchronizing your local repository with the mirror of your choice.

☞ Chapter 5 helps you learn to install and use many of the apt tools from Chapter 4 on RPM-based distributions, such as Fedora and SUSE Linux. Based on the work of Conectiva (now Mandriva) Linux, you can use the tools described in Chapter 5 to create and maintain an apt repository for several different RPM-based distributions.

☞ Chapter 6 supports the use of yum as a client on RPM-based distributions. Many Linux users prefer yum because of its Python-based compatibility with RPM systems. It's now the default update tool for Fedora Linux. You can even install and use yum on RHEL (and rebuild distributions). While GUI tools for yum are not yet stable, the Yum Extender appears to be most promising.

☞ Chapter 7 helps you design, populate, and manage your own yum Repository on a RHEL computer. You can use this repository to maintain Fedora Linux systems. It includes guidelines that can help you minimize the downloads required to create the repository. Finally, if you have authorized subscriptions, this chapter provides instructions on how you create a yum repository for a network of RHEL computers.

CONVENTIONS USED

Command line operations are called out with a monospaced font. The prompt is assumed; for example, the following command would be run at a Linux command line interface:

```
up2date --show-channel
```

Commands are often included in the text of a paragraph in a similar monospaced font. For example, if you see `up2date --show-channel`, you could type that text in a command line interface.

Many URLs in this book do not include a prefix such as http://, unless the context is not obvious. For example, when we refer to the vsFTP home page at vsftpd.beasts.org, we are referring to the associated Web page. But remember, there are other TCP/IP ports and prefixes, such as ftp://, rsync://, and file:///.

Long commands are written on multiple lines for clarity (as shown here), but should be typed on one line. A backslash (\) is inserted in the line to indicate that it is all one line; for example,

```
rsync -av --exclude debug \
rsync://mirrors.kernel.org/fedora/core/updates/3/i386/* \
/var/ftp/pub/yum/3/i386/updates/
```

Notes, Warnings, and Tips appear in the text as follows:

Note
Particular points that need to be emphasized appear in a box to alert you.

WARNING
The warning box is used to emphasize an issue or concern that might be encountered and should be avoided.

Tip
A box labeled with the above denotes information that is specifically useful.

Acknowledgments

While it is my name on the cover, the production of a book is a team effort. Outside of the team, I'd also like to thank Todd Warner of Red Hat, as well as Martin Buckley, Sascha Wessels, Marissa Krupa, and Jasmin Ul-Haque of Novell/SUSE for their help.

Naturally, Linux would not have the world-class patch management tools without its world of dedicated developers. The Debian developers behind apt, the Yellowdog developers behind yum, the Conectiva (now Mandriva) developers who brought apt to RPM-based distributions, as well as those who have added to the associated tools, all deserve special thanks.

Also important to this process are the editors at Prentice Hall: Chris Zahn, Jill Harry, Karen Gettman, Ebony Haight, Michael Thurston, Elise Walter, and Debbie Williams. I could not have made this book into a quality work without the reviews of Elizabeth Zinkann, Joe Brazeal, Matthew Crosby, Bret Strong, George Vish, Aaron Weber, and Fabien Gandon. This book would not have been possible except for the vision of the Open Source Series editor, Bruce Perens.

## CHAPTER 1

Patch Management Systems

It's important to keep Linux systems up to date. Updates can help you keep your systems secure, help you fix problems, and help you incorporate the newest features. Updates in the world of computers are also known as patches.

In this chapter, we'll examine the basics of patch management, how you can apply patches to your computer, and where you should get patches for several Linux distributions. Patch management methods vary by distribution. If you're paying for support from Red Hat or SUSE, you're paying in part for support through their patch management systems. If you're using another Linux distribution, there are solid freely available alternatives.

When you administer a network, you're responsible for updates on a number of computers. You could configure each of these computers to get their updates automatically, but that might overload your network and connection to the Internet. In later chapters, we will show you how to configure a patch management repository for your network.

1.1 BASIC PATCH CONCEPTS

In the world of Linux, patches are more than just something you might apply to the source code of a kernel. They include the updates that can help you keep your systems secure, error-free, and updated with the latest features.

Before we continue, it's important to define the concept of a patch and note the variety of sources from where you can download patches for your computer systems.

1.1.1 What Is a Patch?

A patch is an update. It incorporates changes in source code. Patches are normally applied to specific software components, such as the kernel, or a service, such as vsFTP. Patches may fix bugs, address security issues, or incorporate new features. As an administrator, you're responsible for testing the new software, making sure that it addresses any problems before your users see them on their systems.

In general, when you patch a program, service, or system, you'll be upgrading a package. Some Linux distributions can be configured to warn you when patches for installed software are available. We'll show you how to configure this in later chapters.

Security Fixes

The most important patches address security problems. This is where the Linux development model shines. Developers start working on a patch almost immediately after a security issue is revealed. The process is public, which reassures those concerned about the quality of the patch. As a result, security patches are often available in hours.

If you're administering a Linux computer, you need to keep up to date on the latest security issues. If you've paid for a subscription to a Red Hat or a SUSE distribution, you can get email warnings about security problems with your installed services. Other distributions may make alerts available by email or through their mailing lists. Problems with services are often announced on major Linux news sites, such as www.linuxtoday.com.

Service Upgrades

Users will always demand upgrades. And Linux developers will respond. I suspect that after someone finds a way to use Linux to toast bread, another developer will start working on how to upgrade Linux into a bread maker.

More practically, if someone developed a way to make Samba on Linux emulate a Microsoft Active Directory domain controller (which is in work for Samba 4.0, per http://www.samba.org/samba/devel/roadmap-4.0.html), there would be a lot of demand for that service. You would likely find yourself downloading that package on a substantial number of computers.

In general, programs that are released with new features get a lot of demand. Unfortunately, bugs are most likely to be found when a program is released with new features.

Just remember, the developers of a service are usually different from the developers of a distribution. So if you have a problem with a service, the fault may not be with the developers at Red Hat, SUSE, Debian, and so on.

Bug Fixes

If software were perfect, I think there would not be so much work in computing, especially at Microsoft. A lot of work goes into diagnosing and repairing buggy programs. Fortunately, the same infrastructure which leads to quick security fixes also leads to quick bug fixes for open source Linux programs.

When users report problems, they're likely to demand quick solutions. The previous performance of Linux developers in finding quick solutions leads to increased expectations for quick bug fixes. As an administrator, you'll be expected to roll out patches quickly, reliably, and securely.

Kernel Patches

Patches to the Linux kernel are of a special kind. They include the changes in source code between consecutive versions of a kernel. For example, if you want to upgrade from kernel version 2.6.15 to 2.6.16, you should apply `patch-2.6.16` to your current kernel.

There are special requirements associated with kernel patches. Generally, they work only with the kernel as released through www.kernel.org. The people behind some distributions build their kernels with different features. Native Linux kernel patches may lead to conflicts, lost features, or even kernel panics.

Standard Linux kernel patches require that you adjust perhaps dozens of settings and then compile that kernel in binary format. This process can take hours, and is therefore something that you may not want to repeat. Many Linux distributions include preconfigured kernels in their repositories that you can use to upgrade your systems without having to compile them.

Note

Debian-based Linux distributions make it easy for you to set up a binary kernel from recompiled code, which you can then use to upgrade other Debian-based systems on your network.

Kernel Upgrades

Because the kernel is so important to the operating system, you should not take chances. It's best to upgrade Linux kernels by installing them side-by-side with the current working Linux kernel. If there is a problem, you can still boot that system with the old kernel.

If your users add hardware, modify drivers, or otherwise experiment with the guts of Linux, there's a chance that a new kernel that works on your test equipment may not work on some of the computers on your network.

In recognition, most upgrade services treat `kernel-*` packages differently. Services such as Red Hat's `up2date` and SUSE's YaST Online Update do not install upgraded kernels, unless you authorize the installation.

Risks

Whenever you install a patch, there are risks. For example, many kernel patches may lead to situations where you're unable to boot Linux.

If you run into a situation where a patch leads to a crash, you may be able to restore your system from a backup. If you're unable to boot your system for this purpose, you may need to use a "rescue mode" for your distribution. Rescue modes are available using the first installation CD associated with Red Hat/Fedora and SUSE.

Alternatively, you may be able to use a CD/DVD-based distribution, such as Knoppix. When you boot from a Knoppix CD, you can start a full-featured Linux distribution. You can then connect to backup media and even networks to restore your pre-patch configuration. For more information, see www.knoppix.org.

1.1.2   Patch Sources

There are several sources for patches and upgrades. The best source is generally the upgrade repository preconfigured for your distribution. However, there is often a delay when distribution developers process updates from other sources, such as the kernel, or services, such as the Apache Web server.

If you're in a hurry, you can download packages from the Web site directly associated with your service. While not built for your distribution, it can help you get new features into service as quickly as possible.

Sometimes the developers of a distribution don't bother with every service or upgrade. In some cases, third parties, such as developers of related distributions or even independent developers, configure packages that you can use.

The Native Linux Distribution

When you're upgrading a service, it's usually best to upgrade using the package built by the developers of your distribution. That is the most reliable way to be sure that the package you install copies files into expected locations. It also ensures that the package you install becomes part of that computer's package database.

For example, if you want new features associated with a new version of vsFTP on Red Hat Enterprise Linux 3, you'll want to use the associated vsFTP RPM package built by Red Hat. There are several advantages:

☞ Files associated with the package are installed in locations expected by other programs built for that distribution.

☞ Dependencies for a service may vary between distributions.

☞ Upgrades built for a distribution are included in the package database for that system.

☞ Upgrades can be installed with the native update systems for that distribution.

However, there may be a delay before the employees or volunteers associated with a distribution are able to build and customize a new or updated service.

Service Developers

If you absolutely need the latest update as soon as possible, you can install the package as released by the developer of that service. This may be appropriate if you're testing new features before distributing the package to other users on your network or if you absolutely need the latest security patch.

If you do use a package released by a service developer, you may be able to use the Red Hat Package Manager (RPM) or the Debian Packaging System (DEB) package as built by those developers for your distribution. Sometimes the developers of a service are well-schooled in how to build a package for a distribution, such as Red Hat or Debian. Otherwise, you'll have to download the package in a format such as a tarball and install it yourself.

Unless the developers of a service have specifically built a RPM or DEB package for your distribution, the disadvantages to installing such a service include

☞ Additional work is required to process and install the service.

☞ Files may be installed in directories not consistent with your distribution.

☞ The service is not included in your distribution's database of packages.

To overcome any resulting problems, you can install the service as packaged for your distribution as soon as it is available.

Note

A "tarball" is an archive, usually compressed, typically in tar.gz or tar.bz2 format. For more information on how to decompress a tarball, see the man page for the tar command. When decompressed, installation instructions are normally made available in an included text file, such as README or INSTALL.

Third Parties

There are two kinds of third-party packages available. One is packaged for a different distribution that uses the same package manager. Another is configured by an independent developer or group who may or may not have customized a package for your distribution.

Linux programs are generally processed into one of two major package formats: the RPM and DEB. These formats are used by almost all the major Linux distributions. Some examples include

☞ RPM: Red Hat, Fedora, SUSE, Mandriva, Turbolinux, Yellow Dog

☞ DEB: Debian, Knoppix, Ubuntu, Xandros

For example, if a package has been created in RPM format only for Mandrake, you can use the `rpm` command to install that package on other RPM-based distributions, such as Red Hat and SUSE. However, the risks are similar to installing an uncustomized package released from a service developer.

Note

Mandriva is the company formed from the merger of Mandrake, Lycoris, and Conectiva. Mandriva 2006 (released in late 2005) comes from their combined efforts. For more information, see www.mandriva.com.

There are several databases of RPM packages, from where you can search and download the package for the distribution and version of your choice. They include www.rpmfind.net and rpm.pbone.net.

As you'll see in Chapter 4, "Making apt Work for You," distributions based on the Debian package system are more closely integrated. If you want to install a package from a different distribution with Debian packages, all you need to do is refer to its respective repositories. RPM-based distributions are moving in the same direction with yum.

There are developers who maintain their own distributions. One of the most useful is maintained in apt and yum RPM repositories at dag.wieers.com.

1.1.3   Patch Testing

Critical to the concept of patch management is testing. When applied indiscriminately, patches can override working drivers, break existing software, and change the links to key files. They may introduce new features that override services on which you rely.

Best practices suggest that you test every patch before installing it on production computers. Ideally, you'll have one or more extra computers available for this purpose.

Definitions and Assumptions

In this book, I define production and test computers as follows:

☞   A production computer is a desktop or server system, configured with the services and applications that are actually used to run your business.

☞   A test computer is a desktop or server system that should be used exclusively for testing new software. Ideally, test computers are also configured with the same services and applications that you have on production server and desktop computers. They should be segregated from production computers with a firewall.

Test computers may be a luxury unavailable to administrators of smaller networks. If you're in that position, you should at least test each patch on your own administrative system. Every problem you see on your own system is one less problem that you hear about from *each* of your users.

There is no single method for patch testing. Testing methods are as diverse as available applications and services. I've divided the testing process into three categories: installation, applications, and services. In any case, always follow this maxim: **Do not install a patch on a production computer before testing.**

Testing Patch Installations

The first step in testing a patch is installation. When you use the techniques described in this book, there should be no unmet dependencies. However, dependencies often require you to install more patches. Therefore, when you test a patch installation, you need to know what you're installing to know the scope of the patch.

So, in summary, when checking the installation of a patch on a test computer, check for the following:

☞ When checking a patch, make sure all package dependencies are satisfied. List the packages required to satisfy those dependencies.

☞ If there are dependent packages, include those in your testing.

These are general guidelines that vary with what you're installing. For example, if you're installing a new Linux kernel, test everything on a production-level system. If you're upgrading a stand-alone application, make sure that the upgrade won't break features on which your users depend. If you're upgrading a service, make sure that your configuration file still works as intended. If you're upgrading dependent libraries, make sure they don't affect the application or services which depend on them.

If you have problems with a patch, check the troubleshooting steps described at the end of this section.

Testing a New Kernel

The kernel is the most important patch to test. As the core of the Linux operating system, an upgraded kernel can affect everything. There are several principles that you should follow when testing a new Linux kernel:

☞ Make sure you have a reason to change kernels. Check the release notes for that kernel. You may not need the patch. For example, if a new kernel incorporates a driver for network cards that you don't use, there is no reason for you to go through all this trouble.

☞ Never upgrade to a new kernel—in a way, that overwrites your existing kernel. Do not delete the existing kernel until you're finished testing the new kernel.

Most distributions support side-by-side installations of new and existing kernels. In fact, when you install (and don't upgrade) an existing kernel using a customized binary package, Red Hat/Fedora, SUSE, and Debian all "dual-boot" the new and existing kernels.

☞ Test how the new kernel manages your boot process. Watch as it detects your hardware and starts your services. If there are problems or even unusual delays, the new kernel may have a problem with the associated hardware or service.

☞ Check the log files associated with the boot process. Pay particular attention to services that won't start or hardware that isn't detected.

☞ Test the new kernel on your system, based on the release notes. Make sure the new kernel works as intended on your computers.

☞ Test your services and applications under the new kernel. Pay attention to any changes in behavior. Document these changes.

☞ When you're ready to upgrade the kernel on production computers, tell your users what they can expect.

If you identify a problem with the kernel and absolutely need the upgrade, you may need to recompile the kernel yourself. For more information, see the Kernel Rebuild Guide, available from www.tldp.org. After you rebuild, you can install and start the testing process again.

Testing Application Patches

Many applications are patched frequently. Application patches may incorporate security improvements, additional features, bug fixes, or more. When you see an application patch, don't just blindly upgrade. Consider the following:

☞ Read the release notes. Evaluate the reason for the patch. Does it add any features that you need? Does it address any bugs which annoy you about the application? Does it improve your security in a way that applies to your computers or your network?

☞ If there are configuration files associated with an application, back them up. For example, if a user customizes the look and feel of The GIMP, a patch might overwrite some of the settings in each user's .gimp-* configuration directory.

You may want to use configuration files from users who use the application frequently. Tell them that you're considering an upgrade. They can help identify key features that you will want to preserve.

☞ If you decide that you need the application patch, test it carefully. Download and install it on your test system. Make a list of downloaded packages, especially if there are dependencies.

☞ Test the patch on your system. First, based on the release notes, make sure the patch works as intended.

☞ Identify any changes made to applicable configuration files, and assess their impact on your users. Make notes.

☞ If there are problems with the patch, re-evaluate the changes. Make sure you actually need the patch.

☞ When you're ready to install the application patch in production, make sure your users know what to expect.

If you identify a problem with an application patch and absolutely need it, see the troubleshooting steps identified at the end of this section.

Testing Service Patches

Many services are patched frequently. Service patches may incorporate security improvements, additional features, bug fixes, or more. When you see a service patch, don't just blindly upgrade. Consider the following:

☞ Read the release notes. Evaluate the reason for the patch. Does it add any features you need? Does it address any bugs that annoy you about the application? Does it improve your security in a way that applies to your computers or your network?

☞ If configuration files are associated with the service, back them up, at least to another directory.

☞ If you decide that you need the service patch, test it carefully. Download and install it on your test system. Make a list of downloaded packages, especially if there are dependencies.

☞ Test the patch on your system. First, based on the release notes, make sure the patch works as intended.

☞ Identify any differences from the previous configuration files, and assess their impact on your users. Make notes.

☞ If the service is shared on a network, test the upgrade from another computer. Measure the current network demands on this service. If practical, find some way to simulate these demands on the upgraded service.

☞ If there are problems with the patch, re-evaluate the changes. Make sure you actually need the patch.

☞ When you're ready to install the service patch in production, make sure your users know what to expect.

If you identify a problem with an application patch and absolutely need it, see the troubleshooting steps identified at the end of this section.

Patch Troubleshooting

If you have a problem with a patch, the problem may or may not be with the patch. It could be a symptom of a different problem. Because troubleshooting depends on what you're patching, I can provide only general guidelines here. But as with any troubleshooting, it's best to apply the scientific method:

1. Observe the problem. Identify its symptoms, using log files where applicable.

2. Formulate a hypothesis of the cause. Was it the patch? Is there a configuration setting which conflicts with the patch? Is there something else you might need to install?

3. Test the hypothesis. If correct, you should be able to test the patch in a different way to confirm your hypothesis.

If you're having trouble formulating a hypothesis, get support. If you've paid for support, such as with a subscription to Red Hat Enterprise Linux (RHEL), use it. Otherwise, make use of the documentation. Many Linux administrators have documented their experiences in HOWTOs, FAQs, and more. They may have experienced the problems you're seeing now.

If you can't find the answer in existing documentation, you can try documenting your problem on an appropriate mailing list. They're frequently available for distributions, applications, and services. Identify the problem, the symptoms you've seen, the documentation you've read, and what you've tried to do to address the problem. Many Linux gurus are motivated to "show off" by solving your problem.

1.2   DISTRIBUTION-SPECIFIC REPOSITORIES

Every major Linux distribution includes a repository of installation programs and packages. Distribution developers also maintain patches on these same repositories, and they update these repositories with security patches, upgrades, bug fixes, and new kernels as needed.

In this book, we focus on the releases from the developers of three major distributions: Red Hat/Fedora, Novell/SUSE, and Debian.

Note

The Web and FTP sites associated with a distribution are often very busy. Connections are limited to a certain number of users; even with such limits, downloads may be slow. Most distributions have "mirrors," or second-level repositories, which maintain an exact copy of the original.

1.2.1   Red Hat Enterprise Linux Updates

The current distribution released by Red Hat is known as Red Hat Enterprise Linux 4 (RHEL). With its reliance on older technologies, it is widely regarded as a conservative, perhaps even boring, distribution. Red Hat has stated that it will provide support and updates for at least five years, which makes it an ideal candidate for the enterprise. But even a boring and stable distribution such as RHEL requires frequent updates.

RHEL updates are limited to computers with valid subscriptions on the Red Hat Network (https://rhn.redhat.com). Each subscription allows you to register one computer on the Red Hat Network, which includes the right to download updates and CDs. I explain how you can purchase and activate a subscription in detail shortly.

RHEL updates are often consolidated onto CDs, on a quarterly basis. If you've purchased a subscription to the Red Hat Network, you should be on the email list which notifies you of individual patches and quarterly updates as they're released. While default updates are taken from Red Hat Network servers, Red Hat supports the use of Proxy and Satellite servers to cache that content on your LAN.

Because RHEL is released under the Free Software Foundation's (FSF) General Public License (GPL), the source code is publicly available from ftp.redhat.com. Several groups have built the source code, without the Red Hat trademarks, into enterprise distributions that are functionally equivalent to RHEL. We'll describe some of these "rebuilds," as well as how to use their repositories, in Chapter 2, "Consolidating Patches on a Red Hat/Fedora Network."

Note

The GPL and related licenses are critical to the Linux development process. In fact, this book has been released under a related license, the Open Publication License (www.opencontent.org), an open source compatible book license. For more information on the myriad of GNU licenses, see www.fsf.org/licensing/licenses/.

If you want RHEL, you may have already taken the following steps:

1. Register with the Red Hat Network at https://rhn.redhat.com.
2. Examine available RHEL distributions.
3. Purchase one or more subscriptions for RHEL.
4. Activate your subscription(s).
5. Download or acquire the CDs for RHEL.
6. Install RHEL on your computers.
7. Update your system through the Red Hat Network.

We'll describe these steps (except installation) in detail in the following sections.

Register with the Red Hat Network

If you want to install RHEL on more than one computer, it's best to register first with the Red Hat Network. That will help you manage all your RHEL computers with one Red Hat Network account. If you're setting up a subscription for a corporate account, read Red Hat's Best Practices Guide, available from rhn.redhat.com/help/.

To register with the Red Hat Network, you'll need an account. To create a new account, navigate to https://rhn.redhat.com/newlogin/ and create a new corporate or personal login.

Examine Available Red Hat Enterprise Linux Distributions

Red Hat currently supports several different versions of RHEL. As you can see in Table 1-1, there are several different versions available; pricing varies by system and architecture. For more information, including current prices, see https://www.redhat.com/software/rhel/compare/.

Table 1-1   Red Hat Enterprise Linux systems

Version	System	Architecture
2.1	Advanced Server (AS)	x86
	Enterprise Server (ES)	x86
	Workstation (WS)	x86
3	AS	x86, Itanium, AMD64/Intel EM64T, iSeries/pSeries, S/390, zSeries
	ES	x86, Itanium, AMD64/Intel EM64T
	WS	x86, Itanium, AMD64/Intel EM64T
	Desktop	x86, AMD64/Intel EM64T
4	AS	x86, Itanium, AMD64/Intel EM64T, iSeries/pSeries, S/390, zSeries
	ES	x86, Itanium, AMD64/Intel EM64T
	WS	x86, Itanium, AMD64/Intel EM64T
	Desktop	x86, AMD64/Intel EM64T

Note

You can now subscribe to RHEL for free for 30 days. For details, see www.redhat.com/software/rhel/eval/. Registration on the Red Hat Network is required.

Purchase One or More Subscriptions for RHEL

When you purchase RHEL, you're buying a time-limited subscription to the Red Hat Network, along with some level of Web, email, or phone-based support. There are three ways to get a subscription to RHEL:

☞ Direct from Red Hat; for options, see www.redhat.com/software/rhel/.

☞ As a boxed set from Red Hat or a third party.

☞ Preinstalled on a server or workstation.

Note

If you work for an academic institution, you may be able to get a RHEL subscription at a greatly reduced rate; see www.redhat.com/solutions/industries/education/products/ for details.

Activate Your Subscription

When you purchase RHEL, there are two ways to activate your subscription. If you have a registration number, you can activate your subscription at www.redhat.com/apps/activate; you can also activate a RHEL 4 subscription during the installation process. In either case, make sure to link this subscription to the appropriate Red Hat Network account.

Alternatively, if you purchased your subscription directly from Red Hat in the USA or via www.redhat.com, your subscription should already be active in your Red Hat Network account.

Download the CDs for RHEL

When you have a subscription to RHEL, you can download the CDs from the Red Hat Network. Because you'll be downloading two or more GB of data, you'll need a high-speed Internet connection. You can then download the CDs in ISO format by using the following steps:

1. Make sure you have sufficient room for the RHEL CDs. The four CDs of binary packages alone can easily require 2.5GB of space on a hard drive.
2. Log into the Red Hat Network at rhn.redhat.com.
3. To find the distributions that you can download, select Channels.

   You can download individual packages from available software channels listed on this Web page.
4. To find the ISOs that you can download, select Easy ISOs.
5. Select the desired distribution channel, such as *Red Hat Enterprise Linux AS (v.4 for 32-bit x86)*.

   You can download ISOs directly from the Red Hat Network at a Web page that looks similar to Figure 1-1.
6. Download the ISOs that you need. As shown in the figure, you can click the *Install Disc* links directly or use the `curl` command. Copy and paste the URL for the ISO into the `curl` command as follows:

```
#curl -C --O 'very_long_url'
```

Figure 1-1   Red Hat Network ISO downloads

Of course, if you've purchased a boxed set, you can use the CDs directly from the box. Now you can set up an installation repository for your RHEL distribution. If you have the physical CDs, they're easy to mount. Just insert them into the drive, and run the mount /media/cdrecorder or mount /mnt/cdrom command.

You can mount ISO files as if they were physical CDs. For example, I've downloaded the first ISO for RHEL AS 4 in my home directory and mounted it with the following command:

```
# mount -o loop  /home/michael/RHEL4-i386-AS-disc1.iso /media/cdrecorder
```

You can then copy the files from each CD to the installation directory of your choice. After you share these files with the NFS, FTP, or HTTP protocols, you can then install RHEL from this directory over your LAN. Make sure to copy the hidden .discinfo file from the first installation CD; you can then use this installation repository for Red Hat's system-config-packages utility.

Alternatively, you can configure a RHEL installation repository simply by sharing the directory with the installation ISO files on an NFS network.

Installing Red Hat Enterprise Linux
The steps required to install RHEL are beyond the scope of this book. For more information on RHEL installation, see Red Hat's installation guide, available from www.redhat.com/docs/manuals/enterprise.

If you're installing RHEL on a computer that you intend to use as a local Red Hat Network Proxy Server, keep the packages that you include to a minimum.

The Update Agent

RHEL's Update Agent, also known as up2date, provides a complete system for updating the RPM packages installed on your RHEL computers. It allows you to register with and monitor appropriate Red Hat repositories for updates. In Chapter 2, you'll learn how to configure a Red Hat repository locally on your computer.

You can review a standard RHEL 4 Network Alert Icon in Figure 1-2. It's a circle next to the date in the upper right part of the GUI. There are four options associated with this icon, which is available only in the GUI:

☞ The red exclamation point in the upper-right part of the figure indicates that this system is not fully up to date.

☞ If you see a green icon with arrows pointing in two directions, the Update Agent is currently checking the repository for updates.

☞ If you see a gray icon with a slash through it, RHEL on your computer is unable to connect to the repository. There may be a problem with the connection from your system or to the computer with the repository.

☞ A blue check mark means that your system is fully up to date with the latest patches.

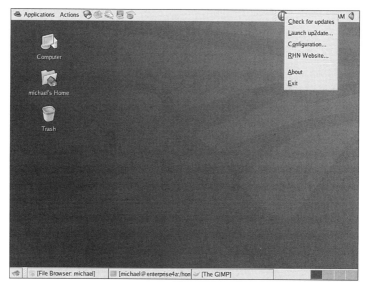

Figure 1-2   Update Agent options in RHEL 4

As you can see in the figure, there are four options associated with the Update Agent:

☞ *Check for updates* allows you to check the versions of packages on your system against those in the RHEL repository. If you see a red exclamation point, updates are available. When you've configured the Update Agent, you can call up the list by clicking the exclamation point; you'll see a screen similar to Figure 1-3.

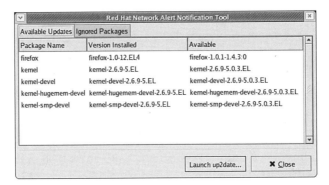

Figure 1-3   The Red Hat Network Alert Notification Tool defines available updates

☞ *Launch up2date* initiates the Red Hat Update Agent. You'll examine the process from a standard computer in the next section.

☞ *Configuration* starts the Red Hat Network Alert Notification Tool.

☞ *RHN Website* opens your default Web browser and navigates to rhn.redhat.com.

There are several things that you need to configure the Update Agent.

If you have a proxy server on your network, you'll need to configure the Red Hat Network Alert Notification Tool. In the GUI, right-click the Update Agent icon, and click Configuration from the shortcut menu that appears. This opens the Red Hat Network Alert Notification Tool window. Click Forward through the Terms of Service to reach the Proxy Configuration page shown in Figure 1-4.

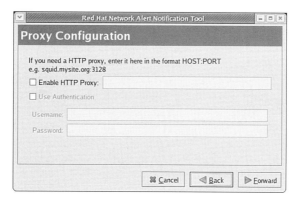

Figure 1-4   Configuring the Red Hat Network for a Proxy Server

---

Note

The Red Hat Network Alert Notification tool warns you of new updates graphically—there is no command line version of this tool available.

Test the result. Right-click the Red Hat Network icon, and then select *Check for Updates*. When you next hover your mouse over the icon, you'll see the number of updates available. You can click the icon to bring up the available updates; you'll see a screen similar to Figure 1-3.

Alternatively, in the command line interface, you can find a list of available updates, along with their dependencies, with the following command:

```
# up2date --dry-run
```

Updating Red Hat Enterprise Linux Using the Update Agent

Now you can update RHEL using the Update Agent. You can start the process in a number of ways; one method that works in both the GUI and text console is the up2date command. We illustrate the process in the GUI for clarity; the process is essentially the same at the text console, and requires the following steps:

1. From the command line, run the up2date command.
2. When the Welcome to the Red Hat Update Agent window displays, click Forward.

   If you see a Login Page, you're prompted to enter your Red Hat Network account. You can then enter a new subscription number or prompt the Update Agent to use an existing active subscription. The Update Agent then sends your hardware information and collects a list of packages currently installed on your computer.

   If you need to change the Red Hat Network account for your computer, such as from a personal to a corporate account, you can force the Update

Agent to reset your account information with the `up2date --register` command. If you're using RHEL 2.1, the command is `rhn_register --configure`.

3. Now you'll see a list of available channels, such as those shown for my server in Figure 1-5. If you have more than one channel available, you can change update selections as desired. When done, click Forward to continue.

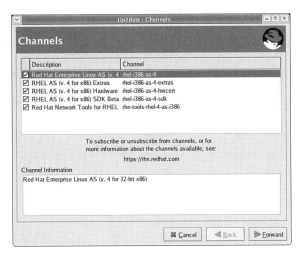

Figure 1-5   Available Red Hat Network channels

4. The Update Agent fetches headers from the repository associated with each channel. By default, it skips downloads of any kernel related packages, as shown in Figure 1-6.

Figure 1-6   The Update Agent avoids downloading kernel packages by default

You can change the list of packages to be skipped with the `up2date --config` command. This opens a Red Hat Network Configuration window. You can change the list of packages under the Package Exceptions tab.

5. Next, you'll see a list of available package updates from your channels. You can select the packages of your choice, as shown in Figure 1-7. Click Forward when ready.

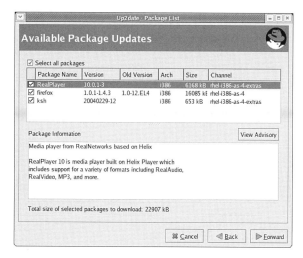

Figure 1-7   The Update Agent lists available updates

6. The Update Agent tests for dependencies. If found, other required packages are added to the update list. The Update Agent then proceeds with retrieving packages. When the process is complete, click Forward to continue.

Updated packages are downloaded by default to the `/var/spool/up2date` directory.

7. The Update Agent proceeds with installing the downloaded packages. When the process is complete, click Forward to continue.

8. The Update Agent lists the packages that it installed or upgraded on your system. Click Finish after you've reviewed these packages.

Configuring the Update Agent Settings

Naturally, Red Hat's Update Agent is much more flexible when started from the command line interface. As an administrator, you may administer a number of your systems remotely; in this case, the command line interface is more efficient.

The Update Agent configuration command is `up2date-nox --configure`. As it opens several-dozen configuration options, it's best to pipe the output to a pager with a command such as

```
up2date-nox --configure | less
```

You can review the settings associated with the Update Agent in Table 1-2; the sequence in this table is based on RHEL 4. Changes are saved in `/etc/sysconfig/rhn/up2date`. Alternatively, if you run `up2date --configure` in the GUI, you'll find many of the same settings in Figure 1-8.

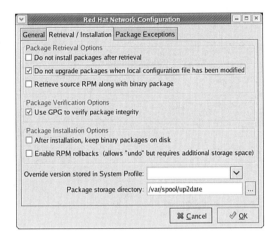

Figure 1-8   Configuring the Update Agent

Table 1-2   Update Agent configuration options

Option	Description
debug	Enables or disables debugging
useRhn	Set to yes if you have and want to use a RHEL subscription or a Proxy/Satellite server
rhnuuid	Specifies the unique Red Hat Network user ID for the computer
isatty	Connects the output to a terminal
showAvailablePackages	Lists all available packages from the repository; disabled by default
useNoSSLForPackage	Allows unencrypted downloads; disabled by default
storageDir	Specifies a directory for headers, RPMs, and other files downloaded from the repository; default is `/var/spool/up2date`
pkgSkipList	Specifies packages that the Update Agent should skip when searching for updates; `kernel*` packages are included by default
retrieveOnly	Sets update retrieval without installation; disabled by default
noSSLServerURL	Specifies the URL for the repository

Option	Description
networkSetup	Sets up the use of the Update Agent network configurator, where you can specify any proxy server on your network; one method is shown in Figure 1-4
networkRetries	Configures the number of times the Update Agent retries when there is a connection problem
pkgsToInstallNotUp	Specifies the names of packages that are not installed automatically with an `up2date --install` or `up2date -u` command
enableProxy	Allows you to update through a local proxy server, which controls your LAN's connections to the Internet
noBootLoader	Disables any upgrades to the boot loader
proxyPassword	Sets a password to use for a local proxy server
updateUp2date	Allows the Update Agent to update itself when an upgrade is available
keepAfterInstall	Stores downloaded packages and headers in storageDir after installation
useGPG	Requires the use of GPG signatures to verify the integrity of a package
headerCacheSize	Configures a maximum number of headers to cache in RAM
forceInstall	Overrides pkgsToInstallNotUp; would install new kernel
systemIdPath	Specifies the file with System ID information
retrieveSource	Configures retrieval of source RPMs; disabled by default
enableRollbacks	Allows you to undo the current update; disabled by default
gpgKeyRing	Specifies the file with the Update Agent GPG key
adminAddress	When the Update Agent is run in batch mode, with the `up2date -u` command, notice is sent to this address
serverURL	Specifies the URL with the repository; may be changed if you've configured an Update Agent Proxy or Satellite server
fileSkipList	Allows you to specify files for the Network Agent to skip
versionOverride	Overrides the version listed in `/etc/redhat-release`
sslCACert	Specifies the file with the SSL Certificate
noReplaceConfig	Packages that would change configuration data are not installed by default
enableProxyAuth	Supports the use of an authenticated proxy server
disallowConfChange	Sets a list of configuration changes not allowed through the Update Agent
headerFetchCount	Sets the maximum number of RPM headers to acquire at a time

continues

Table 1-2   continued

Option	Description
proxyUser	Assigns a username for an authenticated proxy server
removeSkipList	While the Update Agent removes packages from StorageDir by default, this list specifies packages which should not be removed
httpProxy	Specifies the URL of the local proxy server; standard TCP/IP ports suggest an address such as squid.example.com:3128
noReboot	Disables any instruction to reboot this computer

Update Agent Command Line Options

There are a number of other useful actions that you can take with the Update Agent. They're associated with different switches for the up2date command. While a complete list is available in the associated man page, I've listed the more important alternatives here:

```
up2date --configure
```

As described earlier, this command allows you to configure Update Agent options. If you're in the GUI, this opens the Update Agent configuration window shown in Figure 1-9; if you want the full functionality associated with the command line interface, use the up2date-nox --configure command.

```
up2date --register
```

This command allows you to register (or revise your registration) with the Red Hat Network.

```
up2date -d packagename
```

This command downloads specified packages, without installing them. If you already have the most up-to-date version of the packagename, you'll see a message to that effect.

```
up2date --src packagename
```

This command downloads the source package along with the associated binary RPM. If you already have the most up-to-date version of the packagename, you'll see a message to that effect.

```
up2date --show-channels
```

This command lists the channels available for updates to your computer. For more information on Red Hat Network channels, see Chapter 2.

```
up2date --hardware
```

The `--hardware` switch updates the hardware profile for your computer, as documented on the Red Hat Network.

```
up2date --list-rollbacks
```

This switch lists packages that you can restore to their former versions.

```
up2date -u
```

This command automatically updates your system with all upgradeable packages.

```
up2date --installall --channel=rhel-i386-as-4
```

This downloads and installs all packages from the given channel, as defined in the output from the `up2date --show-channels` command. Naturally, you'll want to enable the `KeepAfterInstall` configuration option described in the previous section. Otherwise, the Update Agent deletes these packages after downloading and installing them on your system.

Aggregating Red Hat Enterprise Linux Updates

If you administer just a few RHEL computers on a network, you may choose to configure them to download their updates directly from the Red Hat Network (after you've tested each update, of course). But if you have a substantial number of RHEL computers, their simultaneous updates may overload your connection to the Internet.

There are several methods you can use to manage and maintain control of how you keep your systems up to date.

QUARTERLY UPDATES

Red Hat provides CD-based updates of its RHEL distributions on a quarterly basis. These updates include all upgraded packages otherwise available through the Update Agent. You can store these packages in a local installation repository and upgrade your system with said packages.

PROXY SERVERS

Another way to update a group of RHEL systems is with a proxy server. A Red Hat Network Proxy Server stores content locally and passes authentication requests to the Red Hat Network. It requires a relatively high-powered system; minimum requirements shown in the release notes include

- ☞ Dell PowerEdge 1750 server or equivalent
- ☞ Two or more CPUs
- ☞ 512MB of RAM
- ☞ 3GB of storage for RHEL AS
- ☞ 1.5GB for source and update packages

These are relatively minimal requirements. If you're storing updates for more than one version of RHEL, practical hardware requirements increase accordingly.

The default Red Hat Network Proxy Server is available with 10 desktop subscription entitlements. Other packages may be available; contact Red Hat sales or www.redhat.com for more information.

You can learn how to install and configure the Red Hat Network Proxy Server in Chapter 2, as well as how to configure your RHEL clients to connect to those servers.

SATELLITE SERVERS

If you have a larger network, or one which requires a higher level of security, you may want more control over how your computers communicate with the Red Hat Network. This is possible with the Red Hat Network Satellite Server. Authentication, policies, and profiles are stored on the Satellite Server. Updates can be "pushed" directly to the clients of your choice. A Satellite Server can also serve as an installation server, from which you can automate the RHEL installation process on as many computers for which you have subscriptions.

Nominally, the hardware requirements for a Satellite Server are not significantly greater than for a Proxy Server. But if you have the number of RHEL systems that justify a Satellite server, you'll want to follow Red Hat recommendations, including

- ☞ Dell PowerEdge 2650 server or equivalent
- ☞ Two or more 2.4GHz CPUs
- ☞ 2GB-4GB of RAM
- ☞ 3GB of storage for RHEL AS
- ☞ 5GB for source and update packages—per channel (such as for different hardware-based versions of RHEL)
- ☞ 2GB of storage for database RPMs
- ☞ 36GB of storage in the database repository

These are relatively minimal requirements. If you're storing updates for more than one version of RHEL, practical hardware requirements increase accordingly.

The default Red Hat Network Proxy Server is available with 50 desktop subscription entitlements. Other packages may be available; contact Red Hat sales or www.redhat.com for more information.

CREATIVE OPTIONS

You can create your own repository of available updates. If you enable the `KeepAfterInstall` option, updates that you download are stored in `/var/spool/up2date`. You can then share these updates with other computers on your network. Assuming their configurations are identical, you can upgrade with these same packages. Some administrators have been known to configure downloaded packages in a yum repository, as demonstrated in Chapters 6, "Configuring a yum Client," and 7, "Setting up a yum Repository."

Alternatively, you can point the Upgrade Agent to repositories created by one of the Red Hat Rebuilds that you'll learn about in Chapter 2.

1.2.2   Novell/SUSE

The SUSE distributions, now owned by Novell, have a very different look and feel from the RHEL distributions. Administrative tools are integrated into the SUSE all-in-one tool, known as YaST (Yet another Setup Tool). While YaST is not geared to the command line interface, it does support a low-level graphical screen even from remote consoles, and it has a similar look and feel to YaST in the GUI.

In this section, you'll examine detailed workings of the YaST Online Update tool and get a feel for what you can do with repositories on SUSE Linux Enterprise Server (SLES). Unlike Red Hat, SUSE does not have a dedicated interface for subscriptions similar to the Red Hat Network.

YaST Online Update

In this section, you'll examine YaST Online Update on SUSE Linux Professional 9.3. Unlike RHEL, registration is not required at this operating system level. YaST Online Update, also known as YOU, provides a complete system for updating the RPM packages installed on your SUSE Linux Professional computers. It allows you to monitor appropriate SUSE repositories for updates. In Chapter 2, you'll learn how to configure a SUSE repository locally on your computer.

You can review a standard SUSE Professional GUI in Figure 1-9. You'll see a circle next to the date in the lower-right part of the GUI. A red exclamation point indicates that updates are available.

Figure 1-9   SUSE is watching for updates

To start YaST Online Update, take the following steps:

1. Click Menu -> System -> YaST.

   You're prompted to enter the root password before SUSE opens YaST.

2. In the YaST menu, select the Software option from the left-hand pane, and then select Online Update.

3. You can now configure YaST Online Update, as shown in Figure 1-10.

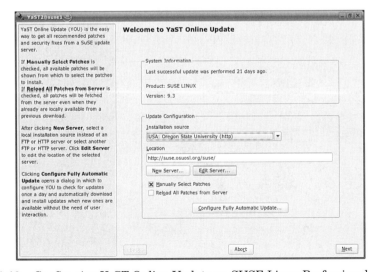

Figure 1-10   Configuring YaST Online Update on SUSE Linux Professional

You can configure YaST Online Update in several different ways. The Installation source drop-down box allows you to choose from several pre-configured SUSE update mirrors from the USA or Europe. You can specify the URL of your choice in the Location text box. Click New Server, and you can select a local source on a directory, CD, or DVD. You can also select a network source from a FTP, HTTP, Samba, or NFS server. For your first update, select a preconfigured Installation source and the Manually Select Patches option.

If your chosen repository requires a user name and password, click Edit Server. You can verify authentication here.

When you're comfortable with YaST Online Update, you can Configure Fully Automatic Update from this window, which allows automated updates on a daily or weekly basis, starting at a time specified by you.

4. When you're finished with this window, click Next to continue.

   YaST Online Update opens a window telling you that it's "Retrieving information about new updates." This process may take several minutes.

5. You can now configure the patches to be downloaded and installed, as shown in Figure 1-11.

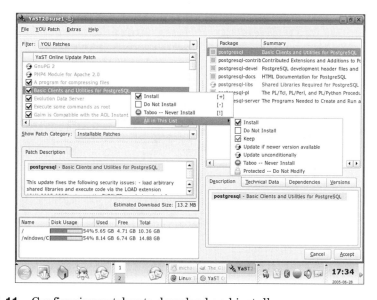

Figure 1-11   Configuring patches to download and install

You can customize what YaST Online Update does with each patch. As shown in Figure 1-11, you can set several conditions on what to do with each patch:

☞ Install

☞ Do not install during this update

☞ Never install this package with YaST Online Update

☞ Keep; retain the current package as is

☞ Update if a newer version of this package is available

☞ Update always; may overwrite previous configurations

☞ Do not modify this package

Review the list of available packages. When ready, press Accept to continue.

6. YaST Online Update now proceeds with downloading the patches you've selected.

If you've included a kernel in the update list, YaST Online Update requests confirmation, as shown in Figure 1-12. As you can see for yourself, a kernel update includes several different packages. Unless you're ready to risk a new kernel, press Skip Patch.

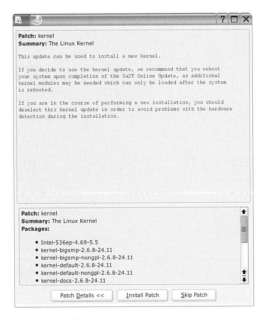

Figure 1-12   Confirming kernel patches

You may also have to confirm installation of other patches for packages, such as databases.

7. When the process is complete, you'll see a message listing the number of patches which have been installed. Click Finish to continue.

8. To complete the process, YaST Online Update writes the system configuration and runs the scripts in the `/sbin/conf.d` directory to integrate patches into your system.

When complete, you can find a repository of download patches in the following directory:

```
/var/lib/YaST2/you/mnt/i386/update/9.3
```

The directory with your patches will vary slightly, depending on your CPU and version of SUSE Linux. This repository includes four different categories of patches, as associated with their subdirectories:

1. Deltas include relatively small changes in the RPM package for installed systems.

2. Patches include text descriptions of the changes associated with each patch.

3. RPMs include new RPM packages; they're generally installed as an upgrade to your current system.

4. Scripts include small text programs that generally apply new drivers to your system.

If you're running SUSE Linux Enterprise Server 9, downloads are divided into SUSE-SLES and SUSE-CORE packages. The SLES packages are associated with the first installation CD; the CORE packages include downloaded updates associated with the remaining CDs. In other words, you can find updates in the following two directories:

```
/var/lib/YaST2/you/mnt/i386/update/SUSE-SLES/9
/var/lib/YaST2/you/mnt/i386/update/SUSE-CORE/9
```

Downloaded RPMs, patches and scripts can be found in the same subdirectories.

SUSE Linux Enterprise Server Updates

SUSE Linux Enterprise Server is designed to hold repositories. In SUSE Linux Enterprise Server 9, there is a YOU Server Configuration option available with the Online Update. When you start this server, you'll see the YaST Online Update Server Configuration screen shown in Figure 1-13.

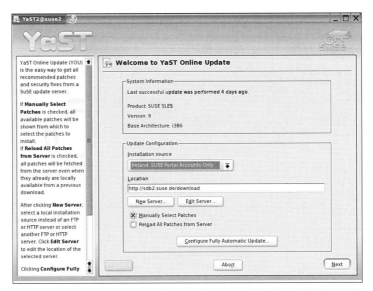

Figure 1-13   SUSE Linux Enterprise Server has more limits on YaST Online Update

If you have a valid subscription for SUSE Linux Enterprise Server, it'll be associated with your SUSE Linux online account. In the Update Server configuration screen, select a server and then click Edit Server. This opens the Authorization window shown in Figure 1-14, where you'll need to enter the username and password for your account. Any SUSE subscriptions should be automatically linked to that account.

Figure 1-14   Authorizing SUSE Linux Enterprise Server Online Update

Downloading SUSE Linux

Two of the flagship distributions in the SUSE Linux line are SUSE Linux Professional and SUSE Linux Enterprise server.

While each version of SUSE Linux Professional is available only for sale during the first few months of each release, it's available for download after that. For more information, see www.novell.com/products/linuxprofessional/. It's best if you use a mirror; links are available from the noted Web site. As of this writing, downloads of SUSE Linux Professional 9.3 are available as a DVD ISO or a standard installation tree. If you download the installation tree, you'll need a boot CD or floppy. Starting with version 10.0, Novell has made an open source version of SUSE Linux Professional available at www.openuse.org.

SUSE Linux Enterprise Server is available with a 30-day evaluation license. More information is available from www.novell.com/products/ linuxenterpriseserver. You'll need a Novell account before you can download this system. SUSE Linux Enterprise Server 9 requires that you download six CDs from the SUSE servers in Ireland or Utah (USA).

As of this writing, with instructions available on the download page, you can extend the evaluation to six months. The license is only required for updates; the server remains functional thereafter.

1.2.3   Debian

For me, Debian offers what I think of as the Heathkit version of Linux. It offers a wide degree of flexibility. Debian repositories offer a wider variety of packages than any other distribution that I know.

Debian hearkens back to the origins of Linux, where it was solely a cooperative arrangement between developers. As you can see at www.debian.org, this distribution is the province of its volunteers. However, there is commercial support available for Debian. Ian Murdock, one of the founders of Debian, started Progeny as a company which provides commercial support for Debian (and several other versions of Linux). For more information, see www.progeny.com.

The current version of Debian Linux is known as Sarge. There is also a "testing" distribution, similar to a beta, known as Etch. The developmental distribution, which includes packages more likely to have problems, is known as Sid. You might recognize these names from the Disney movie *Toy Story*.

Installing Debian

Debian Linux is different. You could download the 14 CDs or 2 DVDs associated with Sarge and install Debian from there. You could store the associated packages in a network repository. I have a fairly speedy cable modem connection, and I still find the thought of downloading this amount of data rather intimidating.

If you don't have a high-speed connection, you can purchase CDs or DVDs from vendors, such as www.cheapbytes.com or www.thelinuxshop.co.uk. I've installed Debian Sarge over a network connection, installing just the packages that I need. For this purpose, a high-speed connection is still the only practical method. I've started with the first installation CD. I was able to install enough of the operating system, including links to Debian repositories in `/etc/apt/sources.list`. For more information on this method, see www.debian.org/CD/netinst/.

Note

Most of the current development work on Debian is on a different release, known as Debian Sid. It is known as an unstable release; in my opinion, it is akin to the Developmental (Rawhide) releases of Fedora Linux. For more information on Debian Sid, see www.debian.org/releases/unstable/.

Many Regional Mirrors

After you've installed the basic Debian distribution, you'll want to configure your `/etc/apt/sources.list` file with one or more appropriate repositories. One list is available in the Debian Web page of mirrors at www.debian.org/mirror/list. I count mirrors available in over 50 countries.

To use a mirror, you'll want to specify the URL, the distribution, and whether you want to be able to download source code. In my case, I've added the following mirrors to my `sources.list` file:

```
deb ftp://debian.oregonstate.edu/debian/ stable main
deb-src ftp://debian.oregonstate.edu/debian/ stable main
```

This points my Debian computer to a mirror at Oregon State University. This is direct from the Debian Web page of mirrors noted previously. As I've installed Debian Sarge on my system, I've listed the `stable` repository. I've also noted the `main` set of packages. If I wanted additional packages contributed by other developers, I'd add `contrib` to these lines. If I wanted to access repositories of proprietary packages, I'd add `non-free` to these lines.

The apt System

The Debian patch management system is very closely integrated with the `apt` series of commands. You'll learn about the `apt` commands in detail in Chapter 4. The strength of `apt` is how it searches for and includes any dependent packages as it installs (or removes) the packages you desire.

The `apt` commands are also in common use on Debian-based distributions, such as Knoppix, as well as some RPM-based distributions, such as Conectiva.

There are two `apt` commands which I use more than others. The first command is the following:

```
apt-cache search searchterm
```

I can check the repositories configured in my `/etc/apt/sources.list` for the package of my choice. All I need is a search term; for example, if I wanted to search for packages related to Linux office suites, I substitute `office` for `searchterm`. My repositories return a wide variety of packages, including the OpenOffice.org, KOffice, and Abiword applications, as well as related programs that might fit in an Office suite, such as `xfonts` and the HP Office Jet driver (`hpoj`).

The other `apt` command I use frequently is

```
apt-get install packagename
```

For example, if I want to install the standard Linux DNS server, I substitute `bind` for `packagename`. The appropriate version of `bind` is installed; if there are dependencies, they are also installed. If additional configuration is required, Debian prompts me for appropriate selections. Alternatively, if I wanted to remove a package with dependencies, I could run the following command:

```
apt-get remove packagename
```

Synaptic offers a GUI front-end to the apt system. As you can see in Figure 1-15, Synaptic allows you to graphically view, install, and remove the packages you desire.

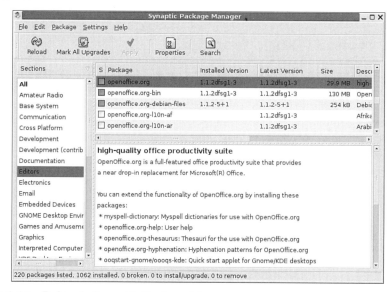

Figure 1-15 Debian's Synaptic Package Manager

1.2.4   Other Linux Distributions

There are hundreds of Linux distributions. Many have their own update
repositories. I'll mention a few of the more important Linux distributions here:

- ☞ **Mandriva Linux**. As of this writing, this company is merging the former
  Mandrake and Conectiva distributions. Mandrake was developed from
  Red Hat Linux and uses RPMs; they have a wide variety of graphical
  tools. Conectiva is the developer of apt for RPMs; before their work, the
  apt tools were most closely associated with Debian-based distributions.
  For more information, see www.mandriva.com.

- ☞ **Yellowdog Linux**. While this distribution was developed for PowerPC
  computers, their update tool, Yellowdog Updater, Modified (yum) is
  widely used on RPM-based distributions, including Red Hat's Fedora
  Linux. For more information, see www.yellowdoglinux.com.

- ☞ **Linspire**. Formerly known as Lindows, this distribution is known for its
  user friendliness and support, which has made it one of the distributions
  of choice at Walmart. For more information, see www.linspire.com.

- ☞ **Knoppix**. This Debian-based distribution has quickly gained fame as the
  "handyman" that can fix numerous problems with Linux (and even Microsoft Windows) computers. For more information, see www.knoppix. org.

It's not fair that I don't really have the space to mention other Linux distributions. There are many other excellent distributions available, with repositories that you can use and even replicate on your own networks. Many of
these distributions use the yum and apt tools that you can learn about in the
last half of this book.

1.3   COMMUNITY-BASED SOURCES

Besides Debian Linux, there are a number of distributions and "rebuilds"
backed by a community of developers and users. This list includes Fedora
Linux, the community-based offering of Red Hat, along with other distributions, such as Slackware Linux.

The most common current examples of rebuilds are the groups that have
taken the source code from Red Hat Enterprise Linux and built their own
binary packages and even downloadable CDs/DVDs.

Note

When I refer to a "rebuild," I'm referring to a distribution that is built from the source code of another distribution. This is in contrast to a "clone" which is an operating system that emulates the functionality of another while using different source code. For example, while Linux is a clone of Unix, CentOS-4 is a rebuild of Red Hat Enterprise Linux 4.

1.3.1   Fedora Linux

When Red Hat moved to a subscription model for its flagship RHEL distribution, it wanted to retain the support of the Linux community. For this reason, it started the Fedora Linux project. Red Hat has stated that Fedora Linux distributions will be released every 4 to 8 months, and it will be the testbed for future RHEL releases. As of this writing, the current version is Fedora Core 4, and we'll be using that version in our examples.

As a community project, Fedora Linux does not have access to the Red Hat Network. However, as a RHEL testbed, it uses the same basic Update Agent as described earlier in this chapter.

Therefore, Fedora Linux needed a community-based repository and update tool. The basic repositories are listed at fedora.redhat.com/download/mirrors. The basic update tool is the tool associated with Yellowdog Linux, yum. Before you can start the update process, you'll need to import the Fedora GPG key into your update system. As it's already available in the /usr/share/rhn directory, all you need to do is run:

```
rpm --import /usr/share/rhn/RPM-GPG-KEY-fedora
```

If you're using Fedora Linux, you should update the files in the /etc/yum.repos.d directory. The default version of this directory includes six files:

- ☞ fedora.repo includes the basic Fedora Core repository.
- ☞ fedora-updates.repo contains the updates associated with Fedora Core.
- ☞ fedora-updates-testing.repo has updates that may not be ready for production for Fedora Core. These are proposed updates.
- ☞ fedora-extras.repo contains additional packages which are tested for Fedora Core, but are not part of the official distribution.
- ☞ fedora-extras-devel.repo has packages that may not be ready for production for the Extras repository of Fedora Core. These updates are incorporated in the Extras repository when they're ready for production.
- ☞ fedora-devel.repo includes the repository with the regular rebuilds of packages; formerly known as Rawhide.

These files include two variables, $releasever and $basearch. They refer to the release version of Fedora Core and the CPU version, respectively.

My version of this file in Fedora Core 4 points to random mirrors. The
first time I ran yum, this file pointed my computer to a repository in Denmark.
As I am in the USA, that is not what I want. So I'll want to change each of the
files in the `/etc/yum.repos.d` directory. For example, if I wanted to use the mirror at North Carolina State University at ftp://ftp.linux.ncsu.edu/, I'd comment out the `mirrorlist` command in each of the six files and substitute in the
following files:

☞ `fedora.repo`

   `baseurl=ftp://ftp.linux.ncsu.edu/pub/fedora/linux/core/$releasever/`
   `$basearch/os/`

☞ `fedora-updates.repo`

   `baseurl=ftp://ftp.linux.ncsu.edu/pub/fedora/linux/core/updates/`
   `$releasever/$basearch/`

☞ `fedora-updates-testing.repo`

   `baseurl=ftp://ftp.linux.ncsu.edu/pub/fedora/linux/core/updates/`
   `testing/$releasever/$basearch/`

☞ `fedora-extas.repo`

   `baseurl=ftp://ftp.linux.ncsu.edu/pub/fedora/linux/extras/`
   `$releasever/$basearch/`

☞ `fedora-extas-devel.repo`

   `baseurl=ftp://ftp.linux.ncsu.edu/pub/fedora/linux/extras/`
   `development/$basearch/`

☞ `fedora-devel.repo`

   `baseurl=ftp://ftp.linux.ncsu.edu/pub/fedora/linux/core/development/`
   `$basearch/`

You should update these files with the mirror-based repositories of your
choice. It's OK to have more than one repository listed in each of the
`/etc/yum.repos.d` configuration files. We'll explore this process in more detail
in Chapter 2.

1.3.2   Red Hat Rebuilds

There are several different groups that have rebuilt the Red Hat Enterprise
Linux source code. This is allowable because Red Hat has released the source
code for almost all RHEL packages under the GPL or related open source
licenses. Before release, each of these groups has modified the source code to
remove Red Hat trademarks. While there are several versions of RHEL 4, the
developers behind the rebuilds have configured a generic rebuild, which can
be configured as a server or workstation. While these rebuilds generally support 32- and 64-bit x86 systems, support for other architectures varies.
   Some of the groups behind RHEL rebuilds include the following:

☞   cAos is the group behind CentOS 4, which is based on the source code for RHEL 4. It has a strong following and is based on a community of volunteers. For more information, see www.caosity.org.

☞   White Box Linux was developed by a group associated with a Louisiana library system; they had the first available rebuild of RHEL 3. For more information, see www.whiteboxlinux.org.

Note

The people behind White Box Linux worked overtime, adding Linux terminals and wireless networks, to help evacuees from Hurricane Katrina (2005) stay in touch with friends and families. Thousands of evacuees have relocated, at least temporarily, to their area. These dedicated Linux hackers have maintained their efforts even after a near-direct hit from Hurricane Rita.

☞   Lineox was built by a company in Finland, the original home of Linus Torvalds. They offer CDs, DVDs, and paid levels of support. For more information, see www.lineox.net.

☞   Fermi Linux was rebuilt by several developers at the Fermi National Accelerator Laboratory near Chicago. Scientific Linux was developed from Fermi Linux and is maintained by developers at similar laboratories including the European particle physics laboratory (CERN). For more information, see www-oss.fnal.gov/projects/fermilinux/ and www. scientificlinux.org.

A more complete list of RHEL rebuilds is available at www.linuxmafia.com/faq/RedHat/rhel-forks.html.

1.4 CONFIGURING YOUR LAN

When you configure a LAN with Linux, you need to consider the demands of patch management along with any other requirements of your users. While you can certainly schedule patch management upgrades during off-hours, there are a number of other demands which are often scheduled for off-hours, including backups, CPU intensive database programs, and more. This includes scripts run in the middle of the night on Linux computers, such as those in the /etc/cron.daily directory.

As an example, there have been around 2GB in updates to Fedora Core 3 over a four-month period. Averaged over this period, that's approximately 20MB of downloads per day. That's a problem only if you connect to updates via telephone modem (nearly half of all Internet connections in the USA still use a telephone modem). Therefore, one practical requirement for Linux patch management is a high-speed connection.

An update of 20MB per day might not be a big problem if you have one or two Linux computers and a typical residential DSL (Digital Subscriber Line) or Cable Internet connection. However, if you're running a network of Linux computers, you need to think about your requirements. If you choose to consolidate patches on a local computer, you'll need a computer that can handle the patch management demands from possibly all the other computers on your network.

The hardware requirements increase depending on whether you need to download source packages—and whether you're planning Linux patch management for more than one architecture on your network.

1.4.1   Linux Patch Management in a Network

If you have a substantial number of Linux computers, it may be cost effective to buy, configure, and dedicate one or more computers to the patch management task. For example, assume that you have a network of 100 computers, and patch management requires that each of these computers downloads 20MB per day. Downloading an additional 2GB per day, every day, can be expensive on business-level Internet connections.

Some packages, such as those associated with the OpenOffice.org suite, require several hundred MB to update. If 100 computers on your network download these packages simultaneously, this can overload many business-level Internet connections. For example, it could take all night for 100 computers to download this amount of data over a "T3" connection. This type of connection can easily cost upwards of $10,000/month.

Note

Common higher-speed connections for business start with dedicated "T1" lines at 1.44 Mbps. T3 connections support 45Mbps. Multiple and fractional connections are available through 620Mbps and even higher speeds. While a certain quality of service is often guaranteed on these connections, prices often start in the hundreds of dollars (U.S.) per month.

If you can configure a proxy server, you could download Linux patch data once from the Internet, and then the 100 computers on your network could download the patches locally. You would then save the additional costs for your Internet connection.

Note

The costs associated with business-level connections to the Internet vary widely. If you're in a country that encourages the market to provide inexpensive high-speed connections, such as the Republic of Korea, you may be able to let your network grow larger before considering a proxy server. On the other hand, if you're in an area where Internet connections are more expensive or less reliable, you may want to consider patch management even if your network includes only two or three Linux computers.

Depending on the number of computers that require updates, you may want to configure more than one patch management proxy server for your network. While details are beyond the scope of this book, you should consider several factors before making this decision:

☞ Marginal costs; what is the additional cost required if all your systems accessed a remote repository through the Internet?

☞ Network capacity; for example, whether your network conforms to Ethernet or faster standards. The Red Hat hardware requirements for proxy servers specify computers with Gigabit Ethernet adapters.

☞ Control; if you have subscriptions to a Linux support service, you may prefer to store those subscriptions on a local server. Some subscription services make this possible.

☞ Frequency of updates; how often do you need to update or synchronize each of your proxy servers with each other and a central repository through the Internet.

You can examine some of these factors in the following sections.

1.4.2 Rigorous Hardware Requirements

Any computer that you configure as a local repository for Linux patch management meets the definitions of a proxy server. It caches content from the Internet for use by multiple computers on your network.

As suggested earlier in this chapter, Red Hat includes some fairly rigorous requirements for Red Hat Network Proxy Servers. It's unlikely that you'll be able to recycle an older workstation for this purpose.

Storage/CPU/Network Specifications

If you're configuring a new computer as a Linux patch management repository, you should first consider any recommendations from your distribution supplier. Among others, Red Hat and Novell/SUSE have experience with caching content from the Internet.

In general, CPU speed is less important on a proxy server. If you've dedicated a computer as a proxy server, you're not expecting it to run many independent programs. However, if your network includes a substantial number of computers which need access to your local repository, multiple CPUs can be useful. The important hardware requirements of a proxy server repository include the following:

☞ **Network connections**. If you have a limited budget for network hardware, it's worth focusing the latest hardware on your repositories. In other words, make sure that computer has the fastest network cards, along with faster hubs, switches and routers nearby, when possible.

☞ **Hard drives**. Naturally, Linux patch management repositories require larger hard drives for the many GB of data associated with each distribution. Access speed, controllers, and caching size are more important on a proxy server.

Hardware reliability may be less important on a Linux patch management repository. After all, this computer is essentially just a mirror of data that is already available. If that computer fails, you can reload the data through the Internet. However, if Linux patches are important and time-sensitive in your organization, your view of this may differ.

Amount of Data

Hard drives don't always have to be large. If you're only storing updates on a Linux patch management repository, all you need on a proxy server is room for the operating system and the package updates. With today's Linux distributions, that amounts to less than 10GB of data (even for SUSE Linux).

But this may grow quickly depending on your needs. As suggested earlier, if you have more than one type of system architecture, such as Intel 32-bit, 64-bit, PowerPC, and so on, data requirements can grow exponentially.

In addition, if you have more than one version of Linux that requires updates, you'll need to keep separate repositories for each. In other words, not only do you need separate repositories for any RHEL, SUSE, and Debian computers, you'll need separate repositories for RHEL 3, RHEL 4, SUSE 9.0, SUSE 9.1, SUSE 9.2, SUSE 9.3, SUSE 10.0, Fedora Core 1 through 5, and more.

1.4.3 Source Packages

The size of your repositories could easily double if your users need access to the source code.

Source code is readily available because of the requirements of the GPL. This allows any developer to take the source code and modify it for their own needs. Developers can modify and redistribute GPL source code, as long as it is still released under the GPL.

But unless you're administering a network with Linux developers, you might think that you don't have to worry about Linux source packages.

You don't have to be a developer to need Linux source code. Anyone who wants to customize the Linux kernel needs the source code. While some distributions make the source code available in a binary package, Red Hat releases its build of the kernel source code as a source RPM.

Linux drivers for many hardware components are still under development. Experimental drivers often work well. But to install many of these drivers, you need the kernel source code.

The need for source code is not limited to the kernel. Regular users can modify the source code of many GPL-licensed programs. All they need is the source code, and they can revise, compile, and rebuild the program of choice.

1.4.4 More Than One Repository

Even if all the Linux computers on your network run the same version of the same distribution using the same CPU, you may need more than one repository. As noted earlier, Fedora Core 4 includes configuration files for six different repositories. While most users don't need to access the Red Hat development, or repositories, you never know when one user might be so desperate for the latest features that he is willing to try a development version of his favorite program.

You might need separate repositories on a Linux patch management server for the following reasons:

☞ Distribution brands; each distribution brand builds its packages differently and therefore maintains separate repositories.

☞ Distribution versions; for example, if you have a reliable server on RHEL 2.1, you might not want to upgrade to RHEL 4, even though a subscription makes this possible. Red Hat has committed to support each of its enterprise distributions for at least five years, which means you might need to maintain local repositories for RHEL 2.1 through at least 2007.

☞ Number of architectures; for each architecture where you have Linux installed on your network, you'll need a separate repository.

☞ Source requirements; if some of your users are Linux developers, you might need to download source packages into a separate repository.

☞ Development packages; if you're monitoring the progress of a program, you'll want access to the development packages so you can monitor improvements as they're made.

☞ Testing packages; some groups make development packages available in a separate repository before declaring them stable and ready for a production environment.

☞ Independent repositories; some developers keep independent repositories on their Web and FTP servers. Many are available for public use.

1.4.5 Keeping Your Repository Updated

There are two basic methods you might use to keep a local repository up to date. Some distributions allow you to store download packages and their headers on a local computer. You can then share the directory with those download packages and point the other computers on your network to that local repository. Red Hat and SUSE make that possible in some cases with their Subscription systems.

Alternatively, you can synchronize your repositories with those available online. This is where the `rsync` command can help. I detail how you can do this in later chapters, especially Chapter 3, "SUSE's Update Systems and rsync Mirrors." While that chapter is focused on SUSE Linux, the use of the `rsync` command described in that chapter applies to repositories for all distributions.

Some administrators prefer to wait until updates are available in a more convenient format. For example, RHEL makes quarterly updates of its distributions available, which administrators can configure into a local repository using the techniques described in the last half of this book.

After you've determined how you'll keep your repositories up to date, automate the process so that it happens during off-peak hours. Remember, you might be downloading hundreds of megabytes of packages, so make sure that the download does not interfere with other scheduled work, such as:

☞ **Computing-intensive programs**. For example, intensive database programs require so much in computer and network resources that they're often run while most users are not at work.

☞ **Administrative programs**. Backups, log rotations, and more in Linux are often configured in scripts in the `/etc/cron.daily` directory.

☞ **Other downloads**. Many Linux users download other distributions. It's best if you can limit large downloads by regular users at least to specific time periods.

☞ **Power outages**. Some networks may limit available power due to costs, availability, or local conditions.

1.5 SUMMARY

When you apply patch management techniques to your Linux computers, you can keep them secure, up to date with the latest services, and nearly bug-free.

In this chapter, you learned to configure repositories and apply patches and updates on RHEL, SUSE, and some other Linux distributions. Subscriptions are required in some cases, which entitle you to keep your systems up to date with the latest patches from specific vendor repositories. As patches can easily run into hundreds of megabytes, it can be helpful to configure a patch management repository on one or more computers on your LAN so that you do not have to pay for an Internet connection where all your computers download updates individually from remote locations.

In the following chapters, you'll learn how to configure and manage local patch repositories on your network.

## CHAPTER 2

Consolidating Patches on a Red Hat/Fedora Network

Patching Linux on one computer is a straightforward process. As you read in Chapter 1, "Patch Management Systems," many distributions include patch management utilities that can keep a single system up to date. Regular patch downloads for one or two computers over a typical high-speed connection are not a problem. Regular patch downloads from dozens of computers from a LAN over a shared Internet connection can be troublesome.

Therefore, you need to know how to configure a central patch management repository for a network. In this chapter, I outline how you can plan a repository by using Fedora Core Linux. In Chapter 7, "Setting Up a yum Repository," I provide the detailed instructions for setting up a repository for Fedora Core. Alternatively, if you're administering patch management for Red Hat Enterprise Linux (RHEL) systems, you can set up a Red Hat Proxy Server. I'll take you through the configuration process for a Red Hat Network proxy and client, step by step.

Finally, I'll describe the basic patch management process for some of the rebuilds of RHEL, specifically CentOS and Lineox. Because they use the yum and apt tools, you can keep them up to date using the repository tools you'll learn about later in this book.

Note

In this chapter, we'll be referring to proxy servers (lowercase) which cache and may sometimes regulate your LAN's communication with outside networks, such as the Internet. We'll also be referring to a Red Hat Network Proxy Server (uppercase), which can be configured as your LAN's repository for RHEL updates.

2.1 CREATING YOUR OWN FEDORA REPOSITORY

In this section, you'll learn the basic process for creating a Fedora repository. It relies on the yum commands, so you'll learn the details in Chapter 7. For the most part, this section is a high-level overview; it can help you contrast the requirements for patch management for networks based on Fedora, RHEL, and RHEL rebuild distributions.

If you're configuring a repository, it's normally best if you create a dedicated partition for that repository. This section assumes that you've installed a new hard drive for this purpose and details the steps that you would take to create a dedicated partition.

2.1.1   Installation Requirements

Unlike with the Red Hat Network Proxy Server, there are no specific hardware requirements for a Fedora repository. Software requirements are fairly minimal. But the demands on a Fedora-based patch repository are the same. Other Fedora computers on your network will pull updates from your local repository on a regular basis. Therefore, on a Fedora-based patch repository, you should consider the following:

Hardware

An ideal Fedora repository computer should meet the requirements associated with a Red Hat Network Proxy Server, as described in Chapter 1. To review, while CPU speed is less important, you should have a computer with the following:

- ☞ Fast hard drive access; because any local cache of patches fills gigabytes of space, you'll want a computer that can pull those updates quickly.
- ☞ Fastest possible network connections; if dozens of computers download updates from your repository simultaneously, they need to share bandwidth on your LAN.
- ☞ Extra RAM cache updates, which can help minimize the requirements on the hard drive(s).

Hard Drive Partitions

When you configure Fedora as a patch management computer, it is best to set up a dedicated partition for the purpose. In this way, other programs that you might install and other services with ever-growing log files won't crowd out your repositories (or vise versa).

Normally, patches are downloaded to the `/var` directory. Red Hat, Fedora, Debian, and SUSE all follow this convention. Red Hat and Fedora patch RPMs are normally downloaded to `/var/spool/up2date` and then deleted after the RPMs are used to update your system. As you learned in Chapter 1, Fedora clients are configured through files such as `/etc/yum.conf` or in the `/etc/yum.repos.d` directory to pull updates from FTP or HTTP servers.

Therefore, most administrators create Fedora repositories on a local FTP or HTTP server. The default directories for associated files are `/var/ftp/pub` and `/var/www/html`. If you want to protect the space assigned to your repositories, you'll want to dedicate a partition for this purpose.

Note

You can also use an NFS server as a repository. I focus on HTTP and FTP because the details are more intricate.

Space Requirements

Compared with the space available on the latest inexpensive hard drives, the space required for a Fedora repository is not terribly significant. All you need is room for the operating system and the repository. However, if you manage multiple repositories for multiple versions of Fedora on more than one architecture, you can still run out of room quickly. It's best if you plan ahead. If you plan to reinstall Fedora on your computers every time a new version is released, the requirements are straightforward; one possible scenario with an installation and update repository for x86 systems is shown in Table 2-1. This is just a hypothetical breakdown; I've tried to be generous with space requirements.

Table 2-1   Possible Fedora repository space requirements: one release, one architecture

Requirement	Space	Description
Fedora Core	3GB	Typical installation with GUI, without all services
Installation Repository	2.5GB	Fedora Core installation files typically require four CDs
Update Repository	5GB	Some packages are patched multiple times during the life of a distribution. It can be helpful to keep older updates in case of trouble

That doesn't seem so bad. With these requirements, it seems like you can install a Fedora repository on an older computer with a 10GB hard drive. As long as you make sure that your network can handle the load, this seems to be sufficient. But you need to consider additional factors:

☞ As noted on fedora.redhat.com, releases are planned every four to eight months. Updates are made available for about a full year afterwards. If you don't install every new version of Fedora, the update repository requirements may double or more.

☞ If you want to maintain a Fedora update repository for more than a year, you'll have to reconfigure your repository for Fedora Legacy updates. The space requirements increase accordingly. You may also need to reconfigure the associated configuration files. For more information, see www.fedoralegacy.org.

☞ As you bring new computers online, you may want to install later releases of Fedora. Each release requires its own installation and update repository, which could double associated space requirements yet again.

☞ Fedora is also available for 64-bit x86-64 systems. If you want to install and maintain Fedora on these computers (and continue to maintain regular 32-bit systems), the requirements on your installation and update repositories might double yet again.

Personally, I enjoy installing Linux on my computers. However, preserving the configuration and personal files associated with older versions can be a tedious process. After Linux is installed, you may not want to reinstall another version until there are significant changes, such as a major new kernel. It's normally two or three years between major kernel releases (such as between versions 2.4 and 2.6). By then, you could be maintaining client computers with multiple architectures. It's easy to see how a repository could grow to hundreds of gigabytes.

Creating a Dedicated Partition During Installation

It's easiest to configure partitions for Fedora Core during the installation process. The Disk Druid screen shown in Figure 2-1 allows you to dedicate partitions or logical volumes to the directory of your choice.

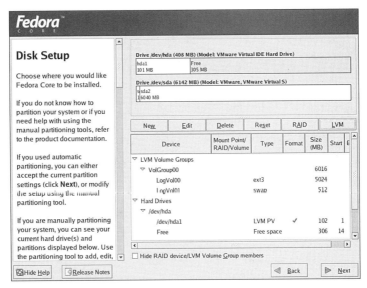

Figure 2-1   You can configure partitions with Fedora Disk Druid

In Disk Druid, just click Add, and then you can assign a directory such as /var/ftp to a partition such as /dev/hda5. Alternatively, if there's room on a Logical Volume Management (LVM) physical volume (PV), you can assign space from that area for your repository.

Creating a Dedicated Partition After Installation

You can still configure a dedicated partition for your repository after Linux is installed. All you need is sufficient free space on an available hard drive. For example, assume that you've added a second hard drive on your computer and want to dedicate that space to a repository. You could then use `fdisk` to create a new partition on that drive. Just take the following steps:

1. Make sure you have sufficient room for your desired repository. The `fdisk -l` command lists available space on attached hard drives.

   As you can see in Figure 2-2, I have an empty 10GB IDE hard drive on `/dev/hda`. I'll want to dedicate this entire drive as a partition for the `/var/ftp` directory.

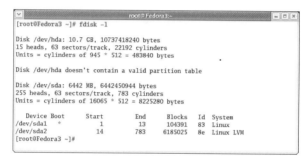

```
[root@Fedora3 ~]# fdisk -l

Disk /dev/hda: 10.7 GB, 10737418240 bytes
15 heads, 63 sectors/track, 22192 cylinders
Units = cylinders of 945 * 512 = 483840 bytes

Disk /dev/hda doesn't contain a valid partition table

Disk /dev/sda: 6442 MB, 6442450944 bytes
255 heads, 63 sectors/track, 783 cylinders
Units = cylinders of 16065 * 512 = 8225280 bytes

   Device Boot      Start         End      Blocks   Id  System
/dev/sda1   *           1          13      104391   83  Linux
/dev/sda2              14         783     6185025   8e  Linux LVM
[root@Fedora3 ~]#
```

Figure 2-2   Finding the current partition table

2. Run the `fdisk /dev/hda` command to open that hard drive to edit its partition table.
3. Run the `p` command; this confirms an empty partition table for this hard drive.
4. Run the `n` command; you're prompted as shown whether you want to create a primary or an extended partition.
5. Press `p`; you're prompted for a partition number between 1 and 4. As this is the first partition on this particular drive, press `1`.
6. Accept the default values for the first and last cylinder; these actions assign the entire hard drive to the new partition.

   If you wanted to limit the size of the new partition, you could have specified a size in kilobytes (K) or megabytes (M). For example, if you wanted a 5GB partition, you could have entered +5000M at the Last cylinder prompt.
7. Press `p` to review the result on this hard drive's partition table. You can review the result in Figure 2-3.

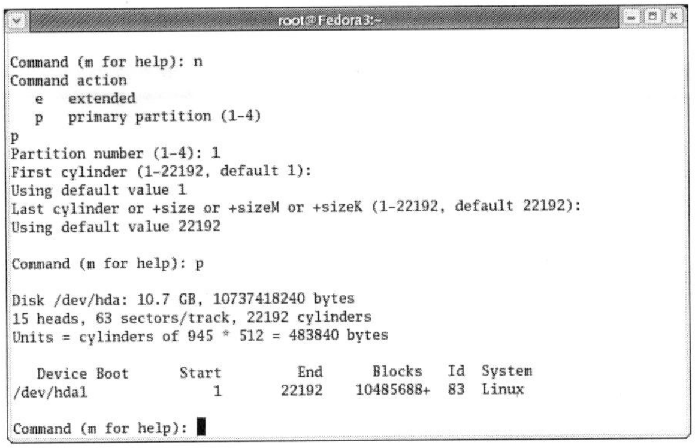

Figure 2-3   Creating a new partition

If you're satisfied, press `w` to write the partition table to the hard drive. For a list of other `fdisk` commands, press `m`.

8. If the partition you create is on a hard drive that's currently being used on your system, you'll have to reboot Linux to reread the partition table. While you could force things, the results could be disastrous for your data.

Note

For more information on `fdisk` and partitions, see the Linux Partition HOWTO at www.tldp.org/HOWTO/Partition/index.html.

After you've created a new partition, the remaining steps are straightforward. All you need to do is format the partition, mount it on a temporary directory, copy existing data, and then bring the result into your partition table. The next time you boot Linux, it'll boot the desired directory on your new partition automatically. For details, take the following steps:

1. Format the new partition. For example, if the new partition is `/dev/hdb1`, you'd run the following command:

```
mkfs.ext3 /dev/hdb1
```

2. If the partition is already mounted on an active directory, Fedora Core won't format the partition; it returns an error message.

Note

Don't run a format command such as `mkfs` or `fdformat` on an active partition. It can destroy data on that partition and possibly more. While distributions, such as the latest versions of Fedora Core, include safety settings that may warn you against formatting a partition, the risk is still there.

---

3. When the format is complete, make sure journaling is enabled. Because the default Fedora ext3 file system is a journaling file system, you may want to make sure journaling is configured on the new partition:

```
tune2fs -j /dev/hdb1
```

4. Now you can mount the new partition on the directory of your choice. For now, you'll want to mount it on a temporary directory; I often create `/mnt/test` for this purpose. To mount the newly formatted `/dev/hdb1` partition, run the following command:

```
mount /dev/hdb1 /mnt/test
```

5. Now you can copy the files from the directory that you want to mount on the newly formatted partition. For example, if you want to create a repository on a local FTP server, copy the files from the local FTP source directory, `/var/ftp` to `/mnt/test`. The `cp -ar` command copies any subdirectories recursively.

```
cp -ar /var/ftp/* /mnt/test
```

6. Document the desired mount in your partition table configuration file, `/etc/fstab`. Open it in the text editor of your choice. Based on the information shown here, you would add the following line:

```
/dev/hdb1            /var/ftp            ext3      defaults        1 2
```

7. Save your changes and reboot.

8. The next time Linux boots, it should mount the `/var/ftp` directory on `/dev/hdb1`. You can verify this with the `mount` command. You can now create a Fedora repository on this partition, with confidence that what you save here won't be crowded out by other services or files that users might save to this computer.

Configuring Fedora for a New Repository Computer

If you haven't already done so, you should run the Update Agent on this computer. Before you use it as a repository for other computers on your network, you should make sure this computer itself is up to date!

The steps are quite similar to those you've seen for RHEL in Chapter 1; one major difference is that you do not have to register your Fedora Linux computer on the Red Hat Network.

2.1.2   Creating a Repository

Now that you have a dedicated partition, you can create the repository that you need for the computers on your network. While we detail the process in later chapters, we describe the basic steps here:

1. Select a Web or FTP server. As discussed in Chapter 1, Fedora clients look for updates on Web and FTP servers.
2. Plan the directory tree for the repository. You'll need separate directories for at least the installation and updates.
3. Download the files for the repository.
4. Synchronize the repository. You may want to create and automate scripts to keep that repository up to date.

Note

If you're creating a repository for Fedora Core 3 or later, the tools have been changed. The standard command is `yum-arch`; those who create yum repositories are moving toward the `createrepo` command. We'll discuss the use of both tools in Chapter 6, "Configuring a yum Client," and Chapter 7, "Setting up a yum Repository."

Selecting a Service

As described in Chapter 1, Fedora clients pull updates from FTP and HTTP (Web) servers. You learned how to point a Fedora client to a FTP or HTTP mirror. You'll want to create your repository on an FTP, NFS, or HTTP server, which is what Fedora users are familiar with. While I personally prefer FTP because the protocol is inherently faster, some prefer the security associated with an HTTP (or even an HTTPS) server.

After you choose a service, you should set up a dedicated partition, as described earlier in this chapter. Then you can install and configure the service of your choice. We'll show you how to configure a yum repository on a vsFTP server in Chapter 7.

Planning the Tree

Next, you'll need to plan the directory structure. The simplest plan is to mirror an existing repository from a server connected to the Internet. But as many repositories are configured for multiple architectures, mirroring may download much more than what you need.

There is a substantial number of directories associated with Fedora Core repositories. If you don't need development, testing, or source packages, you do not need all the standard repository directories on your system. In fact, you may want to discourage users from downloading and installing developmental packages, because they may have unpredictable effects on your system.

For the latest releases of Fedora Core, you may need to justify your use of different repository directories. Some of the options include

- ☞ Core and Extras—Core includes the basic packages associated with Fedora. Extras include additional tools that can be added by individual developers and have often gone through less testing.
- ☞ Different Fedora Core releases—If you are configuring a repository for clients where Fedora Core 2, 3, 4, and 5 are installed, you'll need different repository trees for each. Each release includes subdirectories for source RPMs and released architectures.
- ☞ Development and test releases—As described in Chapter 1, development releases include new features as they're developed, even on a nightly basis. Test releases are the "beta" versions of Fedora. Generally, you can avoid these repository trees completely.
- ☞ Updates—These are key. They include the patches and updates that you want your users to have and install on their systems (after you test and approve them, of course). There are testing and released updates.

Unless you're a Fedora developer, you don't want or need most of these directory trees in your repository.

Downloading and Synchronizing

Now that you know what you want to download, you can proceed with the process. With the right command, such as `rsync` or `wget`, you can download the repository trees of your choice. We'll describe this process in more detail in Chapter 7. There are a number of developers who have automated this process.

Note

You can use the basic directions in Chapter 3, "SUSE's Update Systems and rsync Mirrors," to create a local mirror of any repository with the `rsync` command. While Chapter 3 applies to SUSE, the basic commands apply to any repository on an `rsync` server.

2.2 CONFIGURING A RED HAT NETWORK PROXY

When you're managing patches for a group of RHEL computers, you may not want all of them downloading hundreds of megabytes of patches through the Internet simultaneously. As discussed in Chapter 1, you can configure one or more Proxy or Satellite Servers for patch management.

In this section, you'll learn to configure a Red Hat Network Proxy Server and client. You can then attach other RHEL clients on your network, download the same updates more quickly, and keep the load on your Internet connection to a minimum.

Note

If you're connecting a Red Hat Network Proxy Server to a local Red Hat Network Satellite Server, that Satellite serves as the Red Hat Network for the purpose of this chapter. Substitute accordingly. We have chosen not to cover the Red Hat Network Satellite Server, as that would bias this book too far toward Red Hat and related distributions.

2.2.1   Configuring the Proxy Server

The installation requirements for a Red Hat Network Proxy Server described in Chapter 1 mean that you'll need a dedicated computer. Red Hat suggests that you keep what you install on the Proxy Server computer to an absolute minimum.

In other words, don't install other services on a Red Hat Network Proxy Server computer. This includes a GUI. As a competent Linux administrator, you do not need a GUI to configure or update the Proxy Server.

In this section, you'll configure a Red Hat Network Proxy Server from the command line interface and your administrative account on the Red Hat Network. In the following sections, we'll describe specific installation requirements, and we will then outline everything that you need to do to configure your Proxy Server, which includes the following:

1. Install RHEL in a minimal configuration; even the standard Red Hat minimal configuration supports networking.

2. Configure your firewall to allow communication with the Red Hat Network.

3. Set up a connection to external NTP (Network Time Protocol) servers.

4. Configure the RHEL computer as a router.

5. Register this computer on the Red Hat Network.

6. Get to the Red Hat Network channel with the proxy packages.

7. Install the Proxy Server packages.

8. Provision this computer with a Proxy Subscription.

9. Configure the Proxy Server.

10. Create the certification keys which allow clients to communicate with this Proxy Server.

When this process is complete, you can configure the clients on your network to pull updates from this computer (and not directly from the Red Hat Network).

Note

At any time during the Proxy Server configuration process, you may need to refresh your server and client configuration settings on the Red Hat Network. To do so, navigate to the target computer and run the `rhn_check` command.

Specialized Installation Requirements

Red Hat suggests that what you install on a Proxy Server computer should be kept to a minimum. For RHEL versions 3 and 4, this corresponds to the Base and Core package groups. This does include all packages required to network and configure this computer through the Update Agent. And the network connection allows you to configure this computer remotely through your Red Hat Network account.

Note

Red Hat and related distributions document package groups in an XML file, `comps.xml`. It's available on the first installation CD, in the `/RedHat/base/` subdirectory.

Red Hat also suggests that you should disable the `iptables` and `ipchains` firewall commands on a Proxy Server. While you can configure a Proxy Server between your RHEL clients and the Internet, you should not configure this computer as a firewall.

The Proxy Server packages that you'll install through the Red Hat Network will allow you to configure minimal Web, Proxy, and routing services on this computer. However, it's best if you don't also configure this computer with any other functionality. For example, standard Apache or Squid services could interfere with the Red Hat Network Proxy Server.

After you've configured a minimal installation of RHEL, you'll need to complete the configuration yourself.

Note

This book uses Red Hat Network Proxy Server 3.6 on RHEL 3. You can also use Proxy Server 3.7 or 4.0. If you want to dedicate a RHEL 4 computer for this purpose, you can use Red Hat Network Proxy Server 3.7 or 4.0. In either case, a Proxy Server on a RHEL 3 or 4 server works equally well for both RHEL 3 and RHEL 4 clients.

A minimal installation doesn't load the Red Hat Setup Agent, also known as the First Boot service. Therefore, you may not have a regular user account. You aren't even connected (yet) to the Red Hat Network.

Before you can run this computer as a Red Hat Network Proxy Server, there are a few more things that you need to do. As you configure this RHEL computer, you'll be working from the command line interface. You do remember how to do this, don't you?

First, this computer needs to recognize its own Fully Qualified Domain Name (FQDN). While this can be accomplished through a DNS (Domain Name Service) server, you'll need to update your `/etc/hosts` file with your FQDN. For example, I've added the following line to my version of this file:

```
192.168.1.1     enterprise3d.example.com
```

Note

Please note that configuration details associated with the Red Hat Network have changed from time to time, so you may need to modify the steps listed in this section for your Red Hat Network account.

Configuration Suggestions

To keep your system secure, it's best to disable any services which you don't need. For example, while the CUPS (Common Unix Print System) is enabled by default even on a minimal installation of RHEL, you're probably not going to use this computer as a print server. You can therefore disable this software with the following command:

```
chkconfig cups off
```

It would be even better if you could uninstall all unneeded services, but that isn't always possible. In fact, with a RHEL minimal installation, most services that are installed are due to dependencies. Some of those services you might be tempted to uninstall are necessary for a Red Hat Network Proxy Server. While some of the installed services are not required, detailing those services is beyond the scope of this book.

Firewall Provisions

Because Red Hat does not support the use of a firewall on a Red Hat Network Proxy Server, you should disable any firewall tools such as `iptables` or `ipchains` on that computer. The `iptables` service is installed by default on RHEL 3 and 4. You can disable this service with the following commands:

```
service iptables stop
chkconfig iptables off
```

Because you won't have firewall tools on this computer, it will likely sit behind a firewall. It needs to communicate with the Red Hat Network. To do so, it requires open ports for outbound connections to regular and secure Web services, on TCP/IP ports 80 and 443. It's normal to have these connections open for most computers on an Internet connected network, so your system is probably already set. However, you may need to reconfigure your firewall to open these ports.

However, if your Proxy Server connects to a Red Hat Network Satellite Server on an external network, you'll also need to configure your firewall to allow inbound connections on TCP/IP port 5222. For details on firewalls and using the `iptables` command, see *Real World Linux Security, 2nd Edition* by Bob Toxen (Upper Saddle River, N.J.: Prentice Hall, 2003).

Synchronizing Time

It's important to make sure the clocks on the computers on your network are relatively synchronized. The standard method is with the NTP daemon (`ntpd`), which relies on the Network Time Protocol (NTP).

To configure the NTP service, add at least three active time servers to the associated `/etc/ntp.conf` configuration file and make sure the NTP daemon runs when you start RHEL. A list of public NTP servers is available online from ntp.isc.org/bin/view/Servers/. Many networks depend on these servers. If overloaded, their responses may be delayed, and that's not good for a time server. As described on the noted Web site, the administrators of these servers may require you to notify them, and you often need to get authorization to link to their servers.

Some servers, especially those known as "Stratum 2" servers, are two levels away from official clocks and aren't as heavily loaded. While they are less accurate, the variance is some small fraction of a second, which causes no problems for most network applications, including the Red Hat Network Proxy Server. Stratum 2 servers generally do not get as much traffic. If so noted on the Public NTP server Web site, you may connect to them without notifying their administrator.

To make sure the NTP server is running (and runs the next time you boot RHEL), run the following commands:

```
service ntpd start
chkconfig ntpd on
```

Configuring the Proxy as a Router

In many scenarios, you'll want to configure your Red Hat Network Proxy Server between your LAN and a gateway to the Internet. As the associated software includes the router associated with the jabberd project (jabberd.jabberstudio.org), the process is simpler than it would be for a regular router.

Routing on a RHEL computer allows network communication between networks over that computer. All you need to do is configure forwarding of IP packets. You can do so during the current RHEL session with the following command:

```
echo '1' > /proc/sys/net/ipv4/ip_forward
```

To make sure RHEL enables routing the next time you boot, you'll need to set the following line in your Linux kernel system control configuration file, /etc/sysctl.conf:

```
net.ipv4.ip_forward = 1
```

Registration Required

Before you can download the Red Hat Network Proxy Server software, you need to register that computer on the Red Hat Network. The most straightforward method is with one of the following commands:

```
rhn_register
up2date --register
```

Alternatively, if you have not yet registered this computer, the first time you run the up2date command, the Update Agent runs the registration process automatically.

Even if you've installed RHEL in a minimal configuration, Red Hat supports a low-intensity blue graphical screen for the Update Agent, similar to what you see if you install RHEL in text mode. Before you register, you're taken through

☞ Some of the latest features associated with the Red Hat Network.

☞ The Red Hat Privacy agreement.

☞ A login page; you should already have a registered account on the Red Hat Network, as described in Chapter 1. For more information, see rhn.redhat.com.

☞ Registering a system profile, which includes basic information about your hardware.

☞ Sending a profile with a list of installed packages to the Red Hat Network.

This is an excellent time to make sure this RHEL computer is up to date with the latest packages. You've read about using the Update Agent on RHEL in Chapter 1. Just remember, you don't have the benefit (or curse, perhaps) of the GUI for this process. Now that you've registered this computer, you may be able to complete this process with a command that completely updates the system with all relevant packages:

```
up2date -u
```

When complete, you can download Red Hat Network Proxy Server software. We'll illustrate the process from a Red Hat Network administrative account in the following sections.

Getting to the Right Channel

Before you can administer the Red Hat Network Proxy Server software, you'll need to subscribe to the Red Hat Network Tools software channel. In the next subsection, I'll show how you can even "push" the installation of Proxy Server software. To subscribe to the right channel, you'll need to take the following steps:

1. Log into the Red Hat Network. Assuming you've installed a minimal version of RHEL 4, there would no Web browser on the Proxy Server computer. You can log into the Red Hat Network from any other computer.

2. Click the Systems link. If you've properly registered the Proxy Server computer on your account, you'll see the name of your system on this Web page. Otherwise, return to the Proxy Server computer and try registering it again.

Note

There are other ways to register a computer on a Red Hat Network account. For more information, see the Red Hat Network client configuration guide, available from www.redhat.com/docs/manuals/RHNetwork/.

---

3. Click System Entitlements. You'll need to change the entitlement for your Proxy Server computer to a Base Management Entitlement, and include an Add-On Provisioning entitlement.

4. Select the name of your Proxy Server computer. It should open the subscription and configuration details associated with that computer. You can see mine in Figure 2-4.

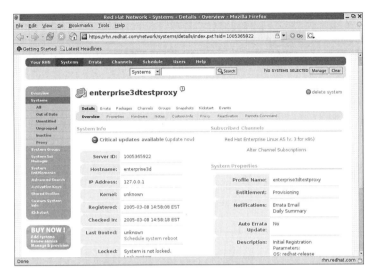

Figure 2-4   Red Hat Network configuration details

5. Under Subscribed Channels, click Alter Channel Subscriptions. Now you can add the Red Hat Network Tools channel.

To install the packages required for a Red Hat Network Proxy Server, continue to the next section. Do not log out of your Red Hat Network account.

Installing Proxy Packages

Now you'll install the packages required for a Red Hat Network Proxy Server. It's available from the Red Hat Network Tools channel that you just configured in the previous section. If you're not already there, log into your Red Hat Network account, and click Systems. Click the name of your Proxy Server computer.

1. Now you'll select the Proxy Server packages. Click Packages, and then click Install. In the Filter by Package Name box, enter rhncfg. This leads to the screen shown in Figure 2-5, which lists the basic packages associated with the Red Hat Network Proxy Server.

If no packages are shown, they may already be installed on your system. For example, you can verify installation of the basic Red Hat Network client configuration libraries with the rpm -q rhncfg command.

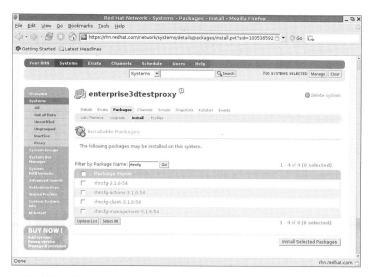

Figure 2-5   Red Hat Network Proxy Server packages

2. Select all `rhncfg` packages shown in Figure 2-5, and click Install Selected Packages. Click Confirm on the next screen. You'll see a message that "…package install has been scheduled…" for your computer.

3. Repeat this process to schedule installation for the `rhns-certs-tools` package, to support SSL certificates for your network.

4. You don't have to wait until the next scheduled update. Return to your Proxy Server computer, and run the `rhn_check` command. The Red Hat Network automatically checks for the new packages that you want to install. It then downloads and installs these packages along with any dependencies. Figure 2-6 shows the messages you'll see after logging in remotely to your Proxy Server computer (via SSH) and running `rhn_check`.

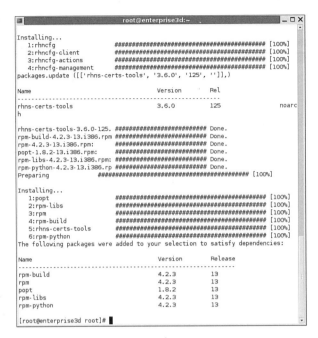

Figure 2-6   Installing packages per Red Hat Network settings

5. Return to your Red Hat Network account. You can confirm installation. Click Details, and then click Events. See what happened in your System History.

6. Before you continue, you'll need to add several files and directories. These commands allow you to configure and control your Proxy Server through your Red Hat Network account:

```
mkdir -p /etc/sysconfig/rhn/allowed-actions/script
touch /etc/sysconfig/rhn/allowed-actions/script/run
mkdir /etc/sysconfig/rhn/allowed-actions/configfiles
touch /etc/sysconfig/rhn/allowed-actions/configfiles/deploy
```

Now you can provision your system as a Proxy Server.

Provisioning a Proxy Subscription

To provision your system as a Proxy Server, log into the Red Hat Network. Click Systems. Select the computer that you want to use. Click Details, and then click Proxy. If you have a valid and available Proxy subscription, you should see a screen similar to Figure 2-7.

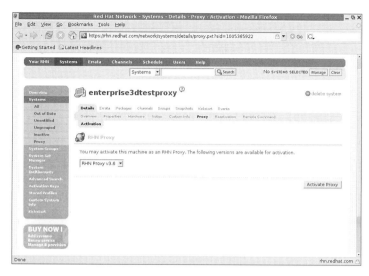

Figure 2-7   Assigning a computer as a Proxy Server

Note

To review your Red Hat Network entitlements, click Channels and then click Channel Entitlements. You'll see a list of software channels to which you can subscribe.

Now you can provision your system as a Proxy Server.

Configuring the Proxy Server

Now that you've installed the required software packages, you can start the Proxy Server configuration process through your administrative Red Hat Network account. Log into that account, navigate to the Proxy Server computer, click Details, and then click Proxy. Click the Activate Proxy button shown in Figure 2-7. This starts the Red Hat Network Proxy Installer. Follow these steps:

1. When you see the "Welcome to the RHN Proxy installer" screen, click Continue.

2. You'll have to agree to the Red Hat terms and conditions; more information is available at www.redhat.com/licenses/. Click I Agree to continue.

Note

If you see errors related to configfiles.deploy or scriptorun, you forgot to create the directories as described in step 6 of the previous section.

---

3. At the Configure RHN Proxy Server screen shown in Figure 2-8, you can configure the following parameters:

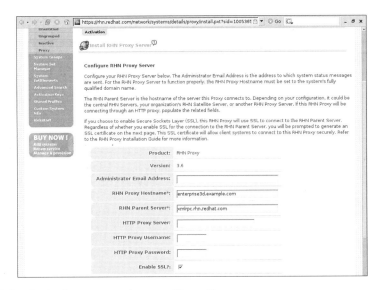

Figure 2-8   Assigning a computer as a Proxy Server

☞ **Administrator Email Address:** The desired administrative email address for critical messages; a substantial number of error-related emails are possible. I get them for every unsuccessful connection to the Proxy Server.

☞ **RHN Proxy Hostname:** The FQDN for this proxy server.

☞ **RHN Parent Server:** The name of the parent server is another Red Hat Network Proxy Server, a Red Hat Network Satellite Server, or the central Red Hat Network Server at xmlrpc.rhn.redhat.com.

☞ **HTTP Proxy Server:** If there is a regular proxy server between your LAN and the Internet, you'll need to enter the name and port of that server. Because proxy services use a different TCP/IP port number (3128) from regular (80) or secure (443) Web services, you should not use the http or https prefixes in the proxy server's FQDN. Use a FQDN in a hostname:port format, such as proxy.example.com:3128.

☞ **HTTP Proxy Username and HTTP Proxy Password:** If your LAN's proxy server requires a username and password, you can enter them in the noted text boxes.

☞ **Enable SSL:** Finally, while you don't have to configure a Red Hat Network Proxy Server using the Secure Sockets Layer (SSL), it's a good idea. It is the default. However, it may be easier to do after you've completed this process.

If you Enable SSL now, the next page you see will be the Configure SSL page shown in Figure 2-9. In that case, you'll have to proceed to the next section, "Creating the Cert Keys," to create a SSL key file to insert here before proceeding. The archive will have a `.tar` extension.

After you've completed your entries, press Continue. You should now see an Install Progress screen similar to Figure 2-10.

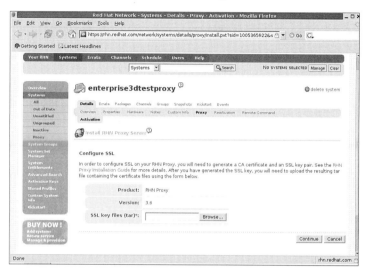

Figure 2-9   Assigning a computer as a Proxy Server

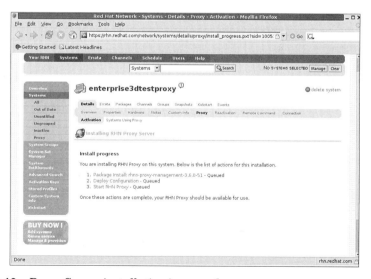

Figure 2-10   Proxy Server installation is queued

4. Return again to the Proxy Server computer. You can wait until the next update, or start the update yourself with the `rhn_check` command.

5. After the `rhn_check` command is complete, return to the Red Hat Network. Refresh your browser from Figure 2-10. The previous steps that were queued should now be listed as Completed.

6. Restart your Proxy Server with the following command:

```
service rhn-proxy restart
```

7. Verify that your Red Hat Network Proxy Server is working; you should see output similar to the following:

```
service rhn-proxy status
squid (pid 5515 5513) is running...
httpd (pid 5551 5550 5549 5548 5547 5546 5545 5544 5532) is running...
jabberd router (pid 5580) is running...
```

Your Red Hat Network Proxy Server system is now ready for clients. If you've configured a SSL Proxy Server, you'll need to create cert keys for the Proxy Server and Web clients.

Creating the Certificate Keys

To secure your Update Agent system, create certificates for your Proxy Server and associated clients. This requires you to return to the Proxy Server and use the `rhn-ssl-tool` command, with several different options. Don't run any of these commands until you understand the whole process as I describe in this section.

The `rhn-ssl-tool` command is part of the `rhns-certs-tools` package that you installed earlier in this process. There are two major command options. The first allows you to create a Certificate Authority (CA) for your network:

```
rhn-ssl-tool --gen-ca [followed by many options]
```

The second option creates Web server CA key sets, which is required for your Proxy Server:

```
rhn-ssl-tool --gen-server [followed by many options]
```

Let's examine these options one at a time. To generate a proper CA for your network, you need to specify appropriate directories for the certificates, using secure passwords with certificates that reflect basic parameters for your organization. You can review some of the switches (which come after `--gen-ca`) in Table 2-2. You don't need to use all the switches shown; however, the more you use, the more unique the CA you create.

Table 2-2   rhn-ssl-tool --gen-ca configuration options

Option	Description
`--gen-ca`	Generates a Certificate Authority key pair and more for your network, also based on options which follow
`-f`	Forces the creation of a new CA key pair
`-d=DIR`	Specifies the directory where CA files are built
`--ca-key=FILE`	Specifies the filename for the private CA key; not required—by default, the command creates a `RHN-ORG-PRIVATE-SSL-KEY` file
`--ca-cert=FILE`	Specifies the filename for the public CA key; not required—by default, the command creates a `RHN-ORG-TRUSTED-SSL-KEY` file
`--set-country=CODE`	Sets a country code
`--set-state=CODE`	Sets a code for your state or province
`--set-city=CODE`	Sets a code for your city or town
`--set-org=ORG`	Defines the name of your organization—your choice
`--set-org-unit=UNIT`	Defines a group within your organization—your choice

For a complete list of switches associated with the `--gen-ca` option, run the `rhn-ssl-tool --gen-ca --help` command. I don't include switches such as `--password=PASSWORD`, because there is no reason to help a "shoulder surfer" by typing your CA password in clear text. The `rhn-ssl-tool` command prompts you for the password if you don't use the `--password` switch.

On my Proxy Server, I run the following command:

```
rhn-ssl-tool --gen-ca --dir="/root/ssl-build" --set-state="Somewhere
Else" --set-city="Nice One" --set-org="Mommabears" --set-org-
unit="home office"
```

This command first prompts for a password. Remember this password. You'll have to use the same password shortly. It then generates a private and public CA key in the `/root/ssl-build` directory, with messages related to your location and organization. My use of this command leads to the following output:

```
Using distinguishing variables:
     --set-country      = "US"
     --set-state        = "Somewhere Else"
     --set-city         = "Nice One"
     --set-org          = "Mommabears"
     --set-org-unit     = "home office"
     --set-common-name  = ""
     --set-email        = ""
```

This command adds several files to the specified `/root/ssl-build` directory, as noted in Table 2-3.

Table 2-3   rhn-ssl-tool --gen-ca generates the following files

Filename	Description
`latest.txt`	Lists files for Proxy Server clients, including the RPMs and the public SSL key
`rhn-ca-openssl.cnf`	Text configuration file for SSL keys
`RHN-ORG-PRIVATE-SSL-KEY`	Not used, unless you generate additional SSL keys
`RHN-ORG-TRUSTED-SSL-CERT`	Key for client use; should be copied to the `/usr/share/rhn` directory on each Proxy Server client
`rhn-org-trusted-ssl-cert-<version>.noarch.rpm`	RPM package for Proxy Server; can be installed on clients
`rhn-org-trusted-ssl-cert-<version>.src.rpm`	Source code package

Now, you can configure the Web server keys. Remember, to have a proxy server, you also need a Web server. The packages that you installed through your Red Hat Network account earlier install a customized version of an Apache and Squid proxy server.

To generate proper Web server keys, specify appropriate directories for the certificates, using secure passwords, with certificates that reflect basic parameters for your organization. You can review some of the switches (which come after `--gen-ca`) in Table 2-4. You don't need to use all the switches shown; however, the more you use, the more unique the CA you create.

Table 2-4   rhn-ssl-tool --gen-server configuration options

Option	Description
`--gen-server`	Generates an SSL key set, along with an RPM and tar archive for that set, and other items based on options that follow
`-d=DIR`	Specifies the directory where CA files are built
`--startdate=YYMMDDHHMMSSZ`	Sets a start date in two-digit format: year, month, day, hour, minute, second, in "Zulu" time, also known as GMT or UTC
`--set-country=CODE`	Sets a country code
`--set-state=CODE`	Sets a code for your state or province

Option	Description
`--set-city=CODE`	Sets a code for your city or town
`--set-org=ORG`	Defines the name of your organization—your choice
`--set-org-unit=UNIT`	Defines a group within your organization—your choice
`--set-hostname=HOSTNAME`	Required only if you're building the key on a computer other than the Proxy Server
`--set-email=EMAIL`	The email address of the certificate administrator

For a complete list of switches associated with the `--gen-server` option, run the `rhn-ssl-tool --gen-server --help` command. I don't include switches such as `--password=PASSWORD`, because there is no reason to help a "shoulder surfer" by typing your CA password in clear text.

On my Proxy Server, I run the following command:

```
rhn-ssl-tool --gen-server --dir="/root/ssl-build" --set-
state="Somewhere Else" --set-city="Nice One" --set-org="Mommabears"
--set-org-unit="home office" --set-email="michael@example.com"
```

This `rhn-ssl-tool` command proceeds to generate SSL keys and certificate files for the Web server, as well as associated RPMs that you can use to build corresponding keys on client computers. The command adds several files to the hostname (enterprise3d) subdirectory of the `/root/ssl-build` directory, as noted in Table 2-5.

Table 2-5   rhn-ssl-tool --gen-server generates the following files

Filename	Description
`latest.txt`	Lists files for Proxy Server clients, including the RPMs and the public SSL tar archive
`rhn-server-openssl.cnf`	Text configuration file for Apaches SSL keys and certificates
`server.crt`	The Web server's public certificate file
`server.csr`	The Web server's certificate request

continues

Table 2-5   continued

Filename	Description
`server.key`	The Web server's private SSL key
`rhn-org-httpd-ssl-archive-<host>-<version>.tar`	An archive of the server keys
`rhn-org-httpd-ssl-key-pair-<host>-<version>.noarch.rpm`	An RPM package for you to install on the Proxy Server, which installs the server* files in the `/etc/httpd/conf/` directory
`rhn-org-httpd-ssl-key-pair-<host>-<version>.src.rpm`	Source code package

Now that you've generated SSL keys for the Proxy Server and Web host, you'll need to install the public CA certificate on each client and the Web service RPM on the Proxy Server.

Note

If you haven't already done so, you can use the archive of the server keys, with the .tar extension, to configure SSL on your Red Hat Network Proxy Server. When available, upload the archive, as shown in Figure 2-9. Then you can return to the Red Hat Network Proxy Server Install Progress page shown in Figure 2-10.

While you're still on the Proxy Server, install the associated Web service RPM. For the commands shown, you can install the Web service SSL certificate RPM package with the following command:

```
cd /root/ssl-build/enterprise3d/
rpm -i rhn-org-httpd-ssl-key-pair-enterprise3d-1.0-1.noarch.rpm
```

Next, make the RHN-ORG-TRUSTED-SSL-CERT file that you created earlier available for clients. Because the software that you've installed has created a Web server on the Proxy Server computer, you can copy this file to the `/var/www/html/pub` directory. To make sure your Proxy Server computer's Web server sees this file, you'll need to restart the Web service with a command, such as

```
service httpd restart
```

One more command; to make the files in the `/var/www/html/pub` directory accessible to Web clients, you'll need to change ownership of these files to the apache user. It's easy to do with the following command:

```
chown apache.apache /var/www/html/pub/*
```

In the next section, we'll install this file on a client.

Note

Alternatively, you can copy and then install the RPM that you created earlier with the `rhn-ssl-tool --gen-ca <lots of stuff>` command. In this case, it's the `rhn-org-trusted-ssl-cert-1.0-1.noarch.rpm` package; if you install this RPM on any client, it will automatically install RHN-ORG-TRUSTED-SSL-CERT in the correct directory.

2.2.2   Configuring the Proxy Client

Now you can set up RHEL 2.1, 3, and 4 clients for your Red Hat Network Proxy Server computer. The process is straightforward. You'll need to reconfigure the update agent to take updates from the Proxy Server (instead of the Red Hat Network). Then, you'll need the cert keys created during the Proxy Server installation process.

If you have a substantial number of RHEL clients, you can automate this process with scripts. Finally, you can make sure RHEL clients are updated on a regular basis, either through the Red Hat Network or with a regular cron job.

Copying the Certificate Key

Before you start configuring the Update Agent, you'll need to copy the right client cert key. It's embedded in the RHN-ORG-TRUSTED-SSL-CERT file described earlier.

If you've followed the instructions described earlier, this file is already available through the Web server on the Proxy Server computer. You need to download the RHN-ORG-TRUSTED-SSL-CERT file. You can do so with a graphical browser. Navigate to this computer with the name or even the IP address of that computer, and you'll see a simple home page, as shown in Figure 2-11.

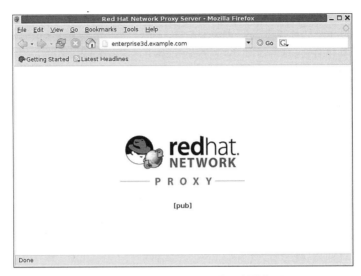

Figure 2-11   The Red Hat Network Proxy Server local Web site

Now the process is easy. Click the [pub] link, and you're taken to a list of files on the Proxy Server's `/var/www/html/pub` directory. You can now download any files that you've loaded to that directory, including `RHN-ORG-TRUSTED-SSL-CERT` .

Alternatively, you can use the `wget` command to download this file from the command line interface:

```
wget http://enterprise3d.example.com/pub/RHN-ORG-TRUSTED-SSL-CERT
```

After you download the `RHN-ORG-TRUSTED-SSL-CERT` file, copy it to the `/usr/share/rhn` directory. Alternatively, if you've loaded the RPM on the Web server, you could install it directly with the following command:

```
rpm -i http://enterprise3d.example.com/pub/rhn-org-trusted-ssl-cert-
1.0-1.noarch.rpm
```

Tip

The previous command may seem too long. In many Web browsers, you can right click a link, select Copy Link from the shortcut menu, and then paste it into the command line.

Reconfiguring the Update Agent

After all this talk about the Proxy Server, there's one possible surprise: it is *not* a proxy server for your clients. (For details, see the note at the beginning of this chapter.) You won't configure your clients' Update Agent for a proxy server (unless you've configured one on a different computer, between your client and your Red Hat Network Proxy Server).

You could partially reconfigure the Update Agent in the GUI with the `up2date-config` command. The GUI interface allows you to modify only some of the settings you need. Alternatively, you could reconfigure the Update Agent from the command line interface using the `up2date-nox --configure` command. But as you can see for yourself, the interface is rather inconvenient.

The best way to fully reconfigure the Update Agent is to open its configuration file, `/etc/sysconfig/rhn/up2date`. In that file, you'll want to change three settings. The defaults are as follows, which pull updates through the Internet from Red Hat's servers:

```
noSSLServerURL=http://xmlrpc.rhn.redhat.com/XMLRPC
serverURL=https://xmlrpc.rhn.redhat.com/XMLRPC
sslCACert=/usr/share/rhn/RHNS-CA-CERT
```

You'll want to change these parameters. For example, my proxy server has a FQDN of enterprise3d.example.com, so I've changed the following parameters in my version of `/etc/sysconfig/rhn/up2date`:

```
noSSLServerURL=http://enterprise3d.example.com/XMLRPC
serverURL=https://enterprise3d.example.com/XMLRPC
sslCACert=/usr/share/rhn/RHN-ORG-TRUSTED-SSL-CERT
```

Automating Updates (Local and Remote)

You can configure updates remotely through the Red Hat Network. Details are beyond the scope of this book. However, the general procedure is straightforward:

1. Log into your Red Hat Network account.
2. Configure the systems that you want to administer in one group.
3. Click Systems, followed by System Groups.
4. Select the group you've configured for this purpose.
5. Select Work With Group.
6. Click Provisioning, followed by Remote Command, which takes you to the screen shown in Figure 2-12.

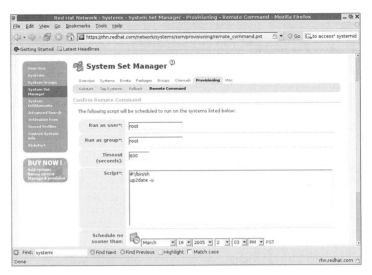

Figure 2-12   Configuring commands for a Red Hat Network group

7. Enter the commands of your choice. As you can see in the figure, I've entered the `up2date -u` command; as soon as each system in this group checks in, it'll automatically update the system per the latest requirements.

Potential Problems

If there are problems after you've followed the instructions described in this chapter, there are a number of things that you can do.

☞ Run the `up2date -u` command from the client command line interface. Check for error messages in the output.

☞ Inspect the log files in the `/var/log/rhn` directory. The `rhn_proxy_broker.log` file notes attempted connections, with possible errors. The `rhn_proxy_redirect.log` file notes requests that are actually redirected to the Red Hat Network.

☞ If you don't see expected entries in the `rhn_proxy_broker.log` file, there may be a problem on your LAN, at least between your Proxy Server and client.

☞ Make sure the services associated with the Proxy Server are running with the `service rhn-proxy status` command. You should see services associated with the Web server (`httpd`), the Proxy Server (`squid`), and the Jabber router (`jabberd`).

☞ Try accessing the Proxy Server Web site. Open a browser from a client, and navigate to the Proxy Server FQDN or IP address. You should see a page similar to Figure 2-11.

☞ Try a `rhn_check` command from your Proxy Server computer. If it successfully connects upstream to a Satellite or the Red Hat Network, it'll run
any pending commands that you may have configured through your Red
Hat Network account.

☞ Rerun the configuration commands described in this chapter. You might
find that you've installed the SSL certificate on the wrong computer.

While this is far from a comprehensive list, I've personally run into a few
problems during this process:

☞ Connection problems noted on a client should have a corresponding message in the `/var/log/rhn/rhn_proxy_broker.log` file. A connection refused
message might indicate problems with the SSL keys that you've installed
on the Proxy Server's `/etc/httpd/conf` directory or the SSL key on the
client's `/usr/share/rhn` directory.

☞ If there's a problem in `rhn_proxy_broker.log`, it should be associated with
an ERROR message in this file. The Web server needs read access to the
`/etc/sysconfig/rhn/systemid` file; you might need to change ownership or
permissions to this file. If there's a problem accessing the upstream Red
Hat Network (or Satellite) server, you'll see it here, and you might have a
network problem on the Proxy Server computer.

☞ A successful connection to the Proxy Server should be shown in the
`/var/log/rhn/rhn_proxy_redirect.log` file.

2.3 CONFIGURING RED HAT REBUILDS

As discussed in Chapter 1, there are a number of groups that have built their
own distributions (without the Red Hat trademarks) from RHEL source code.
As they've built from source code published by Red Hat, their distributions are
known as rebuilds. When Red Hat releases an update, it releases updated
source code. In most cases, you can build your own packages from Red Hat
source code and update your rebuild distribution.

However, this isn't always true. The rebuild groups do not have access to
the same tools as the developers at Red Hat. There are often subtle differences
in the resulting distributions, which go beyond the trademarks.

For example, when I loaded the source code associated with a rebuild kernel, there were dependencies. I had two choices. I could have searched for the
packages built for the rebuild which would satisfy those dependencies. Instead,
I had the packages built by Red Hat handy and used those instead. That did
not work. The source code for the rebuild distribution would not install until I
included dependent packages as customized for that distribution.

In other words, if you administer patch management on a network with rebuild distributions, it's important to configure your updates for repositories with packages built for the rebuild distribution.

Just to give you a feel for this process, I describe how you can configure updates from two of the RHEL rebuilds to the right repositories. Naturally, because the rebuilds do not offer subscriptions to the Red Hat Network, one other major difference is their techniques for patch management. The process is similar to that you learned about in Chapter 1 for Fedora Linux.

Note

Don't use the `rhn_register` command with the rebuild distributions. It tries to register your computer on the Red Hat Network, which requires a subscription. And if you have a subscription, you probably don't want to be running a rebuild distribution in the first place.

Unlike with the other sections in this chapter, I do not describe how you can create a local patch management repository for your LAN. You can learn about this process with the `apt` and `yum` tools in the last half of this book.

In the following sections, I'll show you how you can keep two of the "rebuild" distributions up to date; one uses `yum`; the other user `apt`. You can use the techniques described in Chapters 4 through 7 to create apt or yum repositories as needed for these rebuild distributions.

2.3.1 CentOS

My personal favorite rebuild version of RHEL is CentOS-4. This popular rebuild goes by a number of names. The proper name of the group is The cAos Foundation. CentOS 2, 3, and 4 are rebuilds of RHEL 2.1, 3, and 4 (with Red Hat trademarks removed).

The basic steps are as follows:

1. Identify your Update Agent configuration files; they are associated with files in the `/etc/sysconfig/rhn` directory.
2. In addition, if you want to configure `yum` updates you can do so in the files in the `/etc/yum.repos.d` directory.
3. Find one or more preferred mirror sites for downloads.
4. Identify the repositories that you want to keep up to date.
5. Revise your `yum` configuration files to point to those repositories.

If you want to use `up2date`, as with Fedora or RHEL, you can cite or add repositories to the `/etc/sysconfig/rhn/sources` file.

Alternatively, the cAos rebuilds are configured to use their yum repositories. As of this writing, the default version of CentOS-4's `yum.conf` configuration file cites the repositories in `/etc/yum.repos.d/CentOS-base.repo` file. Some older versions of CentOS linked `yum.conf` to `centos-yum.conf` for repository lists.

Note

Alternatively, `apt` is available with CentOS, and you can use the techniques described in Chapter 4 to update from apt repositories.

As with Fedora Linux, it is in your best interest to revise your `yum` or `sources` configuration files to point to mirrors closer to your location. First, because cAos is a volunteer organization, they've had to ask for contributions to pay for all the downloads from their servers. Second, for the reasons described in Chapter 1, downloads from servers physically closer to your network are faster. You'll have to wait for Chapters 5 and 7 for instructions on how to create apt or yum repositories on your networks.

Before you revise your yum configuration files, find one or more preferred mirrors. The cAos list of mirrors is available from www.caosity.org/download/mirrors. Their "Tier 1" mirrors connect to the Internet at OC3, which corresponds to about 155Mbps. Naturally, this bandwidth is shared with others who may be downloading simultaneously.

Note

If you're downloading a distribution for the first time, you may be interested in Bittorrent, which supports large file downloads from multiple sources. I downloaded a CentOS-4 ISO file with their entire distribution (2GB+) in just over an hour on my home connection. However, not all Linux distributions support Bittorrent. For more information, see www.bittorrent.com.

As an example, inspect the mirror shown in Figure 2-13. The URL is the start of what you can enter as a `baseurl` in your `/etc/yum.repos.d/CentOS-Base.repo` file. The `$releasever` is 4.0. The subdirectories are as shown, and you can (and should) double-check that what you enter corresponds to an available directory on your selected mirror.

If you want to use the `up2date` commands, you'll also want to modify the `yum` commands in `/etc/sysconfig/rhn/sources` to configure updates from the mirror of your choice.

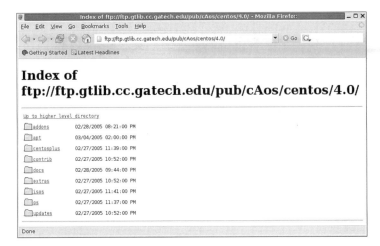

Figure 2-13   A cAos Mirror Site

After you select a mirror, select the repositories that you want to keep up to date. The standard settings in `/etc/yum.conf` refer to `.repo` files in the `/etc/yum.repos.d` directory. For example, for the Georgia Tech updates repository, you can navigate to

```
ftp://ftp.gtlib.cc.gatech.edu/pub/cAos/centos/4.0/updates/i386/
```

You should find RPMS, headers, and repodata subdirectories in each repository. The `$relserver`, as defined from the `centos-release` RPM package, is 4.0. The `$basearch` comes from the `uname -i` command. Thus, you could edit the `[update]` stanza in your `CentOS-Base.repo` file to read

```
baseurl=ftp://ftp.gtlib.cc.gatech.edu/pub/cAos/centos/$releasever/updates/$basearch/
```

You can add URLs from additional `[update]` mirrors below this line, such as

```
http://caos.oregonstate.edu/centos/$releasever/updates/$basearch/
```

When complete, you can use the `yum` command to keep your system updated. Alternatively, if you want to use `up2date`, you'll want to select an appropriate mirror for `/etc/sysconfig/rhn/sources`. For example, you could replace the default Base channel:

```
yum centos4-Base http://mirror.centos.org/centos/4/os/$ARCH/
```

with

```
yum centos4-Base http://caos.oregonstate.edu/centos/4/os/$ARCH/
```

and make parallel changes to the other channels listed in this file.

2.3.2   Lineox

Of all the available RHEL rebuild distributions, I've included Lineox as a contrast to CentOS. I do not claim that Lineox or CentOS are any better in quality or support when compared to other RHEL rebuilds. However, Lineox provides a nice contrast. They are based in Europe, offer paid levels of support, and configure their updates using apt.

One unique feature of Lineox is their paid support for updates and local patch management mirrors. Their patch management system is configured by default to synchronize your repositories on a daily basis. Lineox actually omits the Red Hat Update Agent from its Lineox 4 rebuild distribution.

We'll describe the apt patch management process in Chapters 4 and 5. However, you can configure your /etc/apt/sources.list file using basic methods described in Chapter 1 for Debian Linux. But remember, distributions related to Red Hat use a different package format, the RPM. So the default commands in the /etc/apt/sources.list file include the rpm command, including

```
rpm http://www.raimokoski.com/ pub/lineox/4.0/updates/i386 updates
rpm-src http://www.raimokoski.com/ pub/lineox/4.0/updates/i386 updates
```

You may not want to use the default URL unless you're physically located near the home of Lineox, which is Finland. Lineox makes other options available in various files in the /etc/apt/sources.list.d directory.

2.3.3   Other Rebuilds

As suggested in Chapter 1, there is a wide variety of rebuild distributions created from RHEL source code. There are almost as many variations on patch management as there are rebuilds. But they almost invariably rely in some way either on the yum or apt commands. And you can learn more about these commands and associated repositories in the second half of this book.

2.4   SUMMARY

Patch management is an important tool for keeping Red Hat and related clients up to date. There are a variety of related tools associated with Red Hat patch management updates.

In this chapter, you learned basic patch management techniques on clients that are running Red Hat and related distributions. You can create your own Fedora repositories; however, their frequent updates and new releases make patch management of Fedora clients more problematic. RHEL client subscriptions support patch management through a Red Hat Network account. You can even create your own local Proxy Server repository of patches, which minimizes the load on your network's Internet connection and speeds updates to most RHEL clients on your LAN. Finally, you learned a bit about how patch management varies on rebuild distributions that use RHEL source code.

In the next chapter, you'll learn about SUSE's patch management systems and how they can be adapted for SUSE and RHEL clients.

## CHAPTER 3

SUSE's Update Systems and rsync Mirrors

Just as Red Hat supports patch management systems suitable for one and many computers on a network, SUSE supports similar systems. We briefly explored how you can keep individual SUSE Linux Professional and Linux Enterprise Server systems up to date using YaST in Chapter 1, "Patch Management Systems." In this chapter, we'll explore the process in more detail.

Tip

If you want to know `rsync`, read this chapter, particularly section 3.2.2. The lessons there apply to copying a mirror from any `rsync`-capable update server.

As each version of SUSE Linux Professional becomes publicly available, you can update this distribution using public mirrors. While SUSE Linux Enterprise Server is not publicly available (except for limited evaluation copies), you can still download updates with an authorized subscription. After you've synchronized your updates, you can configure local updates from other SUSE systems on your LAN.

Novell has incorporated Linux update capabilities into its Zenworks Linux Management (ZLM) service. It's more flexible than one might think. You can install ZLM on SUSE Linux Enterprise Server or Red Hat Enterprise Linux. Unfortunately, a full description of how to use ZLM is well beyond the scope of this book.

Note

SUSE Linux Enterprise Server is Novell's subscription enterprise level distribution. SUSE Linux Professional Workstation is SUSE's workstation offering through version 9.3. Newer versions of SUSE for the workstation are known simply as SUSE Linux.

In this chapter, I'll examine the software update options associated with the SUSE Linux distributions. Next, you'll set up an update server for both the Professional and Server SUSE distributions. Finally, I'll examine how to get ZLM up and running on SUSE and Red Hat systems.

3.1   THE YaST UPDATE SYSTEM

While you learned to update a SUSE Linux Professional system in Chapter 1, you were just scratching the surface of how you can manage patches with YaST. To explore what else you can do, open YaST. Click Software on the left screen. In SUSE Linux Professional, you'll see six options. In SUSE Linux Enterprise Server, you'll see slight variations, as shown in Figure 3-1.

Note

If you're using SUSE Linux Professional 9.3/SUSE Linux 10.0, you'll see some additions from SUSE Linux Professional 9.2. It includes *Installation into directory for Xen*, which allows you to create a Xen virtual machine, as described at www.xensource.com. The *Media Check* option allows you to check the integrity of installation CDs or DVDs. Because neither option is related to patch management, details are beyond the scope of this book.

Figure 3-1   SUSE Linux Enterprise Server Update options

You already learned about the Online Update process in Chapter 1. I'll explore each of the remaining options in more detail. While I'm illustrating using the GUI version of YaST, SUSE has made a low-resolution version of this tool available for those who prefer to work from the command line.

As you read through this section, you'll notice that some of the sections are interactive; in other words, the changes you can make for one option may affect what you do with other options. After you've made initial changes, you may want to run YaST Online Update again.

3.1.1 The YaST Package Manager

In this section, we'll examine the Install and Remove Software option, which is known as Software Management in SUSE Linux 10. It allows you to manage the SUSE packages on your system. If you want to install additional packages, the Install and Remove Software option looks by default to the source from where you originally installed SUSE Linux. If you've installed SUSE from a DVD and want to change that to a network source, read the next section.

When you select Install and Remove Software, you're taken to a search screen. If there are any current conflicts in your packages, you'll see them here, as shown in Figure 3-2.

Figure 3-2   This computer wasn't patch managed well

In this case, I have a problem because I downloaded and installed a new version of the GNU mailing list manager, `mailman`, without regard to dependencies. Because I didn't use YaST to manage this patch, SUSE didn't catch this dependency until now. Fortunately, I was able to downgrade the `mailman` package, as suggested during this process. As you can see from Figure 3-2, I could have ignored the dependency. Under the Expert drop-down menu, I could have saved the dependency list to a text file.

Now you can search for the packages of your choice. As you can see in the left pane of Figure 3-3, you can run your search based on any of the following criteria:

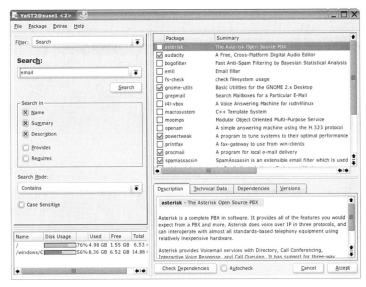

Figure 3-3   Identifying email-related packages

☞ *Name* of the package

☞ *Summary* of the package description

☞ *Description* associated with the package (which is what you see when you run `rpm -qi packagename`)

☞ Files the package *Provides*; may be useful when you have a dependency that cites a specific file

☞ Package that *Requires* what you specify; can help you confirm when you're installing a package that satisfies a number of dependencies

For example, if you're looking for all packages related to "email," you could use it as a search term, specifying Name, Summary, and Description to list all available SUSE packages related to email. As you can see in Figure 3-3, the list probably goes beyond what you might need; for example, YaST includes `asterisk` in this list because the text string "email" is part of the word "Voicemail," which is in the description of the `asterisk` package (which is related to Internet telephones, a.k.a. Voice over IP).

You can change how this works. Click on the Search Mode drop-down text box. It allows you to change how the search term is used. The options include Begins With, Exact Match, Use Wild Cards, and Use Regular Expression. You can also use the Case Sensitive option to make the search term case sensitive.

However, the list also reveals packages that may be useful for the email administrator. As you can see in Figure 3-4, the `ximian-connector` package allows your client's Evolution email managers to act as clients on a Microsoft Exchange network. The package name was changed for SUSE Linux 10.0 to evolution-exchange.

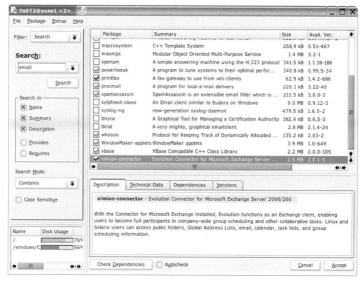

Figure 3-4   More details about each package

You can also review the size and version numbers associated with each candidate package. Size may be important if the target partition is near its limits. Version numbers can help you verify functionality or security.

You can also check for dependencies with the Check Dependencies button at the bottom of the window. For example, when I include the `printfax` package and use this function, YaST identifies dependencies, as shown in Figure 3-5. Alternatively, YaST provides a message that "All package dependencies are OK."

Figure 3-5   Dependencies

Select the Autocheck box at the bottom of the window to automate dependency checking and click Accept. The update process begins. YaST looks to your original installation source. If it's a DVD, it checks your drive. If the DVD isn't there, YaST prompts you to insert it. YaST then installs and removes those packages you've identified (along with dependencies). It then writes the system configuration. In most cases, it backs up any configuration files associated with upgraded packages. When complete, it prompts you as to whether you want to install more packages. If you do, you're returned to the screen similar to that shown in Figure 3-3.

If you've copied your installation CDs to another location (or have configured a different installation source directory), you'll be interested in the next section. When you've changed your installation source, you can return to this menu and make changes without having to find your DVD.

3.1.2   Change Source of Installation

One option that simplifies patch management on a network is a common installation source. In other words, I've copied my installation CDs to a server, which can provide the original installation files for the other SUSE computers on my network. For the rest of this chapter, I refer to the directory where I've copied the installation CDs as the "installation source."

After you copy your installation files to a server, return to the YaST Software module. Select Change Source of Installation (Installation Source on SUSE Linux 10.0). This opens the Software Source Media window shown in Figure 3-6, where you can add your new installation source. YaST allows you to change your source to one of seven different types, which we can divide into five categories: supplementary packages, an authenticated network server, a NFS server, local media, and a local directory.

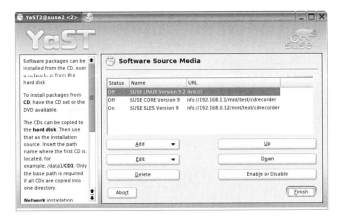

Figure 3-6   Software Source Media

> **Note**
>
> I had to use the CDs to create my SUSE Linux Professional 9.2 network installation source. YaST does not appear to recognize a network installation source created from the SUSE DVD.

Supplementary Packages

In some cases, SUSE makes supplementary packages available online at ftp.suse.com and through mirrors. For example, to update my KDE system, I could use the supplementary packages from a nearby mirror, with a subdirectory such as

```
i386/supplementary/KDE/update_for_9.2
```

Naturally, I can add this to the Software Source Media list. However, this does not work unless the directory includes the `media.1` subdirectory, which you can copy from the first installation CD.

Authenticated Network Server

You can configure your installation source on a network server. FTP, HTTP, and Samba servers may require authentication. If you select any of these three options, you're taken to the Server and Directory window shown in Figure 3-7.

Figure 3-7   Configuring a network installation source

For example, assume that you've configured a local FTP server at IP address 192.168.1.1, in the `pub/` subdirectory. You'd enter the IP address in the Server Name, and the `pub/` subdirectory in the places shown. If you've configured more than one source, you'll see it in the Software Source Media window. You can select the source of your choice in that window and then click Up to make YaST look at that source before others on your list.

If you've configured an authenticated username and password on the FTP server, you can also enter it in the appropriate text boxes shown in

Figure 3-7. Otherwise, FTP and HTTP servers support anonymous authentication. Naturally, unless you actually want others to access your installation source online, you should protect your FTP or HTTP server through your network firewall and other settings detailed in good Linux networking texts, such as *Linux Administration Handbook* by Evi Nemeth, Garth Snyder, and Trent Hein (Upper Saddle River, NJ: Prentice Hall, 2002).

On the other hand, Samba generally requires a username and password, based on how you might configure a Microsoft Windows-style network.

NFS Server

The Network File System (NFS) is native to Unix/Linux computers and is often considered more efficient if your networks are limited to those operating systems. If you configure an NFS share with your Linux computers, you can configure your installation source as a shared NFS directory. All you need is the following:

☞ NFS Server name or IP address

☞ The name of the shared directory from the NFS server

Local Media

If you've installed SUSE over a network, your software source points to that installation source. However, you might want a different software source, such as the SUSE installation DVD, for computers such as laptops.

Insert the CD or DVD. Click Add -> DVD (or CD). YaST mounts the CD/DVD, and then adds the CD/DVD to your Software Source Media list.

Local Directory

If you're experimenting with SUSE at home, you may choose to configure an installation source on a dedicated directory on your local computer. All you need is the name of the directory.

3.1.3   Installation Into Directory

Return to the YaST Software Menu. Select the Installation Into Directory option. You can configure and then install another copy of SUSE Linux into a subdirectory. By default, the subdirectory is `/var/tmp/dirinstall`. You could use this option to create a sample SUSE installation, which you could then copy to other computers on your network. If you do so, keep in mind that standard cron jobs purge files in `/var/tmp` directories on a regular basis. Because this is not really related to patch management, we will not explore it further.

3.1.4 Patch CD Update

If you have a subscription to SUSE Linux Enterprise Server, you can get patch CDs on a regular basis. In the YaST Software Menu, click Patch CD Update. You'll see a window similar to SUSE Online Update, as described in Chapter 1. When you get a patch CD, you can either insert it at this time or redirect this screen to point to a network location for the patch CD.

As with other SUSE Online Updates, you can configure YaST to point to a local directory; an FTP, HTTP, or Samba server; a shared NFS directory; or a CD or DVD. After you connect to the patch CD, whether local or over a network, the process is the same as the Online Update that you learned about in Chapter 1.

3.1.5 System Update

In the YaST Software Menu, select System Update. You're taken to an Installation Settings screen similar to Figure 3-8. This menu allows you to patch applications and services on your system. First, it allows you to update your system based on the current version of the installed distribution. When you select this option, as you can see, there are four parts to the YaST System Update: Update Options, Packages, Backup, and Language.

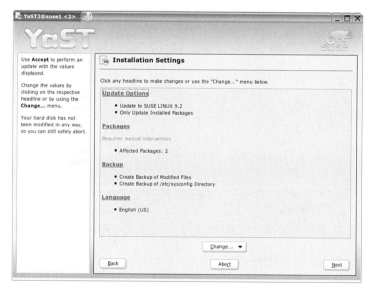

Figure 3-8 Options associated with YaST System Update

Update Options

Update Options allow you to customize how you update and manage patches for your system from appropriate SUSE servers or mirrors.

When you select Update Options, an Update Options screen displays similar to Figure 3-9. By default, YaST allows you to update only those packages which you have installed. However, you can update with other packages associated with your distribution. The options depend on your distribution. If you're running SUSE Linux Enterprise Server, your Update options include the following:

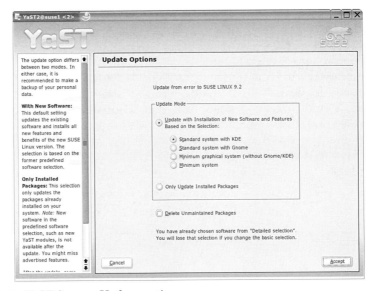

Figure 3-9   YaST System Update options

☞ Default System installs packages associated with the KDE desktop and the CUPS print server.

☞ Full installation adds all packages associated with SUSE Linux Enterprise Server.

☞ A minimal graphical system installs just those packages required for a GUI environment. The standard Linux desktops (GNOME, KDE) are not included in this grouping.

☞ A minimal system includes just those packages required to run a Linux system. This option does not include any graphical desktops and is suitable for a dedicated server.

In contrast, if you're running SUSE Linux Professional, there is no default or full installation option. Instead, you can select

☞ **Standard System With KDE** supports the default SUSE KDE Desktop Environment.

☞ **Standard System With GNOME** allows you to refocus this desktop for users who prefer the GNOME Desktop Environment.

In both cases, the Delete Unmaintained Packages option is economical. If there are packages that won't work after an update, such as older, or superseded services, they are deleted.

Packages

The number of packages listed is the number of packages that will be updated. In many cases, you'll be warned of packages that can't be upgraded or updated automatically. But the number shown is just a summary. Select the Packages link. If you've included some packages not directly associated with your SUSE distribution, you'll probably get a list similar to that shown in Figure 3-10.

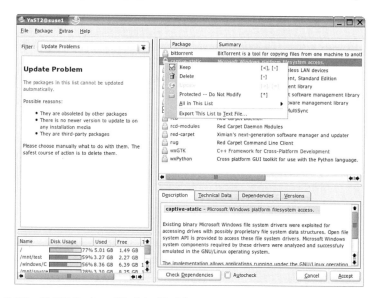

Figure 3-10   YaST System Update Problems

As you can see, most of the packages on the list are protected from changes during this process. They are mostly third-party packages that I don't want changed. However, I can set up each package to be updated or deleted. Right-click the package of your choice to review your options. Additional options are available from the All In This List submenu. Make any desired changes, and select Accept to return to the Installation Settings screen.

Backup

Naturally, when you update applications, it is in your interest to back up associated configuration files. In fact, it is always best to keep a backup of those files, at least those in the /etc directory.

However, YaST will back up configuration files associated with updated packages. You can change what YaST does. Select Backup, and you can make YaST

☞ Create backups of all modified files

☞ Create a complete backup of all files in the /etc/sysconfig directory

☞ Delete any older backups of modified files

Language

You can configure YaST to use the language of your choice during this process. SUSE supports over 20 different languages.

3.1.6 UML Installation

User Mode Linux (UML) allows you to configure virtual Linux machines within SUSE Linux. While it may be useful for you to test specific SUSE features, it is not related to patch management and is therefore not covered in this book. UML has been superseded by Xen in the latest SUSE distribution.

3.1.7 YOU Server Configuration

SUSE Linux Enterprise Server supports one method of caching updates to a LAN, known as YaST Online Update (YOU). When configured, updates are saved to the following directory:

```
/var/lib/YaST2/you
```

By default, it's configured to use your authorized SUSE Enterprise account to cache updates locally, in two channels:

☞ SUSE-CORE, the base packages associated with this distribution

☞ SUSE-SLES, the packages closely associated with SUSE Linux Enterprise Server functionality

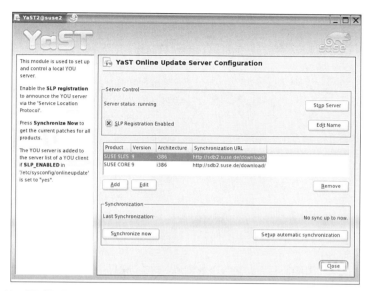

Figure 3-11   YaST Online Update (YOU)

To set this up, first synchronize your SUSE Linux Enterprise Server with one of the available portals. As with Red Hat Enterprise Linux, sites for SUSE updates are limited. You can synchronize with one of two sites, described in Table 3-1. For the latest list, see http://support.novell.com/techcenter/articles/SLES_Updating.html.

Table 3-1   SUSE Linux Enterprise Server Update sites

Location	URL
Germany	http://sdb.suse.de/download/
Ireland	http://sdb2.suse.de/download/

You can edit the update server information as shown in Figure 3-12. You'll need to add at least your authentication information for each channel. Highlight the product, and select Edit. The User Name and Password should correspond with what you use on your Novell account.

Figure 3-12   YaST Online Update (YOU)

The Product Name, Version, and Architecture need not change (unless you've recently upgraded to a new version of this distribution). Enter the Synchronization URL from Table 3-1.

After you've configured your servers, select Synchronize Now. YaST Online Update should now contact your servers. If there's a problem, you'll see a message like "Synchronization failed for..." If you've verified your user name, password, and associated information as shown in Figure 3-12, the problem might simply be related to the download server. I've had problems on occasion connecting to both servers from Table 3-1.

You might not see any results in this window for some time. Remember, you're downloading several hundreds of megabytes of packages, patches, and more. If you want to monitor the progress of the download, monitor changes to the `/var/lib/YaST2/you/mnt/i386/update` directory. For example, i586 RPM packages for SUSE Linux Enterprise Server version 9 downloading through the SUSE-CORE channel can be found in the `SUSE-CORE/9/rpm/i586` subdirectory. Therefore, you can monitor the download with the following commands:

```
cd /var/lib/YaST2/you/mnt/i386/update
ls -ltr SUSE-CORE/9/rpm/i586
```

Naturally, after you've downloaded packages for your update server, you'll want to keep it up to date. Select the Setup automatic synchronization option. This opens the YOU Server Automatic Synchronization Setup window, which allows you to configure updates as a daily cron job. The results are stored in `/etc/cron.d/yast2-you-server`. This file points to a `syncfile` script in the `/var/lib/YaST2/you` directory, which you can run at any time. My version of this script includes the following commands, which synchronizes updates with the SUSE-SLES and SUSE-CORE repositories, as well as a mirror of a SUSE Linux Professional 9.2 update mirror:

```
#!/bin/sh
/usr/bin/online_update -G -p "SUSE SLES" -v 9 -a i386 -u
http://sdb.suse.de/download/
/usr/bin/online_update -G -p "SUSE CORE" -v 9 -a i386 -u
http://sdb.suse.de/download/
/usr/bin/online_update -G -p "SUSE LINUX" -v 9.2 -a i386 -u
http://sdb.osuosl.org/suse/
```

3.1.8   A Local YaST Online Update

After the download is complete, you can update SUSE Linux Enterprise Servers on your local network from this location. All you need to do is point your computer to the appropriate directory. Share the appropriate directory and point your Online Update to this location.

Updating the Local Server

If you've downloaded the cache to a local SUSE Linux Enterprise Server, you may want to update that server. It's a straightforward process. Just follow these steps:

1. Start YaST and select Online Update. This opens the Welcome To YaST Online Update window.
2. Select New Server. This opens the Select Type of URL window.
3. Select Directory and then OK.
4. If you don't know the local directory, you can select Browse. But from the previous section, you've created a repository in the `/var/lib/YaST2/you/mnt` directory. Enter the appropriate directory and select OK.
5. Select Next. If you're successful, you'll see a message that YaST Online Update is "Retrieving information about new updates."
6. You're taken to the YOU Patches screen, similar to that shown in Figure 3-13.

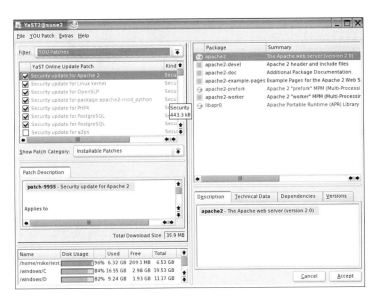

Figure 3-13   Many security patches are available

As you can see, I haven't updated this server for quite some time. There are security patches of several types. Search through your own version of this screen. You may find

☞ Security updates that are not installed by default. If you use the service, you should strongly consider installing the security update. If you do not use the service, you should consider uninstalling that service.

☞ Recommended updates are not security related, but may incorporate improvements to essential services, such as YaST. Some are configured to be installed by default.

☞ Optional updates may include non-essential hardware drivers, language files, and more.

It's worth taking some time to consider what you'll choose to install during this update. You don't have to install everything at once. You can update just a few services, check the result on your system, and update again. You've already done the hard work of downloading the updates to your local SUSE Linux Enterprise Server. They'll still be there when you're done.

7. After you've selected the systems that you want to update, click Accept.

8. If there are patches which affect the functionality of currently running services, you're warned to stop that service.

One example is shown in Figure 3-14. In this case, if you're updating the PostgreSQL database service, updates may boot your users with unexpected results. If you see warnings, you can either continue to Install or Skip installation of the highlighted patch.

Figure 3-14   Update warning

9. YaST Online Update starts downloading and installing the patch, in this case, from your local directory. But the patches are local, so you should not have to wait very long.

   The total progress bar might not reach 100 percent before the process stops. However, you should see a message, such as "Installation finished." At that point, select Finish to continue.

10. YaST Online Update now writes the patches to your system configuration. When complete, you're returned to the main YaST Software Menu.

Sharing the Update Directory

Now that you've updated the local SUSE Linux Enterprise Server, you can share the local repository with other SUSE Linux Enterprise Server computers on your network. As you saw earlier, YaST Online Update allows you to configure updates from local and network sources.

While this is not a networking book, the most straightforward way to share directories with other Linux computers is with a Network File System server. For more information on the NFS, see *Mastering Red Hat Enterprise Linux 3* by Michael Jang (Alameda, CA: Sybex, 2004).The server and client tools are normally available, even in a minimal Linux installation.

To share the directory that you created earlier, follow these steps:

1. Add the following line to the local `/etc/exports` file:

```
/var/lib/YaST2/you/mnt/    192.168.0.0/24(ro,sync)
```

This line assumes that the directory where you synchronized patches is as shown, and your LAN is configured on the private 192.168.0.0 IPv4 network. These computers are allowed read-only (`ro`) access, and changes must be synchronized (`sync`) regularly.

2. If the local NFS Server is not already running, you'll need to start it with a command such as

```
/etc/init.d/nfsserver start
```

If your NFS server is already running, you may need to substitute `restart` for `start`.

3. Make sure you export the share with the `exportfs -a` command.

4. Confirm your exports with the `showmount -e` command.

Updating Neighboring Servers

Now you can proceed to updates of remote SUSE Linux Enterprise Servers on your network. To do so, follow these steps:

1. Confirm your access to the shared NFS directory. If the SUSE Linux Enterprise Server with the repository is suse2.example.com (you can substitute the IP address), you can confirm access with the following command:

```
showmount -e suse2.example.com
```

2. On the remote SUSE Linux Enterprise Server, start YaST. Select Online Update from the Software menu. Select New Server. In the Select Type of URL window, select NFS, and click OK.

3. Enter the name or IP address of the NFS server, as well as the shared directory, and click OK. You'll see the shared directory in the Location text box in a format similar to

```
nfs://suse2.example.com//var/lib/YaST2/you/mnt/
```

If this doesn't work, you can mount the shared directory locally, and use the techniques described in the previous section.

4. Now you can update your system using the techniques described in the previous section.

5. When the process is complete, consider configuring automatic updates. Return to YaST Online Update. Select the Configure Fully Automatic Update option.

3.2   CONFIGURING YaST PATCH MANAGEMENT FOR A LAN

There are two ways to configure an update server for SUSE Linux Professional. You can configure a mirror using a YaST Online Update Server on SUSE Linux Enterprise Server. Alternatively, you can configure a mirror using the `rsync` command. One relative advantage of `rsync` is that it is customizable; if you use the YaST Online Update Server for regular PCs, you'll end up with updates for 32-bit and 64-bit systems.

In either case, you'll need to select a mirror. You can find a current (but not necessarily complete) list at http://www.novell.com/products/linuxprofessional/downloads/ftp/int_mirrors.html. Before you select a mirror, check it out in the browser of your choice. A mirror you see in this list may be redirected to a different URL. For example, the mirror I use, http://suse.oregonstate.edu, is automatically redirected to http://suse.osuosl.org.

3.2.1   Creating a Local Mirror with YaST Online Update Server

If you have a SUSE Linux Enterprise Server, you can create a mirror for SUSE Linux Professional computers on your network by using the YaST Online Update Server. First, select a mirror.

Note

This section assumes you're maintaining updates for SUSE Linux Professional version 9.2. If you're maintaining updates for a different version of SUSE Linux Professional, substitute version numbers accordingly.

Selecting a Mirror

You've seen how this server works earlier in this chapter. To open YaST in the GUI, click Main Menu -> System -> Control Center (YaST). Select Software in the left pane, and select YOU Server Configuration. In the YaST Online Update Server Configuration window, select Add. This opens a window similar to that shown previously in Figure 3-12.

In this unnamed window, you'll need to enter four parameters:

☞ Product Name—SUSE Linux is normally sufficient.

☞ Version—Enter the version number for the distribution, such as 9.2; this becomes the subdirectory with the mirror in the `/var/lib/YaST2/you/mnt/i386/update` directory.

☞ Architecture—Specify the architecture for your distribution, such as i386.

☞ Synchronization URL—Enter the SUSE Mirror of your choice. In my case, I've entered http://suse.osuosl.org/suse/. Depending on mirror availability, some trial and error may be required.

☞ Authentication—In most cases, anonymous authentication is supported on SUSE mirrors associated with SUSE Linux Professional.

Synchronizing
After you've entered the parameters of your choice, click OK. Back in the YaST Online Update Server Configuration window, select Synchronize now. The YaST Online Update Server proceeds through any products configured in this menu. Depending on the timing of your update, you may be downloading several gigabytes of data. This process may take some time.

If there are problems, you'll see a message such as "Synchronization failed." The mirror of your choice may not be available. If successful, you'll find update RPMs and patches in the `/var/lib/YaST2/you/mnt/i386/update` directory. In my case, where I've created an update server for SUSE Linux Professional 9.2, they are located in the following subdirectories:

☞ `9.2/patches`—Includes a list of patches available to YaST Online Update on your SUSE Linux Professional client computers.

☞ `9.2/scripts`—Includes any update scripts, which can help you install specialized components.

☞ `9.2/rpm`—Contains RPMs in the i586, i686, and noarch subdirectories.

YaST Online Update Server Troubleshooting
If you do have problems, you can troubleshoot the YaST Online Update Server. Exit from the server. Check the current version of the associated log file in `/var/log/YaST2/y2log`. If you can't figure out the problem from the log file, there is more that you can do.

By default, YaST Online Update Server settings are stored in the `you_server_settings` file, in the `/var/lib/YaST2/you` directory. If you've configured authentication settings, usernames and passwords are stored in the `password` file in the same directory. For the next troubleshooting step, move these files. The following commands move them to your `/root` home directory (default permissions won't allow you to move these files as a regular user):

```
mv /var/lib/YaST2/you/you_server_settings ~
mv /var/lib/YaST2/you/password ~
```

If you've previously downloaded packages to your system using the YaST Online Update Server, they'll still be there.

Note

By default, the `/var/lib/YaST2/you/password` file is "world-readable"; in other words, associated with 644 permissions. And this file can display your passwords in clear text. You can change the permissions of this file to be readable only by the file owner without affecting the performance of the YaST Online Update Server.

Return to YaST. Reopen the YaST Online Update Server. You'll see the original two products (SUSE SLES and SUSE CORE) in the update list. You'll need to re-edit these products for the required usernames and passwords.

Re-enter the information described earlier for your SUSE Linux Professional mirror. Try the synchronization process again.

3.2.2 Creating a Local Mirror with rsync

One thing to remember when creating a local mirror is that YaST Online Update looks for patches in the `i386/update/9.2/patches` subdirectory. Except for the version number, this is true for all SUSE Linux distributions. So when you create a mirror, make sure updates are downloaded to that subdirectory. Otherwise, YaST Online Update won't be able to find what you've so laboriously downloaded to your LAN.

Therefore, make sure that this subdirectory is part of the tree where you download the update mirror. You might even want to create a separate partition for this mirror, to keep it from crowding (or being crowded out by) other demands on your system. For convenience, I've created this mirror on an external Firewire (IEEE 1394) hard drive, on partition `/dev/sdb3`. I've also created a `/mnt/yast` directory to mount these updates.

For those distributions with mirrors, you can create and then update your systems with a local mirror server. While you could use commands such as `wget` or FTP clients to create a mirror, I prefer the `rsync` command. After you create an `rsync` mirror, updates download only the data that changed since the last download. Therefore, you can keep a `rsync` mirror up to date fairly quickly and keep the load on your Internet connection to a minimum.

> **Note**
> The first time you create a repository mirror, chances are that you'll be download-ing several gigabytes of data. Be sure you have a sufficiently high-speed connec-tion to the Internet before attempting to create a mirror. The first time I downloaded a SUSE repository on my home cable modem (which runs up to 5 Mb/s), the process took approximately 20 hours.

For this purpose, you need a public mirror which accepts `rsync` connec-tions. Some trial and error may be required. Many FTP sites listed in the offi-cial SUSE Linux Professional list of international mirrors also accept `rsync` connections.

The `rsync` command is important for anyone interested in patch manage-ment. It helps the administrator create and maintain a local patch manage-ment server with a minimum of load on the Internet connection. When created, updates download only data that has changed since the last update. This is the briefest of introductions to the world of `rsync`; for more information, see the `rsync` man page, as well as its Web site at http://rsync.samba.org.

In its simplest invocation, you can copy all files, in archive mode (`-a`), from `/home/michael` to `/home/donna` with the following command:

```
rsync -a /home/michael /home/donna
```

When you repeat this command in the future, it only copies what has changed within each file in Michael's home directory, and nothing more. Naturally, this is a powerful tool for backups. You can use `rsync` over a Secure Shell connection. For example, the following command takes the files from the `/home/michael` directory on the computer named remotepc.example.com and copies them locally to `/tmp`:

```
rsync -a -e ssh michael@remotepc.example.com:/home/michael /tmp
```

Now, determine whether your preferred mirror site supports `rsync`, and on what directories. For example, you can find the applicable directories on the distro.ibiblio.org site with the following command (don't forget both colons at the end of the URL):

```
rsync -n mirrors.kernel.org::
```

If the site you try does not have an rsync server, you won't see a response, and you may need to interrupt the command (with Ctrl-C) to get back to the command line.

Watch for hints in the message that you see. For example, this particular command included in the response:

```
suse       Novell SUSE mirror
```

This gives me a hint to the directory structure I need for the `rsync` command. I could synchronize all SUSE related contents, using the `::suse/` subdirectory, but that would download all available SUSE Professional distributions and versions, which might be several dozen more gigabytes than I really need.

With a look at the directory structure at this site, I can find a list of updates with the following command:

```
rsync -n mirrors.kernel.org::suse/i386/update/9.2/
```

As discussed earlier, I've created a separate partition, `/mnt`. I can copy and then synchronize the contents of `/mnt` with this particular server. Don't forget to create the `/mnt/i386/update/9.2` directory. The fastest way is with the following command, which creates all needed directories:

```
mkdir -p /mnt/i386/update/9.2 command.
```

With the following command, I can download patches to the `/mnt/i386/update/9.2/patches` directory. But don't run this command, at least not yet:

```
rsync -a mirrors.kernel.org::suse/i386/update/9.2/.
/mnt/i386/update/9.2
```

While this command should work, you won't know until it's done. There is more that you can and should do with this command. As with most commands, the `-v` switch allows you to watch the progress as `rsync` does its work. Fortunately, `rsync` allows you to "double" the messages; you can expand this command to `rsync -avv <whatever you're syncing>`.

But that's still not enough. If you don't need the source code associated with the download, you can shorten the required time. You know that source code RPMs normally end with the `.src.rpm` extension, so you can exclude those files with the `--exclude=*.src.rpm` switch.

Finally, you can collect statistics associated with the download to make sure you're not getting overloaded. For this purpose, `rsync` supports the `--stats` switch. Finally, we're ready to start the process. If the ibiblio.org mirror is closest, you could start the `rsync` process with the following command:

```
rsync -avv --stats --exclude=*.src.rpm
mirrors.kernel.org::suse/i386/update/9.2/. /mnt/i386/update/9.2
```

When the process is complete, you'll have a mirror, fresh with SUSE updates, ready for use by the other SUSE Linux Professional computers on your network.

Pointing Updates to the Mirror

Now you can point your updates to the local mirror. It's a simple process. If the SUSE Professional or SUSE Linux computer that you want to update is local, all you need to do is point YaST Online Update to the correct mirror directory.

As described in the previous section, I've configured my own SUSE Professional Linux update mirror site in the `/mnt/i386/update/9.2` directory. I know this includes a patches subdirectory. Because YaST Online Update looks for an `i386/update/9.2/patches` subdirectory, all I need to do is point it to `/mnt`.

If I have a SUSE Professional Linux system on the same computer as the update mirror, I can configure the update with the following steps:

1. Start YaST. If you're in the GUI, click the Main Menu button -> System -> Control Center (YaST).
2. Under the Software menu, select Online Update.
3. Under the Installation Source drop-down box, specify User-Defined Location.
4. In the Location text box, specify the directory with the `i386/update/9.2/patches` subdirectory. With the directory defined earlier, that's

   ```
   dir:///mnt/
   ```

   Naturally, if you're working with a different version of SUSE Linux or SUSE Linux Professional, the version number in the directory will change accordingly. Of course, you can use the New Server or Edit Server options to specify the directory.
5. Select Next to continue. You'll see a list of YaST Online Update (YOU) patches similar to that shown in Figure 3-15.

   Review the list of available patches. You'll note that some are upgrades; others are installations of new packages over previous versions. Not all options will be selected. Make any desired changes.
6. When you're ready with your desired patches, select Accept to continue.
7. The Patch Download process provides a warning if there are any critical upgrades, such as those related to the Linux kernel.

   One example of a warning is shown in Figure 3-16. Make appropriate selections related to any warnings that you see.

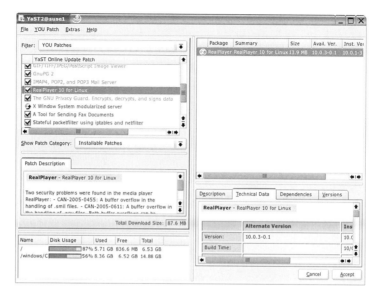

Figure 3-15   Patches on a SUSE professional workstation

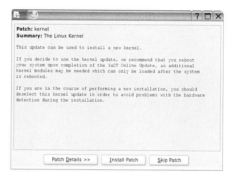

Figure 3-16   Kernel update warning

8. YaST Online Update proceeds with installing the patches and upgrades as you specified. But because the patches are local, you should not have to wait very long.

The total progress bar may not reach 100 percent before the process stops. However, you should see a message such as "Installation finished." At that point, you can select Finish to continue.

9. YaST Online Update now writes the patches to your system configuration. When complete, you're returned to the main YaST Software Menu.

Sharing the Update Directory

Now that you've updated the local SUSE Linux workstation, you can share the local repository with the rest of your network. As you've seen, YaST Online Update allows you to configure updates from local and network sources.

While this is not a book on networking, the most straightforward way to share directories with other Linux computers is with an NFS server. For more information on the NFS, see *Linux Administration Handbook* by Evi Nemeth, Garth Snyder, and Trent Hein (Upper Saddle River, NJ: Prentice Hall, 2002). The server and client tools are normally available even in a minimal Linux installation.

To share the directory that you created earlier, follow these steps:

1. Add the following line to the local `/etc/exports` file:

   ```
   /mnt/i386/update/9.2      192.168.0.0/24(ro,sync)
   ```

   This line assumes that the directory where you synchronized patches is as shown and your LAN is configured on the private 192.168.0.0 IPv4 network. These computers are allowed read-only (`ro`) access, and changes must be synchronized (`sync`) regularly.

2. If the local NFS Server is not already running, you'll need to start it with a command, such as

   ```
   /etc/init.d/nfsserver start
   ```

   If your NFS server is already running, you may need to substitute restart for start.

3. Make sure to export the share with the `exportfs -a` command.

4. Confirm your exports with the `showmount -e` command.

Updating Neighboring Servers

Now you can proceed to updates of remote SUSE Linux Enterprise Servers, Professional Workstations, and later systems on your network. To do so, follow these steps:

1. Confirm your access to the shared NFS directory. If the SUSE Linux Professional workstation with the repository is suse2.example.com (you can substitute the IP address), you can confirm access with the following command:

   ```
   showmount -e suse2.example.com
   ```

2. On the remote SUSE Linux Enterprise Server, start YaST. Select Online Update from the Software menu. Select New Server. In the Select Type of URL window, select NFS, and click OK.

3. Enter the name or IP address of the NFS server, as well as the shared directory, and click OK. You'll see the shared directory in the Location text box in a format similar to

```
nfs://suse2.example.com//mnt/i386/update/9.2
```

If this doesn't work, you can mount the shared directory locally and use the techniques described in the previous section.

4. Now you can update your system using the techniques described in the previous section.

5. When the process is complete, consider configuring automatic updates. Return to YaST Online Update. Select the Configure Fully Automatic Update option.

3.3 ZENworks Linux Management

Novell is selling ZENworks Linux Management (ZLM) as a way to manage the life cycle of Linux systems. Naturally, patch management is a big part of the operating system life cycle, and its functions are integrated into ZLM, formerly known as Red Carpet Enterprise.

Nevertheless, with the skills already described in this chapter, you can still use local mirrors and download patches to help manage Linux computers on your own network. Many of the aforementioned tools can help you manage patches and updates on other Linux distributions. ZLM is a proprietary interface and is also used to manage many non-Linux operating systems. It is feature-rich; full coverage would require an additional book. In this section, you'll learn to install and configure a ZLM 6.6.1 server and client (which was the latest available when this book was drafted).

While this section briefly describes the Web-based interface, more can be done from the command-line interface, using commands such as `rug` and `rcman`. I do not provide detailed descriptions of these tools, as that would refocus this book toward a single proprietary solution that would not work for most Linux distributions. For detailed information on ZLM, see the associated administration guide, which you can download from www.novell.com/documentation/zlm/index.html.

3.3.1 Supported Clients and Servers

If you want to install a ZLM 6.6.1 server, you'll need a computer with SUSE Linux Enterprise Server 9 for Intel 32- or 64-bit computers. Alternatively, you can install ZLM on Red Hat Enterprise Linux 3 AS or ES for Intel 32-bit computers. As of this writing, ZLM 7 was still under development, and we expect that it will be installable as a server on Red Hat Enterprise Linux 4 and work for updates on SUSE Linux Workstation 9.3 and SUSE Linux 10.0 (along with the other clients distributions listed below). If you do not want to install either distribution on your network, you'll have to use the techniques previously described in this chapter to keep your SUSE computers up to date.

You can use ZLM to manage updates for a number of different clients. ZLM 6.6.1 clients are available for the following distributions:

☞ SUSE Linux Enterprise Server version 8 for 32-bit systems

☞ SUSE Linux Enterprise Server version 9 for 32-bit, many 64-bit, PowerPC, and S/390 systems

☞ SUSE Linux Professional Workstation version 9.1 and 9.2 for 32-bit and many 64-bit systems

☞ Red Hat Enterprise Linux 2.1 Workstation for 32-bit systems

☞ Red Hat Enterprise Linux 3 Workstation for 32-bit and many 64-bit systems

☞ Red Hat Enterprise Linux ES (Entry-level Server) 2.1 for 32-bit systems

☞ Red Hat Enterprise Linux ES 3 for 32-bit and many 64-bit systems

☞ Red Hat Enterprise Linux AS (Advanced Server) 2.1 for 32-bit systems

☞ Red Hat Enterprise Linux AS 3 for 32-bit and many 64-bit systems

3.3.2 Installing the ZLM Server

You'll need a license to operate ZLM. You can download a CD from download.novell.com; then use the search terms: `zenworks linux`. You can download the latest available version in ISO format, which you can then write to a CD.

When you have a ZLM CD available, you can install the ZLM server on one of the supported distributions. It includes an installation script, `rce-install`, which you can use to install ZLM server. To install ZENworks, insert and mount the ZLM CD, and then run the `rce-install` script. If the CD is mounted on the `/media/cdrecorder` directory, you can run the script with the following command:

```
/media/cdrecorder/rce-install
```

As shown in Figure 3-17, the script asks you to accept the license agreement. It asks for your activation code, email address, and any proxy information for your network. It then installs at least the Red Carpet Daemon, `rcd`, and the Red Carpet command-line client, `rug`. Support services and packages are also installed, including configuration files that allow you to control the ZLM using a Web server.

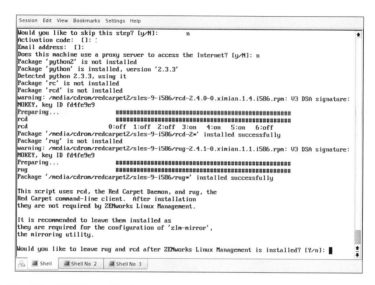

Figure 3-17   The ZLM installation process

Make sure that some essential packages are installed, including

☞ `zlm-server`—The core of the ZLM service

☞ `zlm-mirror`—Mirrors packages or channels to ZLM

☞ `zlm-server-cli`—Adds the `rcman` command, which allows you to administer ZLM from the command line interface.

3.3.3   Configuring the Web interface

When ZLM is installed, you can configure it from the Web interface. It's available through the secure Web protocol, HTTPS. Open the browser of your choice. If the name of the computer with ZLM installed is zlmserver.example.com, navigate to

```
https://zlmserver.example.com
```

Your browser should open up https://zlmserver.example.com/initial.php. At that point, you can configure initial administrative information with

☞ Your name
☞ The email address associated with your Novell account, which also becomes your ZLM username
☞ The password of your choice

You'll also need to configure the `server.key` file, which you should have gotten with your Novell ZLM license. To find the `server.key` file, navigate to your Novell account. It should be associated with the information for your ZLM license. Copy it to the `/etc/ximian/rcserver/` directory. Make sure the ownership of this file is appropriate. On SUSE, it should be owned by the `wwwrun` user and `www` group. On Red Hat, it should be owned by the `apache` user and `apache` group.

Now you can open ZLM locally or remotely. The next time you do so, you'll see a login screen where you'll need the username and password.

3.3.4   Configuring Administrators

In all but the smallest networks, there is normally more than one person who needs administrative privileges. It's easy to add another administrator. Log into the ZLM Web-based interface. Click the Admins link on the left side of the menu. This opens the Account Administration menu. You should see your account on the system. Click Create New Administrator. You can now add another ZLM administrative account, using the same information you just used to create your own account. The only difference is that you do not need to use the same email address you used to register ZLM with Novell.

Alternatively, you could set this up from the command line interface. You can add administrators with the `rce-init` command. For example, if your other administrator's email address is Joe@blow.abc, you'd run

```
rce-init -U Joe@blow.abc -P password -R "Joe Blow"
```

3.3.5   Adding Clients

The ZLM CD also includes the software required to set up ZLM clients. RPM packages for each of the aforementioned client distributions are available in the CD `redcarpet2/` subdirectory. The packages are straightforward; they include the following:

☞ Red Carpet Daemon and associated modules
☞ Red Carpet software updater and manager
☞ Red Carpet command line client (rug)

There are subdirectories under redcarpet2 for each supported client. The directory names are straightforward. The numbers are associated with version numbers of each distribution, as shown in Table 3-2. These directory names are important—you'll need to use them when you specify a target for update packages shortly.

Table 3-2   ZENworks Linux Management Client Categories

Directory	Description
rhel-21as-i386	Red Hat Enterprise Linux 2.1 Advanced Server for 32-bit systems
rhel-21es-i386	Red Hat Enterprise Linux 2.1 Entry level Server for 32-bit systems
rhel-21ws-i386	Red Hat Enterprise Linux 2.1 Workstation for 32-bit systems
rhel-3as-i386	Red Hat Enterprise Linux 3 Advanced Server for 32-bit systems
rhel-3as-x86_64	Red Hat Enterprise Linux 3 Advanced Server for 64-bit systems
rhel-3es-i386	Red Hat Enterprise Linux 3 Entry level Server for 32-bit systems
rhel-3es-x86_64	Red Hat Enterprise Linux 3 Entry level Server for 64-bit systems
rhel-3ws-i386	Red Hat Enterprise Linux 3 Workstation for 32-bit systems
rhel-3ws-x86_64	Red Hat Enterprise Linux 3 Workstation for 64-bit systems
sles-8-i386	SUSE Linux Enterprise Server 8 for 32-bit systems
sles-9-i586	SUSE Linux Enterprise Server 9 for 32-bit systems
sles-9-ia64	SUSE Linux Enterprise Server 9 for Itanium 64-bit systems
sles-9-ppc	SUSE Linux Enterprise Server 9 for Power PCs
sles-9-s390	SUSE Linux Enterprise Server 9 for IBM S/390 systems
sles-9-s390x	SUSE Linux Enterprise Server 9 for IBM S/390x systems
sles-9-x86_64	SUSE Linux Enterprise Server 9 for 64-bit systems
suse-91-i586	SUSE Linux Professional Workstation 9.1 for 32-bit systems
suse-91-x86_64	SUSE Linux Professional Workstation 9.1 for 64-bit systems
suse-92-i586	SUSE Linux Professional Workstation 9.2 for 32-bit systems
suse-92-x86_64	SUSE Linux Professional Workstation 9.2 for 64-bit systems

Additional packages in these directories satisfy associated dependencies. Install the packages from the directory associated with your client distribution, and then start the Red Carpet Daemon with the following command:

```
/etc/init.d/rcd start
```

Now ZLM is configured to use verified SSL certificates. For more information, see the associated Linux HOWTO document at www.tldp.org/HOWTO/SSL-Certificates-HOWTO. If you want to avoid SSL certificates, you can configure your setup as such on each client with the following command:

```
rug set require-verified-certificates false
```

Next, let your ZLM server know that you're ready to connect this client. To do so, add a connection to the ZLM server. Assuming the server name is zlmserver.example.com, you'd run the following commands to connect to the local ZLM server and disconnect from the default Red Carpet server:

```
rug service-add https://zlmserver.example.com/data
rug service-delete http://red-carpet.ximian.com
```

You'll also need to activate each client using a key that you can create in the next section. For example, if you've been told that the activation key is rhel-key, you'd run the following command:

```
rug activate rhel-key Joe@blow.abc
```

3.3.6 Setting Up Activations

To actually connect a client to ZLM, you'll need to set up an activation key. You can configure a single-use key or one that can be used for a whole group of clients. To create a reusable key from the Web-based interface, click Server in the left-hand pane, and then click the Create New Reusable Activations link. You can then enter the key and description of your choice. No special entries are required; for example, I've created the rhel-key for my Red Hat clients.

Alternatively, you can create a key from the command line interface with the appropriate rcman command:

```
rcman act-add --key=susewks-key
```

3.3.7 Creating Groups

After you've installed the ZLM client on a number of computers, you may want to configure some in groups. As you might expect, groups allow you to configure several computers in the same way. While you can create groups in the

Web-based interface, it is (in our opinion) simplest using the command-line interface. The following example creates the susewks group:

```
rcman group-add --desc="SUSE Workstations" susewks
```

All commands in this section prompt for your username and password. As you might remember, the username is the email address associated with the ZLM administrator. While there are switches that allow you to enter the username and password directly to the command, your password would be exposed in clear text.

Before you add members to a group, you'll want to do a few other things. If you want another administrator to have authority over this group, you can add his account with the following command:

```
rcman group-addemail susewks Joe@blow.abc all
```

You're prompted for your authorized username and password. You'll also add the activation key created earlier to the susewks group:

```
rcman act-addgroup susewks-key susewks
```

Now it's time to add the computers of your choice to the susewks group. For example, you could add the suse1 computer with the following command:

```
rcman group-addmachine susewks suse1
```

You can confirm the results. To list the members of the susewks group, issue this command:

```
rcman group-listmachines susewks
```

3.3.8   Configuring Channels

Before you can use ZLM to transfer patches, you need to configure one or more channels. The process is straightforward. For example, to add a PatchMan channel to ZLM, you could run the following command:

```
rcman channel-add "PatchMan" --desc="PatchManagement"
```

Add the following key:

```
rcman act-addchannel susewks-key PatchMan
```

Strangely enough, the `rcman` command returns an error when you have a multiple word description, such as "Patch Management." Now you can add gaggles of RPM packages to your channel. Consider the packages download to the YaST Online Update Server. As described earlier, one of the applicable directories on SUSE Linux Enterprise Server is `/var/lib/YaST2/you/mnt/i386/update/SUSE-CORE/9/rpm/i586`. You could navigate to this directory and then add the download RPMs to your ZLM channel with the following command:

```
rcman channel-addpkg --targets=suse-9-i586 --desc="PatchUpdates"
PatchMan *.rpm
```

You don't have to add every RPM package in a directory, but there are advantages to downloads such as those associated with YaST Online Update Server. There is less concern about conflicts and dependencies from such repositories.

3.3.9   Creating Transactions

Now you can configure transactions. First, make sure that your client is active. From the client, if you haven't already done so, add the service associated with your ZLM server.

```
rug service-add https://zlmserver.example.com/data
```

Activate your system with the encryption key created earlier.

```
rug activate susewks-key Joe@blow.abc
```

If you followed the instructions earlier in this chapter, you should have a PatchMan channel available. To see what channels are available on your system, run the following command:

```
rug channels
```

Now you can activate the channel of your choice. If PatchMan is the channel you want, you'd run the following command:

```
rug subscribe PatchMan
```

Now you can find updates available through your channel. For example, the command shown in Figure 3-18 lists any suggested or urgent updates that may be available through the PatchMan channel.

```
michael@suse1:~ - Shell No. 2 - Konsole <2>                        _ □ X
suse1:/home/michael # rug list-updates

Updates for channel 'PatchMan'
Urg | Name                  | Current Version | Update Version
----+----------------------+-----------------+----------------
sug | freeradius           | 1.0.0-5.2       | 1.0.0-5.4
sug | grip                 | 3.2.0-7         | 3.2.0-7.2
sug | kernel-default       | 2.6.8-24.5      | 2.6.8-24.14
sug | kernel-default-nongpl| 2.6.8-24.5      | 2.6.8-24.14
sug | kernel-source        | 2.6.8-24.5      | 2.6.8-24.14
sug | kernel-um            | 2.6.8-24.5      | 2.6.8-24.14
sug | mysql                | 4.0.21-4.2      | 4.0.21-4.4
sug | openal               | 20040902-2      | 20040902-2.2
sug | postgresql-libs      | 7.4.6-0.1       | 7.4.7-0.1
sug | telnet               | 1.1-41          | 1.1-41.2
sug | xorg-x11-libs        | 6.8.1-15.4      | 6.8.1-15.7

suse1:/home/michael # █
```

Figure 3-18   Available updates through a ZLM channel

You can install the packages of your choice. For example, if you want to install the updated version of `grip` (for recording CDs), just run the following command:

```
rug install grip
```

You're prompted to confirm before the download starts. If you confirm, ZLM downloads and then automatically installs the package you selected onto your computer. But this isn't very efficient. You can download and install all updates from subscribed channels with the following command:

```
rug update
```

But be careful; if you do not want to install all updates, such as a new Linux kernel, you'll have to remove the associated packages from the channel on the ZLM server.

3.4 SUMMARY

In this chapter, you learned to manage updates and patches on SUSE Linux Enterprise Server, SUSE Linux Professional Workstation, and SUSE Linux. With YaST, the process is straightforward for both distributions. The update process may require downloads of hundreds of megabytes or even gigabytes of data.

Naturally, if you're managing multiple SUSE computers, you'll want to keep downloads to a minimum. You can configure your own update server for SUSE Linux Professional workstations using appropriate `rsync` commands. After you have a local repository, you can keep it up to date fairly easily and update all the SUSE Linux Professional computers from that local repository.

While there are no public mirrors for SUSE Linux Enterprise Server, the YaST Online Update Server makes it possible to cache the content locally. That is important because, as of this writing, SUSE Linux Enterprise Server updates are available only from a couple of locations in Europe. With just a little work, YaST Online Update Server can also download and cache content from SUSE Linux Professional and SUSE Linux 10.0 and later mirrors. Finally, ZENworks Linux Management can help you manage patches on various SUSE and Red Hat computers.

## CHAPTER 4

Making apt Work for You

One of the popular Linux patch management systems is based on the Advanced Package Tool, known as apt. While it was developed for Debian Linux, it is the standard patch management tool for a number of Debian and Red Hat-based distributions, including Knoppix, Xandros, and even the Lineox rebuild of Red Hat Enterprise Linux. But if you prefer apt, the associated tools can be installed on most Linux distributions.

In this chapter, you'll learn the fundamentals of apt, including some of its more useful commands. Then you'll see how you can use apt to maintain a Debian client, beyond the fundamental tools that you learned about in Chapter 1, "Patch Management Systems." Finally, you'll see how you can create and maintain a local apt-based repository for your network.

4.1 FUNDAMENTALS OF APT

There are many different commands associated with apt. You reviewed a couple of these commands in Chapter 1. While you can do a lot with apt-cache and apt-get, there are more commands and capabilities.

You should know how to find the best mirrors for your distribution, as well as how to include them in your apt configuration. When you learn how to use various apt commands, you'll learn to appreciate the capabilities of related "all-in-one" tools, including aptitude and the Synaptic Package Manager. If you find apt to your liking, you may need to install it on your chosen distribution. The same apt tools are available for both Debian- and RPM-based distributions.

4.1.1 Installing apt on a Debian-Based Distribution

There are several packages associated with apt. Not all are installed by default. If you want to take full advantage of the apt system, you'll want to install as many apt-related packages as is practical. To find available apt packages on my Debian system, I ran the following command:

```
apt-cache search apt
```

When I ran this command, I got a list of 384 packages. That's too much! As you search through this list, you might realize that it includes unrelated packages, such as `raptor-utils`, because the "apt" string is in its name or description. So you should use a more discriminating search. Without getting too fancy, I find available `apt`-related packages with the following two commands, where I've added a space before and after the search term (in quotes):

```
apt-cache search "apt "
apt-cache search " apt"
```

Because `apt-cache` is part of the `apt` package, this of course assumes that you have previously installed `apt` on your Linux system. These searches reveal a substantial number of packages related to `apt`. (When you install these packages, the `apt` system also installs dependencies.) Some of these packages may be redundant, because they provide different ways of doing the same thing. You don't need to install every `apt`-related package. I've described some of the `apt` packages I consider important in Table 4-1.

Table 4-1 Some important apt-related packages

Package	Description
apt	Installs the basic Advanced Package Tool system
apt-build	Adds a front-end to build and install packages
apt-cacher	Creates a caching system for Debian packages
apt-file	Supports searches within uninstalled packages
apt-howto	Includes a guide to the apt system
apt-listbugs	Incorporates a tool to list critical bugs
apt-src	Configures a source package management tool
apt-utils	Adds important apt commands
apt-watch	Includes an update monitor similar to the Red Hat Network/SUSE watcher applets
apt-zip	Configures apt updates for non-networked computers
aptconf	Provides a front-end for configuring sources.list
aptitude	Adds a terminal-based front-end for apt
cron-apt	Automates apt updates
mini-dinstall	Includes a daemon for updating local repositories
netselect-apt	Helps select the fastest available mirror
synaptic	Provides a GUI package manager interface

Note

The list shown in Table 4-1 is far from complete. It omits packages that are installed as dependencies to those listed here. It also leaves out other packages with tools that you may prefer. This list and chapter encompass just one formula for patch management.

4.1.2   Installing apt on a RPM-Based Distribution

There are a number of RPM-based distributions that can or do use apt as the primary patch management tool. We'll discuss this in more detail in Chapter 5, "Configuring apt for RPM Distributions."

4.1.3   Configuring apt on Your Computer

As discussed in Chapter 1, the key to apt as a patch management tool is the repositories that you select and include in your apt configuration file, `/etc/apt/sources.list`. In that chapter, you used the Debian mirror list at www.debian.org/mirror/list to add appropriate sites for your computer and physical location.

Before you configure `/etc/apt/sources.list`, you should know the different repository categories for your distribution. Debian and other related distributions (e.g. Knoppix, Ubuntu) use different names. You can use the `netselect` tool to help find the repository mirror best suited to your location.

Basic Repository Categories

There are repositories associated with the three current Debian distributions. All three are in use, so you may need to create repositories for each. The three current Debian distributions known are listed here:

☞ Sarge (Debian 3.1)—The current "stable" release. The associated software was released as "stable" in mid-2005. The previous stable distribution was known as Debian Woody (3.0).

☞ Etch (Debian 3.2)—The current beta release. As of this writing, because it was just taken from the unstable release tree, its components may or may not be stable. Etch packages are stored in the Debian `testing` repository.

☞ Sid—The developmental release of Debian, with many packages that may not be ready for production use. Sid packages are stored in the Debian `unstable` repository. Sid was the code name for the developmental release of Debian even before Sarge was released.

Note

While the previous stable version of Debian, known as Woody, is still commonly used, the version before that, known as Potato, is pretty much obsolete. Many mirrors no longer include Potato packages in their repositories.

As of this writing, I use Debian Sarge on my primary laptop computer. I used it even while it was "unstable" and have never had a major problem with associated packages. There are three subcategories associated with each repository, as described in Table 4-2.

Table 4-2   Debian repository subcategories

sources.list subcategory	Description
main	Packages released under open source licenses, such as the GPL, are collected in this category
contrib	Packages that are released under open source licenses and that depend on non-free software are stored here
non-free	Any package that is not released under a qualifying open source license is collected here
non-US	There are a few packages developed in the USA which have limited distribution due to US government export restrictions; if you have a repository outside the USA, you should connect to a non-US repository
main/debian-installer	Includes packages associated with installing Debian over a network

Some `sources.list` options are distribution-specific. For example, Ubuntu Linux (www.ubuntu.com) includes `universe` and `multiverse` repositories that correspond loosely to the Debian unstable and `contrib` / `non-free` repositories. Because the actual contents of those repositories vary, they are far from exact mirrors.

While many Linux users in principle prefer to use free software packages, this may not always be possible on your network. A lot of important Linux compatible software is released under fairly restrictive licenses, such as some versions of Java and RealPlayer.

Repository Selection Tools

There are two basic reasons to select a repository. One is for updates, while the other is for mirroring onto your network. If you're looking for update servers for your `/etc/apt/sources.list` file, it's in your interest to select more than one repository. If one goes down, you can still get the updates you need. On the other hand, if you're looking for a mirror, you may want to find one that supports `rsync` access. Some searching and trial and error may be required.

Depending on your situation, you can use the `netselect` or `netselect-apt` commands to find the repository or repositories best suited to your needs. If you know that there are only a small number of suitable repositories, try `netselect`. For example, if you're in the middle of the U.S. Silicon Valley, you might have noticed that the Debian repositories at the University of California at Berkeley (linux.csua.berkeley.edu) and the University of California at Santa Cruz (sluglug.ucsc.edu) are fairly close. Assuming the bandwidth and demand on both servers is approximately the same (it is up to you to check), you can find the one best suited for your system with the following command:

```
netselect -vv linux.csua.berkeley.edu sluglug.ucsc.edu
```

With the `-vv` switch, you can get measurable results that can help you make a judgment. One possible result is shown here:

```
linux.csua.berkeley.edu     34 ms  13 hops  100% ok (10/10) [   87]
sluglug.ucsc.edu            38 ms  14 hops  100% ok (10/10) [   82]
```

This output lists results in the following order: URL, transmission time, number of hops, percentage and number of successfully transmitted packets, and an overall score based on the transmission time and number of hops. In this case, the scores are close; the results may vary slightly if you repeat this command.

Unfortunately, you can't rely on these tools alone. While distance from a mirror is important, capacity is also an issue. For example, it may be better to connect to a more distant mirror if it has a higher-capacity Internet connection. It may be better to connect to a mirror associated with wealthier sponsors—multi-gigabyte downloads from many thousands of users can be rather expensive. For that reason, Debian strongly discourages downloads direct from the repositories that it owns.

sources.list Results

Based on the information so far in this section, you can now customize your `/etc/apt/sources.list` file with the mirrors best suited for your Debian system. In Chapter 1, you read about adding the following mirrors to this file:

```
deb ftp://debian.oregonstate.edu/debian/ stable main
deb-src ftp://debian.oregonstate.edu/debian/ stable main
```

As you now know, the stable distribution is associated with Debian Sarge. The main repository includes only a part of the available packages for this distribution. If you want all Sarge-associated repositories, access the contrib and non-free repositories, as follows:

```
deb ftp://debian.oregonstate.edu/debian/ stable main contrib non-free
deb-src ftp://debian.oregonstate.edu/debian/ stable main contrib non-
free
```

I've selected additional repositories for my Debian computer, just in case the Oregon State repository goes down. But if you're in the Silicon Valley, you probably do not want to connect to a repository all the way in Oregon. Based on the mirrors described earlier, you might add the following lines to your sources.list file:

```
deb ftp://linux.csua.berkeley.edu/debian/ stable main contrib non-free
deb-src ftp://linux.csua.berkeley.edu/debian/ stable main contrib non-
free
deb ftp://sluglug.ucsc.edu/debian/ stable main contrib non-free
deb-src ftp://sluglug.ucsc.edu/debian/ stable main contrib non-free
```

We'll show you how to use different commands to download a Debian repository for your network later in this chapter.

You can point your /etc/apt/sources.list to a repository on your local network. After you create your own repository using one of the methods described later in this chapter, you can point clients on your local network to that repository. For example, based on the current version of Debian's apache2, Web server files can be stored in the /var/www/apache2-default/ directory. Therefore, if I have a repository on my local web.example.com computer's pub/ subdirectory, I could add the following line to my sources.list file:

```
deb http://web.example.com/pub/ testing main contrib non-free
```

You can even use locally available sources; for example, if the source is mounted on a shared /var/debian NFS directory, you could use the following line in your sources.list file:

```
deb file:/var/debian/ testing main contrib non-free
```

In either case, *be careful*. Before configuring a locally cached repository on your clients, test it. Back up any clients before testing that repository.

4.1.4   The Basic apt Commands

Before using apt, you should learn more about the basic commands than you may have read about in Chapter 1. This section is far from comprehensive. An excellent place to start is the APT HOWTO, available online from www.debian.org/doc/manuals/apt-howto/index.en.html.

One key command is `aptitude`. While I described `apt-get` in Chapter 1, `aptitude` is in many ways an enhanced version of this command. If you're familiar with `apt-get`, you can use most of the same options with aptitude. What you use or prefer depends on you.

apt-get and aptitude

Not all Debian-style distributions include aptitude. But for all commands in this section, you can substitute aptitude for `apt-get`. In fact, you may want to try both versions to see which you prefer.

As described in Chapter 1, the basic command that you can use to install the package of your choice is

```
apt-get install packagename
```

But what you get might not be up to date. To keep your databases up to date, download the `Packages.gz` file, which includes the latest package information from each repository. You don't have to download the file directly. You can update your databases with the help of this file by using the following command:

```
apt-get update
```

Note

Sometimes you may see an error in the output from `apt-get update`. Don't panic. Run the command again. Sometimes the updates that you download the first time fix problems that allow you to complete the update the second time you run that command.

As a systems administrator, you might want to remove some packages on occasion. For example, if you don't want users recompiling their kernels, you could run the following command:

```
apt-get remove kernel-source
```

If you want to keep your system up to date, you'll want to become familiar with the following command (the `-u` switch doesn't work with `aptitude`):

```
apt-get -u dselect-upgrade
```

This is an important command. The `-u` switch forces `apt-get` to tell you what is planned for the upgrade. The `dselect-upgrade` option includes recommended options for packages that are downloaded and installed. This switch is not available for `aptitude`; the aptitude upgrade mode works just as well.

When you download packages with `apt`, they're download as `.deb` packages to the `/var/cache/apt/archives` directory. As you install and patch your system, the space used by this directory can build into the gigabytes. You should keep this directory clean on a periodic basis. If you just want to purge packages that are now obsolete, you could run the following command:

```
apt-get autoclean
```

If you have obsolete packages in your archives, you'll see a series of messages listing the files that are now deleted, such as

```
Del acroread 5.10-0.2 [9171kB]
```

If you're really pressed for space, and do not want a patch management repository on this computer, you could run the following command:

```
apt-get clean
```

Just remember, this command deletes all files in what you could potentially use as a local patch management repository. (For that reason, if you create a mirror, you may want to use a different directory.)

apt-cdrom

If you've downloaded the CDs associated with your distribution, you can use those as sources for your updates. For example, if you've inserted a Debian CD, all you need to do is run the `apt-cdrom` add command. But that's not too helpful, as there are more than a dozen CDs associated with Debian Linux.

However, if you've mounted a CD ISO file on a specific directory, such as `/mnt/inst1`, you could use that information; the `-d` allows you to specify the mount point:

```
apt-cdrom -d /mnt/inst1 add
```

apt-file

If you want to search for a file within an uninstalled package, the `apt-file` command can help. Before you run this command, make sure that your databases are up to date. You can do so with the `apt-file update` command.

Naturally, with the right switches, you can search through and list the files associated with a specific package. As an example, assume that you're looking for the package associated with the OpenOffice.org Writer. You've heard that it starts with the `oowriter` script. To find the associated package, run the following command:

```
apt-file search oowriter
```

The more information you have, the more closely you can find the appropriate package. In this case, you might search using the full path to `oowriter`:

```
apt-file search /usr/bin/oowriter
```

Alternatively, you can list the files associated with an uninstalled package. For example, if you were interested in the files associated with the `lokkit` firewall configuration package (developed by Red Hat and adapted for Debian), you could run the following command:

```
apt-file list lokkit
```

apt-ftparchive / dpkg-scanpackages

To mirror a repository is not enough. You need a package index to allow apt to search through your repository. If you've mirrored a true Debian mirror, you may already have the package index in the repository. Normally, packages are indexed in the `Packages.gz` file.

You can use either the `apt-ftparcive` or the `dpkg-scanpackages` command to generate your own `Packages.gz` file. You should also set up a configuration file. After you have a proper configuration file, you can configure a package index with the following command:

```
apt-ftparchive generate config.file
```

The commands required to create an appropriate apt-ftparchive configuration file are beyond the scope of this book. For more information, search online for `apt-ftparchive.conf`; several developers have documented their own examples in this file.

Alternatively, you can create your own `Packages.gz` file. Navigate to the directory with your download packages. For example, if you wanted to create an archive of data for the packages you've downloaded to update your system, run the following commands:

```
cd /var/cache/apt/archives
dpkg-scanpackages . /dev/null | gzip -9c > Packages.gz
```

Now you can copy or move these files to an appropriate directory on your Web server and then use them to update other similarly configured systems on your network.

apt-howto

If you want to refer to the APT HOWTO, and have installed the associated package, all you need to do is run the `apt-howto` command to call up this document in the default browser for your system.

apt-listbugs

If you want to check a package that you're interested in installing for bugs, you can do so with the `apt-listbugs` command. For example, if you want to check for bugs on the current `apache2` package, run the following command:

```
apt-listbugs list apache2
```

4.1.5   The aptitude System

The aptitude command provides a low-level graphical front-end to various apt and aptitude commands. A key advantage is the high-level view it supports of what you have and can do. For example, the aptitude interface provides a list of the packages that you have installed, can upgrade, and may want to remove because they're obsolete. When you start aptitude, you'll see a screen similar to Figure 4-1.

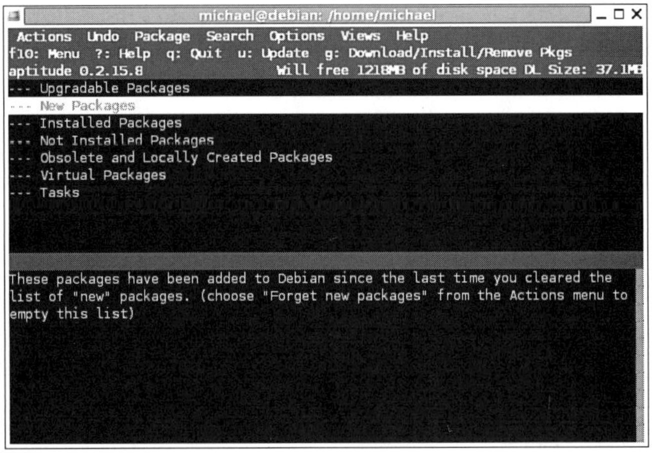

Figure 4-1   The aptitude menu

First, we'll review how the `aptitude` menu is organized, and then you'll see how you can use commands in this menu to keep your system up to date. For detailed information on aptitude, see the associated user's manual, available as part of the `aptitude-doc-en` package or online from http://doc2.inf.elte.hu/doc/aptitude/html/en/.

Some trial and error may be required. After you configure `aptitude` and make package selections, you may get errors, or you may need to make changes. But if you work out the kinks on your own computer, you can more reliably automate the patch management process on other similar computers on your network.

Be careful. In some cases, aptitude may remove packages that you wanted to keep. When I first ran `aptitude` on my laptop, it deleted the basic configuration package for my PCMCIA card. Fortunately, I had a current backup. Be careful to read through the list of packages that would otherwise be removed.

Note

If you use aptitude's feature that removes "unused" packages, be careful. Back up your system. If you lose some features you consider essential, you'll be glad that you took the time to update your backup.

Running Aptitude

As it's a great way to administer remote systems, you'll want to learn to navigate around aptitude. By default, you can use your cursor to move between the aforementioned categories. Highlight the category of your choice, and press Enter. Check out the different categories. As shown in Figure 4-2, you can find out more about each package.

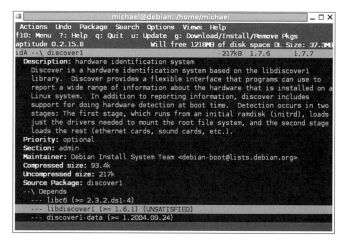

Figure 4-2 Detailed information in Aptitude

The first three letters of the description can tell you a lot. As shown in Figure 4-2, the letters associated with the `discover1` package are idA. The first letter is the current state. The second letter, if present, specifies the action that Aptitude will take. The third letter, A, is shown when the package was automatically installed, such as to satisfy a dependency. The options for the first letter are shown in Table 4-3.

Table 4-3   Aptitude package state labels

Label	Description
I	The package is installed; all dependencies are satisfied
B	The package is installed with broken dependencies
c	The package was removed; configuration files are still installed
C	Package installation was interrupted during configuration; reinstallation may be required
H	Package is partially installed
p	The package and configuration files are not present
v	This is a virtual package

The options for the second letter, the action flag, are shown in Table 4-4.

Table 4-4   Aptitude package action labels

Label	Description
i	The package will be installed
B	The package is broken; dependencies cannot be satisfied
d	The package will be deleted; configuration files will remain
F	No upgrades of this package will be allowed
h	The package will not be upgraded until this hold is canceled
p	The package and configuration files will be deleted
u	The package will be upgraded

If you have problems getting back to the original display, press q. If you want to study the options available through the menu bar, press F10 and use your cursor. As you can see, there are a number of shortcut keys. Some are shown in Figure 4-1; they include F10, ?, q, u, and g. When you press ?, you can go through a number of other shortcut commands that can help you navigate or specify how to manage the packages of your choice.

Note

You could use your cursor and mouse if you have Aptitude open in the GUI. However, you may need to manage systems remotely and may not have access to a GUI, so you need to know how to use the Aptitude switches and command options.

Aptitude Menu Organization

As you can see from Figure 4-1, Aptitude organizes packages into seven different categories. (It's a bit different from the figure. The Virtual Packages category includes no real packages, and if there are security updates pending, there will be another category by this name.) Under each category, you can select the packages of your choice to upgrade, install, or remove:

☞   Security Update

Packages for which security-related updates are available.

☞   Upgradeable Packages

Those packages for which upgrades are available.

☞   New Packages

Lists software that has been made available for your distribution since installation or the last time you've run the Forget New Packages command. There is little or no overlap between this category and "Not Installed Packages."

☞   Installed Packages

Those packages that are currently installed on your computer.

☞   Not Installed Packages

Specify packages which are not new and not currently installed on your computer.

☞   Obsolete and Locally Created Packages

Includes installed packages not available from a repository specified in your `/etc/apt/sources.list`. Some may be obsolete; others may be created by your users.

☞   Virtual Packages

These are usually amalgamations of others that simplify dependencies. For more information, see the `apt-cache` man page and the `debian-policy` package.

☞   Tasks

Tasks correspond to package groups, which can help you select the packages that you may need. For example, you may find a Localization Korean Desktop package group which can help you configure a desktop environment in that language.

Under the first four categories, packages are organized into several different groups. Debian specifies 36 different groups at packages.debian.org/unstable/.

One critical skill with Aptitude is the search for a specific package. The forward slash key (/) opens the "Search for" text box. You can search for the package of your choice.

Configuring Aptitude Patch Management

There are two basic menus where you can configure how Aptitude manages updates. To see how aptitude manages dependencies, navigate to the Options menu and select Dependency Handling. You'll see five configuration options:

☞ Automatically resolve dependencies of a package when it is selected

Any dependencies of a selected package are automatically included in any list of packages to be upgraded or installed.

☞ Automatically fix broken packages before installing or removing

Any unsatisfied dependencies are addressed.

☞ Install Recommended packages automatically

Any packages that are recommended are installed as if they were dependencies.

☞ Remove unused packages automatically

Normally includes obsolete packages that are no longer included in mirrors.

☞ Automatically remove unused packages matching this filter

This list may not match what you see. As Aptitude has evolved, the ways you can use it to implement patch management have changed. Also important are the miscellaneous options. To review them, navigate to the Options menu and select Miscellaneous, which opens the menu shown in Figure 4-3. The options are described in the following list.

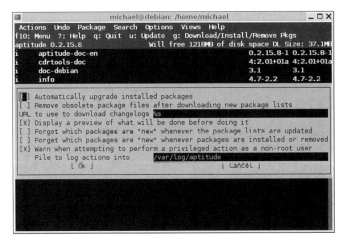

Figure 4-3   You can specify how Aptitude updates your system

☞ Automatically upgrade installed packages

Disabled by default. You don't want your services upgraded unless you're sure that they won't break what you've built with so much hard work.

☞ Remove obsolete package files after downloading new package lists

   Disabled by default. When new package lists are installed, they are compared to existing packages. If there are some which are now obsolete, they are deleted.

☞ URL to use to download changelogs

   By default, changelogs are downloaded from the mirror sites specified in your `sources.list` file.

☞ Display a preview of what will be done before doing it

   You'll see displays of what aptitude will remove, upgrade, and install, before anything is done.

☞ Forget which packages are "new" whenever the package lists are updated

   Disabled by default. New packages will include those currently on your list, and those revealed by your next update.

☞ Forget which packages are "new" whenever the package lists are installed or removed

   Disabled by default. New packages will include those currently on your list, and those revealed by your next package list installation or removal.

☞ Warn when attempting to perform a privileged action as a non-root user

   Except for those actions which solely get information, most actions related to the apt and aptitude commands require root access.

☞ File to log actions into

   By default, the aptitude log file is `/var/log/aptitude`.

Patch Management with Aptitude

Now that you've learned about Aptitude, you can use it to keep your system up to date. Before you start, you'll want an up–to-date package database. To do so, run the Actions -> Update menu or press u. You're prompted for the root password. You'll see a series of messages as your system connects to the repositories listed in your `/etc/apt/sources.list`. If there are errors or problems with a connection, you may need to repeat the process. With a little luck, you won't have errors the second time through.

Before you let aptitude do its thing, you should review what it will do. Make sure that the Miscellaneous options enable Aptitude to "Display a preview of what will be done before doing it." As described in the previous section, this should be supported by the default configuration. Then, when you press g to run the *Download/Install/Remove Pkgs* command, it will open a list similar to that shown in Figure 4-4. You can now review what aptitude will do to your system, in a variety of categories:

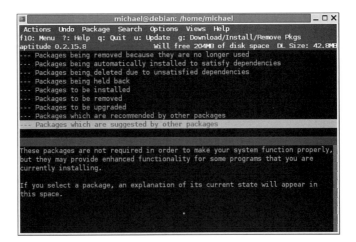

Figure 4-4   What Aptitude will do

☞ Packages being removed because they are no longer used

Sometimes packages are installed to satisfy dependencies. If they're no longer required, for instance, because the original package has been removed, it is added to this list. For example, if I've removed the abiword word processor, I don't need the abiword-common package on my system.

☞ Packages being automatically installed to satisfy dependencies

Just as this suggests, this lists packages that are being installed to satisfy dependencies.

☞ Packages being deleted due to unsatisfied dependencies

Sometimes, packages that satisfy dependencies become obsolete and are removed from available mirrors. Sometimes, there are updates that conflict with such packages.

☞ Packages being held back

Many packages receive regular updates. You may not want to update those packages, because upgrades can sometimes break your configuration. If you did not activate the "Automatically upgrade installed packages" setting described earlier, there will probably be a long list in this section.

☞ Packages to be removed

Sometimes, new versions of a package mean that others no longer work. If these packages are dependencies, they are candidates for removal.

☞ Packages to be upgraded

Even if you haven't activated the "Automatically upgrade installed packages" setting, many packages are still upgraded. Some upgrades are required to satisfy new dependencies.

☞ Packages that are recommended by other packages

While not required, some packages help provide full functionality for others. Such packages are listed here.

☞ Packages that are suggested by other packages

While not required, some packages help enhance functionality for others. Such packages are listed here.

Making Changes with Aptitude

If you want to make changes to this list, you can use the options under the Package Menu. You can change the status of each package, which corresponds to the second letter in the code. For more information on the current status, see Table 4-4.

After you make your changes, run the update (u) command. Not only will it update the package status relative to your configured mirrors, it updates the packages in the noted categories. For example, if you choose to install a package, it will be added either to the "Packages to be installed" or the "Packages to be upgraded" lists.

When you're satisfied with the result, you can press g to run the Download/Install/Remove Pkgs command again. Only after you execute this command a second time does the local computer connect to the mirrors listed in /etc/apt/sources.list and perform the actions which you've just reviewed.

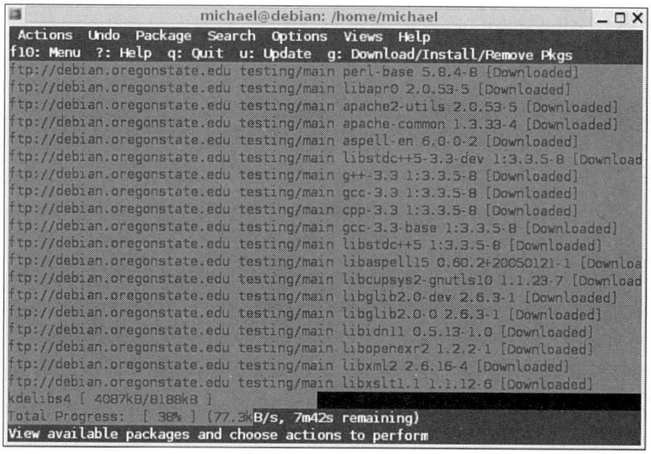

Figure 4-5   Aptitude at work

When Aptitude finishes downloading packages, you're prompted to continue or cancel. By default, packages are downloaded to `/var/cache/apt/archives`. If you cancel, the packages are still stored there. If you continue, Aptitude exits from its graphical menu and then installs those downloaded packages. If there are problems, you may have to make some choices; one example on my computer is shown in Figure 4-6.

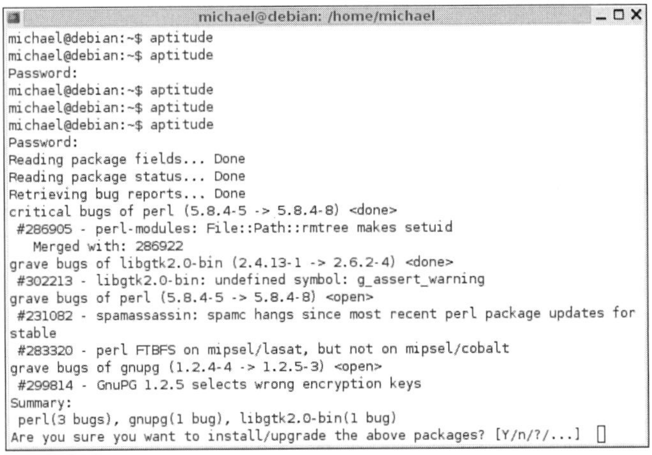

```
michael@debian: /home/michael                               _ □ ✕
michael@debian:~$ aptitude
michael@debian:~$ aptitude
Password:
michael@debian:~$ aptitude
michael@debian:~$ aptitude
michael@debian:~$ aptitude
Password:
Reading package fields... Done
Reading package status... Done
Retrieving bug reports... Done
critical bugs of perl (5.8.4-5 -> 5.8.4-8) <done>
 #286905 - perl-modules: File::Path::rmtree makes setuid
   Merged with: 286922
grave bugs of libgtk2.0-bin (2.4.13-1 -> 2.6.2-4) <done>
 #302213 - libgtk2.0-bin: undefined symbol: g_assert_warning
grave bugs of perl (5.8.4-5 -> 5.8.4-8) <open>
 #231082 - spamassassin: spamc hangs since most recent perl package updates for
stable
 #283320 - perl FTBFS on mipsel/lasat, but not on mipsel/cobalt
grave bugs of gnupg (1.2.4-4 -> 1.2.5-3) <open>
 #299814 - GnuPG 1.2.5 selects wrong encryption keys
Summary:
 perl(3 bugs), gnupg(1 bug), libgtk2.0-bin(1 bug)
Are you sure you want to install/upgrade the above packages? [Y/n/?/...] []
```

Figure 4-6   Aptitude installing, updating, and more

Remember, Aptitude might be installing hundreds of megabytes of data. That takes time.

Note

When you run `aptitude`, *be careful*. When I ran `aptitude`, I wasn't too careful about the list of packages that were to be uninstalled. As a result, aptitude removed the OpenOffice.org writer package while I worked on this chapter. The results were disconcerting.

4.1.6   Running the Synaptic Package Manager

If you really prefer a fully GUI package manager, Debian provides the Synaptic Package Manager. As you can see in Figure 4-7, Synaptic includes many of the same options available for aptitude. While the descriptions may vary, the effect is the same.

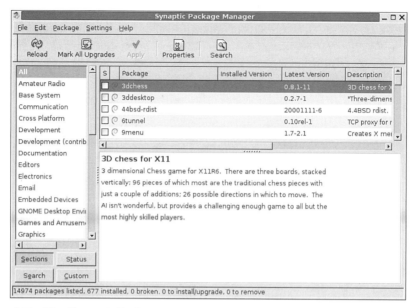

Figure 4-7   The Synaptic Package Manager

Note

This section is based on Synaptic version 0.56. More information is available from www.nongnu.org/synaptic/.

Remember, most every Linux graphical tool is a front-end to one or more commands. Therefore, most of what you see in this section should be familiar. Different perspectives can help you gain insight into the options available for the apt commands.

Because GUI applications are more familiar to most users, we won't go into the same details on how to navigate through Synaptic. However, we will show you how you might configure Synaptic to keep your system up to date.

Note

You can also use a GUI to administer a remote computer with synaptic. All you need is the Secure Shell daemon (SSH). With current versions of SSH, all you need to do is log in to the remote computer with the right switch. For example, if the remote computer is debian1.example.com, the following commands should allow you to use the Synaptic Package Manager to configure updates to the remote computer.

```
ssh -X root@debian1.example.com
synaptic
```

Keeping Synaptic Updated

As with aptitude, it's important to keep the apt configuration database up to date. It's quite simple with Synaptic; the Reload button (or Edit -> Reload Package Information) downloads the latest package lists from your selected repositories.

Configuring Synaptic

Synaptic allows you to customize how you mark your upgrades. With the `dist-upgrade` switch associated with the `apt-get` command, Synaptic supports smart upgrades, which attempt to resolve conflicts and fulfill all dependencies. Press the Mark All Upgrades button. If you haven't already done so, you can choose between Default and Smart Upgrade. Alternatively, you can configure the upgrade mode; click Settings -> Preferences, and select your preferred option from the System Upgrade drop-down box.

The Synaptic Preference dialog box is shown in Figure 4-8. As you can see, this version includes six tabs. Columns and Fonts as well as Colors do not affect the functionality of Synaptic, and are therefore not covered in this book.

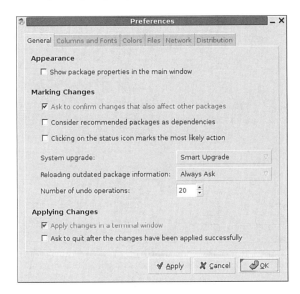

Figure 4-8   Synaptic Preferences

Synaptic Preferences, as shown in Figure 4-8, are significant. They include

☞ Show package properties in the main window

I normally activate this option because it provides more information on each package. However, it could slow performance, especially if you're running Synaptic remotely.

☞ Ask to confirm changes that also affect other packages

If there are dependencies, you'll need to confirm configured changes.

☞ Consider recommended packages as dependencies

As described earlier, recommended packages can enhance functionality. If you activate this option, recommended packages are installed just as if they were dependencies.

☞ Clicking on the status icon marks the most likely action

The status icon is shown in Figure 4-7 as the "S" column to the left of each package name. The most likely action may be installation, upgrade, or removal.

☞ System Upgrade

As described earlier, you can configure a default Smart or Default upgrade for all upgradeable packages.

☞ Reloading outdated package information

If there are outdated packages, you can configure Synaptic to ignore or always reload such packages. In many cases, you may prefer to reload outdated packages, especially if you want to be careful with your current configuration.

☞ Number of undo operations

Synaptic stores your actions and can undo them when you press Ctrl+Z. This option specifies the number of commands you can undo.

☞ Apply changes in a terminal window

By default, Synaptic opens a terminal window to provide messages related to downloads, updates and any configuration issues that may require your input.

☞ Ask to quit after the changes have been applied successfully.

If active, Synaptic allows you to exit after making changes. It's a good idea to check what happened; if there are problems, you can restore your configuration from a backup.

Under the Files tab, you can configure the cache and the Synaptic log files. Under the Temporary Files area, you can manage the cached packages in the `/var/cache/apt/archives` directory:

☞ Leave all download packages in the cache

☞ Delete download packages after installation

☞ Only delete packages which are no longer available

There's also a button that deletes the files in the cache. There are also options with respect to the history files. As Synaptic requires, the root user account, synaptic history, and configuration files are stored in the `/root/.synaptic` directory. You can keep all Synaptic history or delete history files older than the number of days you select.

Under the Network tab, you can configure a connection through any Proxy Server which might govern your network's connection to the Internet.

The Distribution tab is important. It governs package upgrade behavior. The three options are

☞ Always prefer the highest version

We recommend that you do not activate this option unless you're willing to test the latest versions of many packages. The "highest version" may not be stable or production-ready.

☞ Always prefer the installed version

This option can help you maintain many services in a working configuration.

☞ Prefer versions from [possibly several options]

If your `/etc/apt/sources.list` file includes several optional types of repositories (such as stable - Sarge / testing - Etch / unstable - Sid), you can choose between those options.

After you've made your preferred changes, click OK to return to the main Synaptic screen.

Selecting Packages

In the main Synaptic screen, click the Status button. In the left pane, you'll see packages divided into six different categories. When you configure certain packages, you may see a seventh category:

☞ All—Lists all packages, installed and available. With the mirrors that I've selected, there are nearly 15,000 packages available.

☞ Installed—Lists all installed packages, including those in the two categories that follow.

☞ Installed (local or obsolete)—Lists all installed packages that were either built on the local computer or are not available on configured mirrors.

If you see a package in this list, an upgrade may still be available. Perhaps no developer has created a Debian version of the package, or the name of the package may have changed

☞ Installed (upgradable)—Lists those packages for which newer versions are available on configured mirrors. You may want to avoid upgrades, especially for important services, until you know that your configuration files will work with the upgrade.

☞ Not installed—Lists all packages from configured sources that have not been installed on this computer.

☞ Not installed (residual config)—Lists packages that are not installed, but where associated configuration files exist on the local computer. This is typically associated with a package which has been uninstalled. In many cases, you can reinstall the noted package with the existing configuration file.

☞ Pinned—Includes packages that you've selected as "Recommended for Installation to add features," "Suggested for Installation to enhance features," or "Locked to prevent upgrades."

Take a package on the list. Highlight it. Right-click it. It opens a shortcut menu similar to that shown in Figure 4-9.

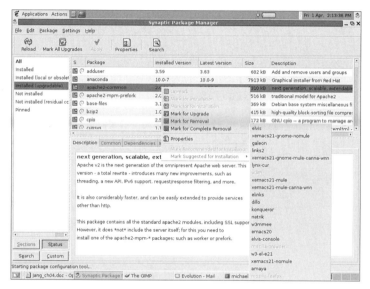

Figure 4-9 Synaptic Package options

As you can see, there are a number of things that you can do with the currently installed `apache2-common` package. Inactive options won't work; you can't install or reinstall an upgradeable package. You can highlight some or all packages in a category. The options are straightforward:

☞ Unmark—If you've selected an option for a package, you can unmark it.

☞ Mark for Installation—You can select an uninstalled package and mark it for installation via Synaptic.

☞ Mark for Reinstallation—For those installed packages where upgrades are not available, you can select and mark them for reinstallation, in case you want a fresh copy of associated files.

☞ Mark for Upgrade—For those installed packages where upgrades are available, you can select and mark them for upgrade via Synaptic.

☞ Mark for Removal—For installed packages, you can mark them for standard removal via Synaptic. Generally, configuration files will not be erased.

☞ Mark for Complete Removal—For installed packages, you can mark them for complete removal via Synaptic. Configuration files will be erased.

☞ Properties—Opens a window that includes a brief description, dependencies, any installed files, and available versions.

☞ Mark Suggested for Installation—Marks packages for installation that add functionality to the target software.

☞ Mark Recommend for Installation—Marks packages for installation that enhance functionality of the target software.

If you absolutely want to prevent upgrades of a certain package, highlight it. Run the Package -> Lock Version command to lock the package at the current version level.

Alternatively, you can force Synaptic to install or upgrade a specific package to a version available on one of your configured mirrors. For example, if you know a certain version of the apache2-common package, highlight it and press Ctrl+E. You'll see a window similar to Figure 4-10, where you can select the version you want to force with the Force Version drop-down box.

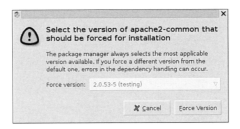

Figure 4-10   Forcing a Synaptic Package version

Making Changes

Take your time as you work with packages in Synaptic. If you choose to use one of the upgrade options described earlier, analyze the Installed (upgradeable) options carefully! If you upgrade a service, anything you've customized for that service may be at risk. If you're allowing Synaptic to delete "unused" packages, analyze that list carefully as well.

When you're ready, press Ctrl+P. This action opens a window that summarizes the actions to be taken. It includes packages to be upgraded, installed, or removed. If you've made changes to the list of packages to be upgraded or removed, those changes will be added to an Unchanged category. One example of this window is shown in Figure 4-11.

Figure 4-11 Reviewing planned changes

If you find an error in your review, this is your last chance to cancel the process. Don't be afraid to go back and review the lists of packages again. When you're ready, press Apply. This starts the process where Synaptic downloads the associated packages. Depending on the megabytes of files you've selected and the speed of your Internet connection, this process may take some time.

When the packages are downloaded, you'll see terminal output. You may be asked some configuration questions associated with specific services during this process. If you're trying to install some problematic packages, find out during this process. For example, Figure 4-12 illustrates some problems with the upgrade. At this point, you can accept the problems and install the packages as they are, or refuse the installation, and return to Synaptic.

Figure 4-12 Upgrade problems

Based on the errors shown, I've either unchecked the installation of related new packages or locked the version of existing packages to avoid upgrades. Sometimes, new packages or upgrades can have bugs. Avoiding upgrades can help you avoid problems in this area.

For example, the messages shown in Figure 4-12 reveal problems associated with the available newer version of the Evolution email manager. Before upgrading my system, I locked Evolution in its current version. While I used these steps, other methods can work equally well:

1. Click Edit -> Search to open the Find window.
2. In the Search box, type in the package of your choice (in this case, evolution), and then click Search.
3. In the upper-right package window, you should see all available packages with `evolution` in the name.
4. Highlight the `evolution` package. Select Package -> Lock Version. Now Synaptic will not upgrade the Evolution email manager.
5. Repeat this process for the packages of your choice. I've also locked the version associated with the other Evolution-related package, `evolution-data-server`.

When you've finished your modifications, click Apply again. If you've made appropriate choices, you should at least see fewer errors. Continue the process until you can update without unacceptable bugs or fatal errors.

If you've saved your downloads, you may be able to use them to update other identically configured Debian computers on your network. If your Debian computers require the same updates, they won't need any additional packages.

4.2   CREATING YOUR apt REPOSITORY

In Chapter 3, "SUSE's Update Systems and rsync Mirrors," you learned how to create an update repository for computers loaded with SUSE Linux by using appropriate `rsync` commands. You don't need and do not have to configure a complete repository on your local network. Debian includes packages for the widest variety of architectures, so you need to know how to limit the downloads—to help manage the demands required on your time, bandwidth, and disk space.

4.2.1   Debian Repository Mirror Options

There are several different tools that you can use to create a local repository for apt-based updates for distributions such as Debian Linux. Most of these tools use either rsync or other commands that follow the same principles. The advantage of such commands is during updates; only changes to individual packages are downloaded, so updates are quicker. The options are outlined in the following list:

☞ Anonymous FTP was the traditional method for setting up a mirror. With the right client, you can select the directories to mirror and limit updates to newer packages. However, any package that is installed must be completely installed.

☞ The basic `rsync` command may be a bit complex, but when configured you can repeat the same command again to keep your mirror up to date. Shortly, you'll examine some appropriate switches to use with `rsync`.

☞ You can configure a partial mirror. For more information, see people.debian.org/~debacle/mirror.html.

☞ The `apt-proxy` package is functionally similar to the Red Hat Network Proxy Server described in Chapter 2, "Consolidating Patches on a Red Hat/Fedora Network." As of this writing, however, `apt-proxy` is available only for the now obsolete Debian Woody. While work on `apt-proxy` version 2 is in progress, there is no *working* Debian version available. For the latest information, see `apt-proxy.sourceforge.net`.

While you might also read about `apt-cacher` and the `aptcached` daemon, some of the domain names associated with these daemons, including www.apt-cacher.org, were unused as of this writing.

☞ The `debmirror` package can help you download complete or partial mirrors. You can read more about the associated commands later in this chapter.

☞ The `apt-mirror` package is one more option for creating the mirror that you need for your local network. You can read more about the associated commands later in this chapter.

These are just a few of the available packages which can help you create a local repository for your network. For more information, see www.debian.org/mirror/ftpmirror.

4.2.2   A Complete Debian Repository

Most Debian repositories include directories for each of the active distribution versions, as well as a substantial number of different computer architectures. Unless there are computers on your network that run different Debian distributions on each of the available architectures, you might not want to mirror the complete repository. If you do, you might need well over 100GB of free space on your hard drive. Downloading this much data may overload most small business Internet connections for days.

Note

If you want to configure a complete Debian mirror to share on the Internet, the people behind Debian ask that you register your mirror at www.debian.org/mirror/submit.

Debian Directories

The major Debian directories correspond to available distributions and architectures. Before you create a mirror, it may be helpful to review what's available in each category on the mirror of your choice. Where there are several names for the same distribution, you may find more than one directory, each pointing to the same set of packages. The current major Debian distributions include Debian Woody, Debian Sarge, Debian Etch, and Debian Sid.

☞ Debian Woody is now the obsolete distribution. As of this writing, the current version of this distribution is 3.0r6. There may be directories on a Debian mirror known as woody, oldstable, or Debian3.0r6. (Debian Potato came before Debian Woody.)

☞ Debian Sarge, as of this writing, is now the most recent stable version of Debian Linux. As of this writing, the current version of this distribution is 3.1r0. There may be directories on a Debian mirror known as sarge, stable, or Debian3.1r0.

☞ Debian Etch, as of this writing, is now the beta, or testing version of Debian Linux. There may be directories on a Debian mirror known as etch or testing.

☞ Debian Sid is the developmental version of Debian Linux. There may be directories on a Debian mirror known as sid, or unstable.

Under each distribution directory, Debian maintainers and developers build and incorporate binary and source packages for a number of different architectures, as noted in Table 4-5.

Table 4-5 Debian architectures

Architecture	Description
alpha	For computers with the HP (formerly Compaq/Digital) CPU.
arm	Associated with computers with Advanced (formerly Acorn) RISC (Reduced Instruction Set Computing) Machine processors; commonly available on handheld computers.
hppa	Short for Hewlett-Packard Precision Architecture; associated with HP's line of RISC CPUs.
i386	The standard architecture associated with 32-bit Intel and compatible CPUs.
ia64	Associated with Itanium and Itanium-2 64-bit CPUs developed by Intel.

Architecture	Description
m68k	The architecture for Motorola's 68000 series of CPUs; not developed beyond 32-bit.
mips	Another RISC CPU commonly used in consumer electronics. Sometimes associated with SGI Indy/Indigo2 workstations. MIPS is short for Microprocessor without Interlocked Pipeline Stages.
mipsel	Also for the MIPS CPU; but customized for HP/Cobalt workstations.
powerpc	One more RISC CPU, developed by Motorola, IBM, and Apple; available in a variety of different computers.
s390	Also known as the Z-series of CPUs; developed by IBM originally for the System 390 servers.
sparc	Associated with the Sparc CPUs developed for SUN workstations.

If the right distribution or architecture is not available on your preferred mirror, you'll need to select and configure a different mirror.

A Basic rsync Script

Debian makes a basic `rsync` script available at www.debian.org/mirror/ftpmirror. The script helps you create a mirror for the distribution and architecture of your choice. Debian recommends that you run the `rsync` command with at least the following switches:

☞ `--recursive`—Downloads and synchronizes all files from subdirectories.

☞ `--times`—Preserves the date and time associated with each file.

☞ `--links`—Recreates any existing symlinks from the mirror.

☞ `--hard-links`—Preserves any existing hard links from the mirror.

☞ `--delete`—Removes any files on your computer that no longer exist on the target mirror. (If you have sufficient space for multiple versions of a package, use `--delete-after`.)

If you don't have computers with all the Debian architectures on your network, you might not want to download every directory from your preferred Debian mirror. The following `--exclude` switches make it possible to limit your download. As you can see from the `rsync` man page, the following switches `--exclude` the noted directories and packages with the noted extensions. Be careful. While a Debian mirror is supposed to use directories, such as `binary-i386`, your selected mirror may not use the same directories. If in doubt, search around using the `rsync` commands described in Chapter 3.

```
--exclude binary-alpha/ --exclude *_alpha.deb
--exclude binary-arm/ --exclude *_arm.deb
--exclude binary-hppa/ --exclude *_hppa.deb
--exclude binary-i386/ --exclude *_i386.deb
--exclude binary-ia64/ --exclude *_ia64.deb
--exclude binary-m68k/ --exclude *_m68k.deb
--exclude binary-mips/ --exclude *_mips.deb
```

```
--exclude binary-mipsel/ --exclude *_mipsel.deb
--exclude binary-powerpc/ --exclude *_powerpc.deb
--exclude binary-s390/ --exclude *_s390.deb
--exclude binary-sparc/ --exclude *_sparc.deb
```

Don't include every switch and option in this list; if you do, you're excluding the directory and package extensions associated with every current Debian architecture. You've read about some of these directories along with those related to major repositories earlier in this chapter. See Table 4-2 for some of the options.

4.2.3   Creating a Debian Mirror

You may not want to use rsync or the associated script just described. You can use the packages you've downloaded and installed on your own computer with commands such as `apt-get -u dselect-upgrade`. If you've followed the instructions associated with the `dpkg-scanpackages` command described earlier in this chapter, you can create a local repository with those packages.

In this section, we'll also use two alternative tools. One is `debmirror`, which allows you to download and synchronize part of a mirror to your own repository with a minimum of configuration. The other is `apt-mirror`, which uses configuration files similar to the standard `/etc/apt/sources.list` configuration file.

Note

Before you change the `/etc/apt/sources.list` to point to the local mirror on your network, you should test your configuration on at least one client. Back up that client before updating your system.

Using Local Packages

If you've upgraded your system with download packages, you may still have them stored in the default download directory, `/var/cache/apt/archives/`. With these packages and the `dpkg-scanpackages` command, you can create your own local repository.

Assuming you've installed the Debian `apache2` Web server (and associated packages), you could configure a repository on Debian Linux (Sarge) with the following commands:

```
cd /var/cache/apt/archives
dpkg-scanpackages . /dev/null | gzip -9c > Packages.gz
mkdir /var/www/apache2-default/pub
cp -ar /var/cache/apt/archives/*  /var/www/apache2-default/pub/
```

Don't forget the dot (.) after `dpkg-scanpackages`; it applies the command to all files in the current directory.

You could then configure your Apache Web server for that specialized repository. To do so, you could point your clients to that repository. Test it first! If you were to point a client to a repository on web.example.com, you would add the following command to your `/etc/apt/sources.list`:

```
deb http://web.example.com/pub/
```

If you limit clients to that repository, you deny access to those Debian mirrors available on the Internet. But in some cases, that may be exactly what you want to do.

Configuring debmirror

The `debmirror` package, developed by Joey Hess and Joerg Wendland, is very simple, which makes it a popular option among many Debian users. Before you can configure `debmirror`, you should download this package, available from the main Sarge repository. Assuming that you've configured `/etc/apt/sources.list` appropriately, you can download and install it with the following commands:

```
apt-get update
apt-get install debmirror
```

As you can see from a `dpkg -L debmirror` command, this package contains six files. Only two of them are important. The `/usr/bin/debmirror` file is a script written in Perl that performs three basic steps:

1. Download packages and source files associated with your selected architecture.
2. Delete any local files and directories not on the remote mirror.
3. Download all other files associated with your selected architecture.

These steps are based on default settings in `/usr/share/doc/debmirror/debmirror.conf`, which downloads a complete mirror associated with the i386 architecture from ftp.debian.org. But as we've emphasized before, it's best for all concerned if you download from a mirror closer to your location.

To override these settings, make a copy of this file in `/etc/debmirror.conf`. If you configure `debmirror`, all you need to do is run the `debmirror` command to synchronize the mirror to the directory of your choice. For example, the following command synchronizes the mirror to the Debian directory associated with a standard FTP server:

```
debmirror /srv/ftp/pub
```

That looks easy. Yes, you can add options as defined in the `debmirror` man page. But it isn't necessary. First, copy the configuration file:

```
cp /usr/share/doc/debmirror/debmirror.conf /etc/
```

Now open `/etc/debmirror.conf` in the text editor of your choice. The settings that you see in this file should correspond to defaults, which you can change to meet your own requirements. Let's examine these defaults, starting with the output options, which correspond to the `-v`, `-p`, and `-debug` switches. At least until I'm sure that the settings work, I like to change the `$verbose` variable:

```
$verbose=0;
$progress=0;
$debug=0;
```

If you don't want to change these variables, you can use the switches associated with `debmirror`. Next, there are download options. While download mirrors generally support anonymous access, you should change the host to the Debian mirror of your choice. Make sure that the `$remoteroot` directory corresponds to the Debian mirror, and make sure that you're accessing the correct distribution (`woody`, `sarge`, `etch`, or `sid`):

```
$host="ftp.debian.org" ;
$user="anonymous";
$remoteroot="/debian";
$download_method="ftp";
@dists="sid";
```

Make sure that you download the correct sections as defined in Table 4-2, and work with the appropriate architecture. The following default downloads all base sections (except `non-US`). While you're testing `debmirror`, you may want to limit the download to one specific section:

```
@sections="main,main/debian-installer,contrib,non-free";
```

The settings that follow correspond to the `--skippackages` switch, which avoids repeating the download of packages or source files; `--getcontents`, which downloads the compressed contents archives; and `--source`, which downloads source packages and avoids limits on the number of files to download. I normally change the `$do_source` variable because I don't normally download source packages:

```
$skippackages=0;
$getcontents=0;
$do_source=1;
$max_batch=0;
```

You can configure how debmirror checks downloaded files. The following settings check for a Release.gpg file, a Release file, and report all errors. However, the defaults do not check MD5 sums of each file:

```
$ignore_release_gpg=0;
$ignore_release=0;
$check_md5sums=0;
$ignore_small_errors=0;
```

By default, debmirror deletes files and directories no longer on the remote mirror during the download process, not after the download is complete:

```
$cleanup=1;
$post_cleanup=0;
```

If you're using debmirror on a rsync server, the default options download up to 200 files at a time and use the rsync -aIL and --partial options. Downloads are performed in passive mode; the dry run option is disabled.

```
$rsync_batch=200;
$rsync_options="-aIL —partial";
$passive=0;
$dry_run=0;
```

When you've configured /etc/debmirror.conf to your liking, you can test the result, by downloading your selections to the directory of your choice with a command, such as

```
debmirror /srv/ftp/pub
```

Afterwards, you can check the result in the appropriate /srv/ftp/pub subdirectories, and download as complete a mirror as you need for your network.

Configuring apt-mirror
There are several other excellent packages that can help you create a local mirror for your network. The other one we'll explore here is apt-mirror; for more information, see http://apt-mirror.sourceforge.net. One advantage of apt-mirror is the preconfigured daily cron job which keeps your mirror up to date. As of this writing, apt-mirror is not available from the standard Debian

repositories. Therefore, if you want to download apt-mirror, you'll need to download it from its Source Forge home page or use the associated apt repository.

To install `apt-mirror` using the apt interface, you'll need to take the following steps:

1. Add the `apt-mirror` repository to your `/etc/apt/sources.list` file. To do so, add the following line:

```
deb http://apt-mirror.sourceforge.net/ apt-mirror/
```

2. Update your database:

```
apt-get update
```

3. Install `apt-mirror`:

```
apt-get install apt-mirror
```

Now you can configure how `apt-mirror` works. The configuration file, `mirror.list`, by default, is installed in the `/etc/apt/` directory. Let's examine what you should do with this configuration file.

By default, the base directory is `/var/spool/apt-mirror`. The mirror files are downloaded to the `mirror` subdirectory. Indexes are downloaded to the `skel` subdirectory. Logs, MD5 checksums, and URLs are stored in the `var` subdirectory. If you want to change these defaults, activate and modify the following commands appropriately in `mirror.list`:

```
# set base_path /var/spool/apt-mirror
# set mirror_path $base_path/mirror
# set skel_path $base_path/skel
# set var_path $base_path/var
```

The default version of this file points to Woody and Sid mirrors in Finland. Unless you're located in or near that country, and have Debian Woody and Sid workstations on your network, you should change at least some of the defaults. Remember, the current standard is Debian Sarge.

Note

The `apt-mirror` package requires the use of the HTTP protocol. While most Debian mirrors are configured for FTP, many work using identical URLs with HTTP. For example, while the Debian mirror list points to ftp://debian.oregonstate.edu/debian, you can use http://debian.oregonstate.edu/debian. Type the URL in your browser to make sure it works on the mirror of your choice.

If you've updated your `/etc/apt/sources.list` to point to faster mirrors closer to your location, you can generally copy this list to your `/etc/apt/mirror.list` file. For example, the following list may be suitable for many users in the Northwest region of the USA:

```
deb http://debian.oregonstate.edu/debian stable main contrib non-free
deb http://security.debian.org/ stable/updates main contrib non-free
deb http://debian.oregonstate.edu/debian stable main/debian-installer
```

Note

Because security updates are sporadic, Debian encourages direct updates from security.debian.org. There are few public mirrors available for Debian security updates. Nevertheless, you may still want to mirror those updates for your own network for all the reasons described in this book.

The remaining lines in this file come into play only if you're upgrading your version of Debian Linux, such as from Woody to Sarge. They allow `apt-mirror` to delete those directories associated with the older version of Debian Linux. Naturally, you should modify the URLs to match those that you use in other parts of this file.

If you've properly configured `/etc/apt/mirror.list`, all you need to do is run `apt-mirror` to start the mirror synchronization process. Some trial and error may be required, as your favorite mirror may not include a critical database file, such as `Packages.gz` and `Sources.gz`.

When you run `apt-mirror`, it starts two threads for each of the directories you've specified in your `/etc/apt/mirror.list`, as shown here:

```
Downloading 18 index files using 18 threads...
Begin time: Wed Apr  6 10:55:31 2005
[18]... [17]... [16]... [15]... [14]... [13]... [12]... [11]...
[10]... [9]... [8]... [7]... [6]... [5]... [4]... [3]... [2]...
[1]... [0]...
End time: Wed Apr  6 10:55:51 2005

Proceed indexes: [PP]

9458573242 bytes will be downloaded into archive.
Downloading 9629 archive files using 20 threads...
Begin time: Wed Apr  6 10:55:55 2005
[20]... [19]...
```

Note the number of bytes to be downloaded. From what I specified in my `/etc/apt/mirror.list`, that's over 9GB! That download will take some time.

After you've run `apt-mirror`, keep the mirror on your network up to date. To this end, the `apt-mirror` package includes a daily cron job. If you activate the embedded command in `/etc/cron.d/apt-mirror`, it runs `apt-mirror` by default at 4 a.m. every day. Make sure the update time is appropriate, relative to any other cron jobs on your system. Don't worry, `apt-mirror` downloads only those packages that have changed since the last update.

Finally, update the clients on your network to get their updates from your local mirror. That means revising the `/etc/apt/sources.list` configuration file on each of your Debian client computers.

4.3   SUMMARY

In this chapter, you explored the ins and outs of the apt commands. When you configure an appropriate mirror, you can use apt, aptitude, or the Synaptic Package Manager to keep your system up to date. But if you use aptitude or the Synaptic Package Manager, be careful. The defaults could easily delete packages that you consider essential.

You also explored how to configure a local `apt` mirror in three ways: based on download packages that you used to update your local computer, with the `debmirror` package, and by using the `apt-mirror` system. All three methods can help you reduce the load on your Internet connection and speed the patches you need on the different Debian (and related) clients on your network. In the next chapter, you'll learn how to configure the `apt` system for RPM-based distributions, such as Fedora Linux.

## CHAPTER 5

Configuring apt for RPM Distributions

There are many Linux users who believe that `apt` is the best available tool for keeping Linux distributions up to date. The developers behind the Conectiva (now Mandriva) Linux distribution have brought `apt` to RPM-based distributions. Although the number of `apt`-enabled repositories is growing, it's quite possible that you'll have to create your own if you want to use `apt` on your Linux computers.

In this chapter, you'll learn a bit about the history and status of `apt` for RPM distributions, how to configure `apt` for RPM distributions, such as Fedora Linux and SUSE Linux Professional, and how to create your own apt repositories from an update database. When configured, you can use most of what you learned in Chapter 4, "Making apt Work for You," to manage patches on your network.

Note

By the time you read this, it is quite possible that the Smart package manager will supersede apt for several RPM-based distributions. The lead developer for Smart, Gustavo Niemeyer, also maintained the RPM port of apt during his time with Conectiva. For more information, see www.smartpm.org.

Some of the problems associated with the `apt` for RPM distributions are problems associated with mixed 32-bit and 64-bit packages. The `apt` system works well for RPMs only if repository architectures aren't mixed. As of this writing, a number of applications on 64-bit RPM-based distributions require 32-bit libraries. Therefore, `apt` for RPM is not viable for most 64-bit Linux systems.

5.1   A HISTORY OF APT FOR **RPM**

One of the problems associated with RPMs is sometimes known as "dependency hell." This phenomenon is associated with failed attempts to install an RPM. You've probably seen messages specifying dependencies. You try to install that "dependency," but that fails because another package isn't installed. Frustration can reign when these messages continue for several levels. The developers behind what was Conectiva Linux "ported" apt to their RPM-based distribution because they wanted to make it easier to manage patches.

5.1.1   Reduced Dependency Trouble

In this book, we've explored some of the methods you can use to manage patches and upgrades on your Linux computers. Much of the work involves different techniques that can help you ensure that all package dependencies are satisfied.

It seems as though every distribution has a different method of patch management. Red Hat Enterprise Linux uses up2date on the Red Hat Network. Fedora uses up2date with yum, and is moving toward using pup with yum. While SUSE uses the YaST Online Update tool, it is moving to accommodate those who want to use the Smart package manager. Debian uses apt. The tool that is best for you depends on your distribution and experience. This book is designed to help you judge what is best for you and your network.

Unfortunately, some of these patch management tools have limited use. Until recently, YaST was limited by license to SUSE distributions. While it's available for other distributions, the up2date tool is closely associated with Red Hat. You can use the Red Hat Network to manage your patches only with a paid subscription to Red Hat Enterprise Linux.

5.1.2   The Conectiva Approach

When the developers of what was Conectiva (based in Brazil) wanted a Linux distribution, they wanted one with a recipe for commercial success. Red Hat and its RPM system was already more commercially successful than the Debian-based distributions.

One perceived weakness of the RPM system is how its installation and upgrade commands don't even look for, much less install or upgrade, any dependent packages. Options such as up2date did not yet exist. While the developers behind the former Conectiva Linux decided to base their distribution on an older version of Red Hat Linux, they had concerns about how to automate upgrades.

Several of the maintainers of apt live in Brazil. It was natural for Conectiva to look to them to help develop their update systems. To manage patches on Conectiva Linux, they developed a port of apt repositories for

RPM-based distributions, known as `apt4rpm`. Conectiva has shared its work under the GPL, and work continues through the SourceForge project. For more information, see http://apt4rpm.sourceforge.net.

Note

Apt for RPM is the client; `apt4rpm` is the associated repository creation tool. For more information on the philosophy, see freshmeat.net/articles/view/182. Claudio Matsuoka's article on the subject, while dated, is still instructive.

Unfortunately, the `apt4rpm` software does not include all the features associated with `apt` on Debian-based distributions. RPMs are built somewhat differently. In most cases, they do not include the pre- and post-installation scripts that can help you configure a DEB package and get it running on your system immediately. While most RPM-based distributions save existing configuration files, that functionality is still less common than with a DEB package.

As of this writing, Conectiva is in the process of merging with Mandrake and Lycoris. The combined company is known as Mandriva, and the process of integrating their knowledge continues.

Conectiva repositories are straightforward. As suggested by Conectiva's version of `/etc/apt/sources.list`, two basic repositories have been configured: `all` and `updates`. As you can see, Conectiva commands have a similar format to those you see in the Debian version of `/etc/apt/sources.list`, as discussed in Chapter 4.

```
rpm [cncbr] ftp://ftp.conectiva.com/pub/conectiva 9/i386 all
rpm-src [cncbr] ftp://ftp.conectiva.com/pub/conectiva 9/i386 all
rpm [cncbr] ftp://atualizacoes.conectiva.com.br 9/i386 updates
rpm-src [cncbr] ftp://atualizacoes.conectiva.com.br 9/i386 updates
```

The differences are straightforward. Instead of `deb` and `deb-src`, which are associated with binary and source packages, Conectiva repository commands start with `rpm` and `rpm-src`. Conectiva repositories are digitally signed; the `[cncbr]` tells apt to look for the signature. As of this writing, it is supported through a mailing list available from http://distro.conectiva.com.br/mailman/listinfo/apt-rpm. With the merger, and the emergence of the Smart Package Manager, this list may be ending. But will the move of SUSE 10.0 to `apt-rpm` give it new life?

Note

Mandriva already has an excellent patch management tool, known as urpmi. I do not cover it in this book, because it is used only for Mandriva Linux. For more information on urpmi, see the related HOWTO at http://developer.skolelinux.no/~zerodogg/rpmhowto/RPM-HOWTO.html.

5.1.3   An Overview of apt for RPM-Based Distributions

There are several other RPM-based distributions that use `apt`. In many cases, `apt` is not the primary patch management system for the distribution. In some cases, developers have processed apt repositories for certain distributions and have made them available for public use. These distributions include the following:

☞ Fedora supports the use of `apt` (at least as of Fedora Core 4). In support, several third-party groups have configured `apt` packages and repositories for this distribution. You can read more about this later in this chapter.

☞ The Polish Linux Distribution, PLD, supports the use of `apt` along with its primary patch management system, known as `poldek`. For more information, see www.pld.org.pl.

☞ Vine Linux, based in Japan, supports `apt`. For more information, see www.vinelinux.org. Originally derived from Red Hat Linux, upgrades are also supported with `apt`. An English language version of this Web site is available at www.vinelinux.org/index-en.html.

☞ Alt Linux is a Russian language distribution that uses RPM packages and supports apt updates. For more information, see www.altlinux.ru. It is based on Mandrake and uses `apt` as its primary update system.

☞ Yellowdog Linux is the distribution designed for the Power PC CPU closely associated with the Apple Macintosh. While they developed the yum commands that you'll learn about in Chapter 6, "Configuring a yum Client," and Chapter 7, "Setting Up a yum Repository," they also support the use of `apt` for updates.

☞ Mandriva allows the use of `apt` as an option to its `urpmi` update system.

☞ SUSE supports the use of `apt`. While YaST Online Update is the primary tool for managing patches on that distribution, SUSE has included `apt` for the first time in SUSE Linux Workstation 10.0. Several `apt` repository URLs are listed at http://linux01.gwdg.de/apt4rpm/home.html. You can read more about this later in this chapter.

There are several groups that support the use of `apt`. The developers behind freshrpms.net have configured `apt` repositories for Fedora, Yellowdog, and older versions of Red Hat Linux. For more information, see apt.freshrpms.net. Dag Wieers has created a number of apt and yum capable repositories. For more information, see http://dag.wieers.com/home-made/apt/.

Note

With recent improvements to yum, it's likely that the Fedora project will no longer support apt repositories starting with Fedora Core 5. Support may still be available from noted third parties, however.

A slightly out-of-date list of repositories for several RPM-based distributions is available as of this writing at http://apt4rpm.sourceforge.net/repos.html. In many cases, you may find up-to-date repositories at the servers indicated for the noted distributions. Some searching, some common-sense directory substitutions (e.g., SUSE version 10.1 for 10.0) as well as trial and error may be required. Interestingly enough, although Fedora appears to be moving away from apt, SUSE seems to be increasing support for the apt system. As of this writing, it appears they may also include support for yum repositories—starting with SUSE 10.1.

5.2   CONFIGURING APT FOR RPM

Generally, if you want to configure apt for RPM, you'll need to download and install it, along with any dependencies. You may also want to install one of the front-end apt package management systems described in Chapter 4, such as aptitude or the Synaptic Package Manager.

If there's one or more apt repositories available for your distribution, you'll want to configure your computer to take updates from that system. Naturally, because there are fewer apt repositories for RPM-based distributions, chances are good that updates will take longer. It is then more important to configure a local apt repository.

If remote apt repositories are available, you can create a local mirror using the techniques described in Chapter 3, "SUSE's Update Systems and rsync Mirrors," and Chapter 4. Otherwise, you may need to create your own apt repositories based on regular package repositories available for your preferred distribution.

5.2.1   Package Options

If you're planning to use apt to manage patches on your system, you may have had trouble in the past with RPM dependency hell, as noted earlier. When you install apt, you may have to deal with the RPM dependency problem one more time.

The packages required for apt vary by RPM-based distribution. Some trial and error may be required. If you're working with Fedora Linux 3 or later, apt RPMs may be downloaded from your favorite repository mirror, in the Extras directory. Related packages are listed in Table 5-1.

Table 5-1   Fedora's apt-related packages

Package	Description
apt	Installs the basic Advanced Package Tool system; includes the `apt-cache`, `apt-cdrom`, `apt-config`, and `apt-get` commands
apt-devel	Adds developmental tools if you want to extend the `apt` commands
apt-groupinstall	Supports searches and retrievals with `apt-cache` and `apt-get`, using the groups defined in `comps.xml` in the `/usr/share/comps/i386` directory
apt-python	Supports a python interface to `apt`; useful for some scripts
synaptic	Provides a GUI package manager interface

Naturally, each of these RPMs includes dependencies. Until you've installed and configured at least the basic `apt` RPM package and encounter dependencies, you'll have to resolve them the old-fashioned way: with patience and hard work.

If you're using an older (pre-10.0) version of SUSE Linux, navigate to ftp://ftp.gwdg.de/pub/linux/suse/apt/SuSE/9.3-i386/RPMS.suser-rbos/ for `apt` packages. The packages listed on this server may require other RPMs already available on the SUSE installation CDs/DVD.

5.2.2   Configuring apt

Next, you can modify the `apt` configuration files to meet your needs. As with Debian Linux, these files are stored in the `/etc/apt` directory. While `apt` relies mainly on the `sources.list` file to find repositories, the locations and details of other `apt` configuration files vary.

Ideally, you'll have access to some local or nearby network repository and can point your `sources.list` file to the appropriate URL. You can mirror the `apt` repository for other computers on your network, and patch management will be a breeze! Well, almost. I hope you're all so fortunate.

5.2.3   Selecting Sources

You might be surprised at the number of apt repositories available for RPM-based distributions. Unless your distribution uses `apt` as its primary means of updates, there are usually fewer `apt` repositories available, and they are likely to be further away from your network.

When selecting a source for an apt repository, check the documentation associated with your distribution. You may be pleasantly surprised. For example, one of the rebuilds of Red Hat Enterprise Linux 4, Lineox, uses `apt` by default for their updates (www.lineox.com).

Note

Lineox also maintains yum repositories for its 64-bit distribution, which avoids the previously described mixed-architecture problem associated with apt. Because there are a number of third parties who create apt repositories for the popular RPM distributions, you may end up associating your `sources.list` file with several different repositories.

5.2.4   Configuring apt for Fedora Linux

Red Hat has stated that Fedora Linux is the development platform for its enterprise distribution. As such, Fedora Linux evolves quickly. New versions are released every four to eight months, and the patch management tools may change just as frequently. As of this writing, there is no single collection of apt repositories and mirrors for Fedora Linux. After all, because this distribution uses `yum` by default for patch management, Fedora developers do not maintain apt repositories. One incomplete list of `apt` repositories is available from www.fedora.us/mirrorlists.

If you're using Fedora Core 4 or later, you'll need to point your `apt` sources to a third-party repository, such as apt.freshrpms.net. This Web site includes links with `apt` (and `yum`) downloads for the released versions of Fedora Core, Yellowdog Linux, as well as several Red Hat Linux versions. More importantly, it includes a list of mirrors you can use in your `/etc/apt/sources.list` configuration file.

Alternatively, you may find `apt` repositories for the latest Fedora Core and Red Hat Enterprise Linux (including rebuild) distributions at http://rpmforge.net. While detailed information was not available as of this writing, the RPM Forge team includes luminaries who've created third-party repositories, including Dag Wieers, Matthias Saou, and Dries Verachtert.

If available third-party repositories are not to your satisfaction, continue reading. Later in this chapter, you'll learn how you can create a dedicated repository for your distribution.

After you've configured repositories, you can run all the commands you've read about in Chapter 4. But there is more. If you're familiar with Red Hat or Fedora, you know that packages are organized in groups. You can find a list of groups on your chosen repositories with the following command:

```
apt-cache groupnames
```

If you ever want to install all the packages in a specific group, make a note of the group name. If you want a list of packages associated with a group, you can find it in the `comps.xml` file described earlier. For standard 32-bit systems, you can find this file in the `/usr/share/comps/i386` directory.

For example, the `ftp-server` package group includes one package, `vsftpd`, which is the default FTP server for Fedora. But the `comps.xml` file may be confusing. You can cut through the clutter by listing the members of this group with the following command:

```
apt-cache showgroup ftp-server
```

You can install all packages in this group with the following command:

```
apt-get groupinstall ftp-server
```

The packages, along with any dependencies, are installed just as they are when you run the `apt-get` command on a Debian system. Packages that are marked as optional in `comps.xml` are not included. You can also remove package groups along with dependencies. For example, if you want to remove the `office` package group, run the following command:

```
apt-get groupremove office
```

As you can see in Figure 5-1, this command specifies the packages to be removed, upgraded, and installed, as well as the results in disk space on your system.

Note

The aforementioned `apt-cache` and `apt-get` commands do not work with Debian Linux. They don't even work with the Lineox rebuild of Red Hat Enterprise Linux 4. However, all but the `apt-get mirror-select` command works with SUSE Linux Professional. Just remember, SUSE organizes package groups differently from Fedora or Red Hat.

```
michael@Fedora3:/home/michael
[root@Fedora3 michael]# apt-get groupremove office
Finding packages belonging to group(s)  office...
Reading Package Lists... Done
Building Dependency Tree... Done
The following packages will be REMOVED:
    ggv (2.8.0-1)
    gpdf (2.8.0-5)
    openoffice.org (1.1.2-10)
    openoffice.org-i18n (1.1.2-10)
    openoffice.org-libs (1.1.2-10)
    planner (0.12.1-1)
0 upgraded, 0 newly installed, 6 removed and 0 not upgraded.
Need to get 0B of archives.
After unpacking 906MB disk space will be freed.
Do you want to continue? [Y/n]
```

Figure 5-1   Removing a package group

However, dependencies that may have been installed with the original installation are not removed. Unlike the result with Debian Linux, the dependencies remain on the computer. That is one flaw with `apt` on RPM-based distributions that still exists today.

Synaptic with Fedora

You can install the Synaptic Package Manager described in Chapter 4. To do so, run the `apt-get install synaptic` command. After you do, it should be accessible in the GUI if you click Main Menu -> System Settings -> More System Settings -> Synaptic Package Manager. Alternatively, just run `synaptic` from a GUI command line interface. As you can see in Figure 5-2, the result is a bit different from what you saw in Chapter 4. By default, the left pane includes the different Fedora package groups.

Figure 5-2 Removing a package group

There is one major difference. In the Fedora version of the Synaptic Package Manager, you can select Edit -> Mark Packages by Task (or Ctrl+G), which opens the window shown in Figure 5-3. If you've run the `apt-cache groupnames` command described earlier, you'll recognize this window as a list of package groups that you can install with the `apt-get groupinstall groupname` command. You can mark the group of your choice; Synaptic configures installation of that group, along with any dependencies.

Figure 5-3   Marking package groups for installation

Then you can Apply Marked Changes with Ctrl+P or the Edit -> Apply Marked Changes command. This action opens a window similar to Figure 5-4, where you can and should check those packages that may be installed, upgraded, or removed, to make sure your needs are addressed. You should also make sure that any packages which are to be removed will not alter the basic configuration of your system. When you're satisfied, click Apply. Synaptic begins the process of downloading and then installing the selected packages, just as you've witnessed for Debian Linux in Chapter 4.

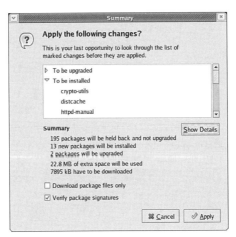

Figure 5-4   Confirming changes

When all required packages are downloaded, Synaptic uses the appropriate apt commands to install and or apply them as upgrades to existing packages. You can monitor the progress of the download, as shown in Figure 5-5. After the changes are complete, you can exit the Synaptic Package Manager.

Figure 5-5   Synaptic progress

5.2.5   Configuring apt for SUSE Linux

The SUSE Linux implementation of apt is similar to that for Fedora. While the packages you install differ, the results are similar in terms of the commands that you can run, as well as the way Synaptic interacts with your system. Naturally, you'll need apt-enabled mirrors configured for your version of SUSE Linux.

As with Fedora Linux, you'll have to configure the mirrors yourself. You could use the directives in the default /etc/apt/sources.list file:

```
rpm ftp://mirrors.mathematik.uni-bielefeld.de/pub/linux/suse/apt/
SuSE/10.0-i386 base update security rpmkeys
rpm ftp://ftp.gwdg.de/pub/linux/suse/apt/ SuSE/10.0-i386 base update
security rpmkeys
```

This would connect your computer to the base repository, as well as updates and security-related changes for your distribution.

If you're into experiments, you could use the sample /etc/apt/sources.list file available from ftp.gwdg.de. For SUSE Linux Professional 10.0, you can find this file in the following subdirectory: pub/linux/suse/apt/SuSE/10.0-i386/examples/. This file includes the following very long command line:

```
rpm      file:/ftp/pub/linux/suse/apt SuSE/10.0-i386 suser-guru
packman packman-i686 kernel-of-the-day suse-projects rpmkeys base java
update-drpm update-prpm update extra kde gnome mozilla openoffice
samba3 suser-agirardet suser-rbos suser-crauch suser-jengelh suser-gbv
usr-local-bin suser-tcousin suser-scorot suser-scrute suser-jogley
kraxel wine suse-people kde3-stable kde-unstable security-prpm
security
```

Note

Now that SUSE has committed to support apt, at least in SUSE 10.0 the number of alternative repositories will soon hopefully increase. The one alternative apt repository available as of this writing is ftp://opensuse.linux.co.nz.

As you've probably observed, the commands in `/etc/apt/sources.list` follows a specific format:

```
Package type / URL / Subdirectory / Repository section / Repository
section ...
```

In this case, the package type is `rpm`; the URL is the FTP site shown; the repositories are stored in the `SuSE/10.0-i386` subdirectory. If you want to create your own repository, you'll need to learn more. Navigate to the subdirectory on the noted URL, in this case, ftp://ftp.gwdg.de/pub/linux/suse/apt/SuSE/10.0-i386/. You'll find subdirectories for each of the noted repository sections.

You normally won't configure `apt` to acquire updates from all sections. In fact, several sections may have no files. Many of these repositories include test packages from specific developers; some of them are SUSE employees.

Therefore, you might want to limit the repository sections in your `/etc/apt/sources.list` to *some* of those suggested in Table 5-2. (These sections are subject to change; you might not see every section shown in the Table in the repository list for SUSE 10.0.) You might want to review all sections; SUSE might include important packages in other sections.

Table 5-2   Sample sections from SUSE's apt repository

apt Repository Section	Description
kernel-of-the-day	Lists the daily SUSE build of the current kernel
misc	Includes a variety of packages
mozilla	Browser and email packages related to Mozilla/Firefox
packman	Adds a variety of packages; many related to multimedia applications
samba3	Connects to a section with Samba-related packages
security	Lists security-related updates
security-prpm	Lists security-related Patch RPM (prpm) updates
update	Adds RPMs normally associated with SUSE updates
update-prpm	Includes update patches relative to existing RPMs
wine	Adds packages related to the Wine Is Not an Emulator (wine) system; for more information, see www.winehq.org

If your concern is obtaining stable updates, ignore this list. Accept the default `/etc/apt/sources.list` file.

After you've configured this file, you can use the Synaptic Package Manager to download and install the latest updates, using these steps:

1. Open Synaptic. In the GUI, click Main Menu -> System -> Configuration -> Package Manager. Enter the root password when prompted. The Synaptic Package Manager should open in your GUI.

2. In Synaptic, click Settings -> Repositories. You should see the repositories that you configured in /etc/apt/sources.list in this window. Any changes you make here are immediately written to this configuration file.

3. Click Edit -> Reload Package Information. This is equivalent to the apt-get update command, which makes sure that your system database is up to date with your configured repositories.

4. Click Edit -> Mark Packages by Task. If you want to install all default and mandatory packages in a group, you can check the package groups of your choice. If you want to learn more about a package group, highlight it and click Description.

5. Configure a smart upgrade. Click Settings -> Preferences, and navigate to the General tab. Under the System Upgrade drop-down text box, select Smart Upgrade.

6. Mark All Upgrades. Click the menu button by that name.

7. Click Apply. This opens the Summary window shown in Figure 5-6. Analyze this window carefully! If there are packages that would change your system, consider your options carefully. In Figure 5-6, the kernel is included in the list. Kernel upgrades can have unpredictable results.

Figure 5-6   Synaptic has marked packages for upgrade

8. Be careful! If the packages are what you want to upgrade, click Apply. Otherwise, click Cancel.

9. Make any changes to the upgrade list that you desire. I do not want to upgrade my kernel, so I clicked the Search icon, where I could call up all kernel-related packages, as shown in Figure 5-7.

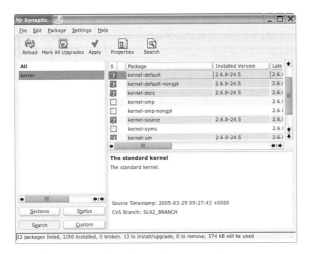

Figure 5-7   Synaptic has marked packages for upgrade

    10. I've unmarked the `kernel-default` package. Because there are dependencies, Synaptic highlights them for any corresponding changes, as shown in Figure 5-8.

Figure 5-8   Synaptic has unmarked packages

    11. In this case, when I unmarked the `kernel-default` package, Synaptic has unmarked all other suggested upgrades for this computer. I can no longer click the Apply button. However, if you still have upgrades to download and install, you can click Apply and return to step 8.

After Synaptic completes the update process, the job isn't done. You may need to update a number of SUSE configuration files in the `/etc/syconfig` directory. You can do so after an `apt`-based update with the following command:

```
SuSEconfig
```

Note

YaST Online Update runs the `SuSEconfig` command automatically after downloading and installing new packages.

Alternatively, you can use the specialty `apt` commands associated with
Fedora Linux to manage packages by groups. You may have read about the following commands in the previous section:

```
apt-cache groupnames
apt-cache showgroup groupname
apt-get groupinstall groupname
apt-get groupremove groupname
```

Be careful when you run these commands. Don't just blindly accept the
defaults! The effects of the `apt-get groupremove` command, for instance, may be
unpredictable. For example, I tried to run the following command on my
system:

```
apt-get groupremove Games-9.2-62.noarch
```

This command proposed that I accept the removal of key packages, such
as `evolution`, `gnome-desktop`, and `kdebase3`. If I had accepted the defaults, I
probably would have had to restore the files associated with these packages
from backup in order to run the KDE Desktop Environment.

5.2.6   Configuring apt for a Red Hat Rebuild

There is at least one rebuild of Red Hat Enterprise Linux 4 that relies prima-
rily on `apt` for updates. Lineox is somewhat unique for a rebuild distribution
of Red Hat Enterprise Linux. It is backed and supported by a separate company in Finland and supports free and paid updates using `apt`-based tools.
Naturally, `apt` packages are already installed by default on this rebuild distribution. (Lineox includes yum repositories for its 64-bit distribution versions.)

Note

There are other Red Hat rebuilds that have apt repositories available, such as
CentOS 4. For more information, see www.caosity.org.

Lineox supports a variety of mirrors worldwide. While the list is not extensive, it makes it possible to use `apt` to keep this rebuild up to date. The default version of Lineox's `/etc/apt/source.list` includes the following URLs:

```
rpm http://www.raimokoski.com/ pub/lineox/4.0/updates/i386 updates
rpm http://www.raimokoski.com/ pub/lineox/4.0/i386/os/Lineox os
```

The mirrors available for Lineox are complete; in other words, you can substitute the base URL of the mirror closest to you and use them to manage patches on your system. For example, the Lineox mirror in the U.S. is located at the Georgia Institute of Technology, at ftp://ftp.gtlib.cc.gatech.edu/. If you're located in the U.S., you should be able to substitute that URL for http://www. raimoski.com/.

The Lineox `apt` configuration files include suggestions for other repositories. We describe them here in some detail, as they may be useful for any Red Hat or Fedora distribution. These suggestions are located in files in the `/etc/apt/sources.list.d` directory and are listed in the following sections. All the suggested repositories in this directory are "commented out." You'll need to remove the comment character (#) if the repository noted is suitable for connections to your network.

While you should be able to connect to mirrors customized for your distribution, don't just change version numbers from the configuration files. Check the mirrors for yourself. Make sure that they contain the repositories that you need.

Note

The repositories described in the following sections may be superseded by those associated with the RPMForge.net project. Check the associated Web sites for the latest information.

---

atrpms.list

You may already be familiar with the repositories available from atrpms.net. The `atrpms.list` file includes the mirror of these repositories, based in Germany. For example, this file for Lineox 4.0 includes the following link to a Fedora Core 2 repository:

```
#rpm http://apt.physik.fu-berlin.de fedora/2/en/i386 at-testing
```

The mirrors listed at http://atrpms.net/mirrors/ are all on the European continent. You should be able to substitute their base URL for http://apt.physik.fu-berlin.de, as shown previously. While the examples in the version of Lineox 4.0 available as of this writing list only Fedora Core 1 and 2; Fedora Core 3 and 4 and Red Hat Enterprise Linux 3 and 4 repositories are also available. If later versions of these distributions have been released, check the mirror of your choice. You may be pleasantly surprised.

There are four different directories available from this repository: at-good, at-stable, at-testing, and at-bleeding. They are sequentially inclusive; in other words, all packages in the at-stable directory are included in the at-good directory; all packages in the at-good directory are included in the at-testing directory; all packages in the at-testing directory are included in the at-bleeding directory. Therefore, you do not need to specify more than one directory when you specify an atrpms.net repository. For example, if you do not want to include any unstable packages for a Fedora Core 4 repository, you could substitute the following line in the atrpms.list file:

```
rpm http://apt.physik.fu-berlin.de fedora/4/en/i386 at-good
```

dag.list

As noted earlier, Dag Wieers is a prominent developer who has built a number of binary packages that might otherwise be unavailable. For example, the still popular pine email reader is no longer included with the standard installation packages for some distributions, including Red Hat Enterprise Linux. You can find a pine RPM customized for Red Hat Enterprise Linux 3 and 4 in the associated dag.list repository.

For example, the following example points to an apt repository for Red Hat Enterprise Linux 3 packages:

```
rpm http://apt.sw.be redhat/el3/en/i386 dag
```

As documented at http://dag.wieers.com/home-made/apt/FAQ.php#B, separate repositories are available for Red Hat Enterprise Linux 2.1 and 4 at

```
rpm http://apt.sw.be redhat/el4/en/i386 dag
rpm http://apt.sw.be redhat/el2.1/en/i386 dag
```

freshrpms.list and os.list

As noted earlier, the developers behind freshrpms.net, including Matthias Saou, have created their own apt repositories. You can find a list of mirrors at apt.freshrpms.net. There may be additional apt mirrors available from the list at freshrpms.net/mirrors. I was able to find a suitable repository at one of these mirrors; I've added the following line to my version of /etc/apt/sources.list:

```
rpm http://ayo.us5.freshrpms.net fedora/linux/4/i386 base core extras
updates
```

Different `apt` repositories are listed in the `freshrpms.list` and `os.list` files in the `/etc/apt/sources.list.d` directory. But these files do not include a complete list of repositories available from freshrpms.net. As you can see from the Irish mirror at http://ayo.ie.freshrpms.net/fedora/linux/4/i386/, there is a substantial number of ayo repository directories available.

newrpms.list

Two developers from Germany, Rudolf Kastl and Dennis Huschens, have created their own repositories for some Red Hat and Fedora Linux updates. For more information, see newrpms.sunsite.dk. As of this writing, their repositories include only untested packages and are not being maintained.

5.3   Setting Up a Local Repository

Ideally, you won't have to go through the steps required to convert a group of RPMs into an `apt` repository. If you find a suitable mirror, you should be able to use the techniques described in Chapters 3 and 4 to download and synchronize your mirror to the `apt` repositories of your choice.

However, many repositories do not include `apt` databases. If you want an `apt` repository on your local network, you may need to download a regular mirror and then create the `apt` package databases from the files copied to your system. That becomes a local repository that you can use to keep your systems up to date.

Note

In this section, we assume that all you need to do is configure binary RPM packages into local repositories. If you have a need to configure source RPMs into an `apt` repository, the techniques are similar; generally, the Web sites mentioned in this chapter provide more information.

5.3.1   Mirroring a Remote Repository

If you're running Fedora Linux, there are several repositories that accept `rsync` connections. The master list of Fedora mirrors is available at fedora.redhat.com/download/mirrors.html. Read through the list, looking for the URLs that start with `rsync`. As an example, I can synchronize my repository with those available from mirrors.kernel.org in San Francisco. If you want to create a repository in the local `/mnt/repo` directory, you can use the command format described in Chapter 3.

First, make sure your chosen mirror still supports `rsync` connections. The following command, if successful, confirms `rsync` access and lists directories available for synchronization (don't forget the two colons at the end of the command):

```
rsync -n mirrors.kernel.org::
```

Now you can see fedora.us as part of the list. To find the appropriate subdirectory, you can do some searching. Generally, `rsync` directories on a mirror are structured in the same way as the HTTP or FTP server for that mirror. I've found the `apt` repositories for Fedora Core 3 at the following URL:

```
http://mirrors.kernel.org/fedora.us/fedora/fedora/3/i386/
```

Now you see the subdirectory associated with the desired apt repository:

```
fedora.us/fedora/fedora/3/i386/
```

Next, you can add this subdirectory to the `rsync` command. As you've seen in Chapter 3, the `-avv` switch adds appropriate levels of information. The dot (.) at the end of the following command points to all of the files in that directory. Now you can synchronize those files to a local directory of your choice; I use `/mnt/repo` in the following command:

```
rsync -avv mirrors.kernel.org::fedora.us/fedora/fedora/3/i386/.
/mnt/repo
```

If you don't want to use `rsync`, one alternative for RPM-based distributions is the `ftpcopy` command. Binary versions are available for Red Hat, Fedora, SUSE, and Yellowdog Linux. If you're using another RPM-based distribution, you can download and install the package from the `ftpcopy` home page at www.ohse.de/uwe/ftpcopy.html.

As an example, assume you want to use the `ftpcopy` command to synchronize a local `/mnt/repo` directory with the SUSE mirror at ftp://suse.osuosl.org/pub/suse/suse/i386/9.3/suse. In that case, you would run the following command to synchronize with the noted server subdirectory:

```
ftpcopy ftp://suse.osuosl.org/pub/suse/suse/i386/9.3/suse /mnt/repo
```

As with `rsync`, you can use the `--exclude` switch to customize what you download. For example, if you don't want to download any of the SUSE 64-bit RPMs, you could modify the command accordingly:

```
ftpcopy --exclude '*.x86_64.rpm'
ftp://suse.osuosl.org/pub/suse/suse/i386/9.3/suse /mnt/repo
```

If you weren't able to find an `apt` repository, you might have downloaded a regular repository of files and updates. Read on to see how you can reconfigure that download into an `apt` repository for your network.

Note

If you want to limit what you have to keep synchronized, analyze the mirror. Look for the directories and files that are updated on a regular basis. For example, Fedora Linux limits new stable packages for a distribution to the Updates directory; in that case, all you have to synchronize is the Updates part of the Fedora repository.

5.3.2 Creating an apt Repository

Now we'll see what you can do to configure an `apt` repository for your network. If you're starting with a set of RPMs downloaded for your network, you'll have to configure the directories you need. While not required, it can help to use the same directory structure that you might find in an `apt` repository for your distribution.

When you configure a repository, you'll want to create it in a partition with sufficient space. It may be helpful to configure a separate partition for your repository, to ensure that there is sufficient space on your system, and to keep updates from crowding out the space required by other services on your server.

Organizing a Repository Like a Mirror

If you've downloaded the RPMs from a standard Fedora repository, you can organize them in that distribution's basic categories: Core, Extras, and Updates. If you're creating an apt repository for standard 32-bit PC workstations, you'll want to start with an `i386/` subdirectory.

As an example, assume that you've configured a separate hard drive and mounted it on the `/mnt/repo` directory. To create the directory structure that you need, you'll run the following commands:

```
mkdir -p /mnt/repo/i386/RPMS.core
mkdir /mnt/repo/i386/RPMS.updates
mkdir /mnt/repo/i386/RPMS.extras
```

Next, you'll copy the appropriate RPMs to the noted directories. For Fedora Linux, you don't have to download the regular Fedora installation files. If you have the DVD mounted on `/media/cdrecorder`, you can copy the RPMs directly with the following command:

```
cp /media/cdrecorder/Fedora/RPMS/* /mnt/repo/i386/RPMS.core/
```

Naturally, you'll also want to copy the RPMs that you've presumably downloaded from a Fedora mirror. But the structure of Fedora mirrors is not consistent. For example (as of this writing), if you've connected to the mirror at Portland State University at http://fedora.cat.pdx.edu/linux/core/, the Extras directory is not readily visible. You actually have to navigate up and down the server to get to the extras RPMs at http://fedora.cat.pdx.edu/linux/extras/4/i386/. On the other hand, the regular and extras RPMs are right there when you navigate to the University of Oregon mirror at ftp://limestone.uoregon.edu/fedora/.

Stable changes to Fedora are stored in the Updates directory. It's important to keep this part of any Fedora repository up to date. You can do so with an appropriate cron job that uses a command, such as `rsync`, to keep your local update repository synchronized with your selected public mirror.

Fedora includes other repository directories. Whether you choose to make them part of your repository depends on the needs of you and your users. However, unless your users are developers, there is no reason to download or synchronize the `development/` or `updates/testing/` directories. In fact, because these packages are not stable, access can be dangerous for those who link to these repositories.

Organizing a Customized Repository

It might not be easy to configure an apt repository for your distribution. It's not fun to analyze the many different directories in the SUSE apt repository.

When you create your own apt repository, you can create your own `apt` directories. For example, for my SUSE computers, I've created a simple two directory repository. One group consists of the operating system files, which I've copied to my `/mnt/test/i386/RPMS.base` directory. The other group includes the updates I've downloaded via the YaST Online Update Server described in Chapter 3. I've copied those files to my `/mnt/test/i386/RPMS.updates` directory.

Processing an RPM-based Repository

Now you have RPMs (and perhaps SRPMs) in appropriate directories. Unfortunately, for Red Hat, Fedora, and SUSE, there is no `apt-ftparchive` or `dpkg-scanpackages` command as described in Chapter 4. These commands allowed you to create generic compressed package databases for `apt` repositories on Debian-based distributions. However, if you do have the `apt-ftparchive` command available on your distribution, you can use this command as described in Chapter 4 to make your repository useful. But there are alternatives.

For some RPM-based distributions, you'll need the `apt4rpm` and `apt-server` packages. If you've previously configured apt on your system, and this package is available from the repositories defined in your `/etc/apt/sources.list`, you can download it along with associated dependencies by using the following command:

```
apt-get install apt4rpm apt-server
```

Alternatively, you may need to download some other packages to satisfy dependencies. For guidance, see http://apt4rpm.sourceforge.net/dl-instruction.html.

When these packages are downloaded and installed, you'll have the tools you need to process the RPMs that you've copied to directories earlier in this section. The key is the `genbasedir` script. You can read it for yourself in the `/usr/bin/genbasedir` file. For the directory created earlier, you could create the `apt` databases with the following command:

```
genbasedir --progress --flat --bz2only --bloat /mnt/test/i386
```

These options aren't absolutely necessary. All that is required is that you cite the directory with the RPM subdirectories. In other words, the following command is sufficient:

```
genbasedir /mnt/test/i386
```

However, I've added the `genbasedir` command options shown for the following reasons:

☞ The `--progress` option allows you to monitor the progress of the command.

☞ The `--flat` option tells the script that the RPMs or SRPMs are in the directory defined.

☞ The `--bz2only` option tells the command to generate only compressed versions of the package database. Without it, you'll find both compressed and uncompressed versions of the database in the `base/` subdirectory.

☞ The `--bloat` option keeps the package file list as part of the database.

Whenever you update the RPMs, you'll need to update the associated database. You don't need to update all databases in your repository. For example, if you update the contents of the `/mnt/test/i386/RPMS.updates` directory, you could update the associated database with the following command:

```
genbasedir --progress --flat --bz2only --bloat /mnt/test/i386 updates
```

Naturally, if you synchronize your RPM directories with a mirror on a regular basis, you'll want to make this command a regular part of that job.

5.4   THE APT COMMANDS IN DETAIL

The `apt` commands are important. You can do more from the command line interface. If you want to take full advantage of the `apt` system, you'll learn how to use the basic `apt` commands. While we do not cover all available `apt` commands in this book, two are critical to anyone interested in patch management for RPM- and DEB-based distributions: `apt-cache` and `apt-get`.

There are certainly more `apt` commands of interest, some of which were covered in Chapter 4. Some are largely limited to Debian-style distributions.

5.4.1   Analyzing apt-cache in Detail

It's worth some trouble to examine what you can do with the `apt-cache` command. You can review most available options with the `apt-cache -h | less` command. This list is not complete; you learned about the `showgroup` and `groupnames` options earlier in this chapter, as well as `search` in Chapter 4. Several options are rarely used because other commands may be more useful. For example, while the `apt-cache add package` command adds a package to the cache, it's best to keep your entire database up to date with the `apt-get update` command. Therefore, several `apt-cache` options are not covered in this book.

apt-cache showpkg

When you run the `apt-cache showpkg packagename` command, `apt-cache` searches through available package databases, as download from servers and locations specified in `/etc/apt/sources.list`. One sample with the `synaptic` package is shown in Figure 5-9.

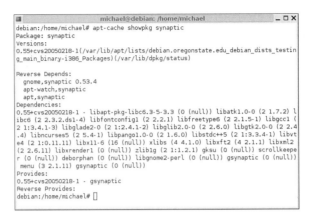

Figure 5-9   Listing versions and dependencies with apt-cache

Data associated with `synaptic` is divided into the following five categories:

☞ Versions specifies the different versions of the `synaptic` package that are available from your repositories.

☞ Reverse depends lists those packages that depend on `synaptic`, or whatever you're planning to install.

☞ Dependencies specifies those packages that are required before you can install `synaptic`.

☞ Provides lists packages and key files provided by the package.

☞ Reverse provides specifies packages that depend on what you're installing.

apt-cache showsrc

When you run `apt-cache showsrc packagename` command, `apt-cache` searches through available source package databases, as downloaded from source repositories specified in `/etc/apt/sources.list`; the source repositories in that file should be associated with the `deb src` or `rpm src` commands.

Among other things, the output includes the name of the source files required to build the binary packages and the `Build-Depends`, which include those packages and libraries required to build the specific package.

apt-cache show

If you want more information on available packages, the `show` option is for you. When you run the `apt-cache show packagename` command, the package does not have to be installed. All you need to do is specify the name of the package and apt-cache searches through the downloaded cache of available packages for dependencies, conflicts, and basic package information. Try it with the package of your choice.

apt-cache depends / rdepends

If you want more information on dependencies, the depends option is for you. When you run the apt-cache depends packagename command, the package does not have to be installed. All you need to do is specify the name of the package and apt-cache searches through the downloaded cache of available packages for dependencies. Try it with the package of your choice.

The rdepends option is relatively straightforward—it provides a list of reverse dependencies, those packages that depend on the package which you've specified.

apt-cache pkgnames

The apt-cache pkgnames command by itself is not useful. It scrolls a very long list of every package available from your repositories. But as a database, it can be powerful. For example, if you want a list of every package with gimp in its name, you'd run the following command:

```
apt-cache pkgnames | grep gimp
```

5.4.2   Analyzing apt-get in Detail

It's worth some trouble to examine what you can do with the apt-get command. You can review most available options with the apt-get -h | less command. This list is not complete; you learned about the mirror-select, showgroup, and groupinstall options earlier in this chapter, as well as update, install, remove, dselect-upgrade, clean, and autoclean options in Chapter 4. Several options that are rarely used are not covered in this book.

Default apt-get options are available either in /etc/apt/apt.conf or the /etc/apt/apt.conf.d directory. Naturally, you can override any defaults in these files with the correct switches.

apt-get switches

Before we discuss options, there are a number of switches available for apt-get, as shown in Table 5-3. You can use it with the options associated with apt-get, as described in this section and elsewhere in this book.

Table 5-3   apt-get switches

Switch	Description
-d	Performs downloads without installing any packages
-f	Attempts to repair broken dependencies
-m	Ignores and does not download any missing packages or those which are download with errors
-q	Silences any messages during the download and installation process
-s	Simulates the download and installation
-y	Answers all prompts with a "yes"
-u	Lists all upgraded packages
-v	Displays full version numbers (current and future) for upgrades
--no-upgrade	Does not perform upgrades
--purge	Purges packages to be deleted, including applicable configuration files
--reinstall	Reinstalls packages which are already at the latest version; replaces all but missing configuration files
--no-remove	If packages are to be removed, the process aborts automatically
--config-file	If you've set up an alternative to apt.conf, specify it with this switch

apt-get upgrade

I don't generally recommend the use of the apt-get upgrade command, because it leads to upgrades to newer versions of most currently installed packages. However, this option does not remove any installed packages; any upgrades which require removals aren't run.

apt-get dist-upgrade

If you're prepared to upgrade your system, the apt-get dist-upgrade command may be for you. It provides the "smart upgrade" option described in Chapter 4 available through the Synaptic Package Manager. Detailed options involve the use of the apt-preferences command available only for Debian-type distributions. Because upgrades often involve hundreds of packages, some conflicts may be inevitable. With the smart upgrade features, upgrades of more important packages take priority.

In some cases, the -f switch can help by repairing broken dependencies. Other switches described in Table 5-3 may also help.

apt-get check

If you're having problems with dependencies, run the `apt-get check` command. It updates the current cache of packages and lists any unmet dependencies.

5.4.3 Debian-Only apt Commands

There are several apt-related commands generally available only for Debian-type distributions. While Conectiva has ported most of these commands to its RPM-based distribution, they are generally not available for other RPM-based distributions. They include several commands described in Chapter 4, including

- ☞ `apt-build` downloads source and build packages associated with a specific download, optimized for a specific architecture.
- ☞ `apt-ftparchive` generates index files for apt-based archives. The corresponding RPM-based command, as described earlier, is `genbasedir`, which is part of the apt-server RPM.
- ☞ `apt-howto` includes the latest version of the APT HOWTO; it is also available from www.debian.org/doc/manuals/apt-howto.
- ☞ `apt-listbugs` is normally not run by itself; when installed, it's automatically invoked by other `apt` commands to download available bug reports.

5.4.4 RPM-Only apt Commands

There are three `apt` scripts available only for RPM-based distributions. As of this writing, they have not been ported to Debian-based distributions. Depending on the distribution, they may be available as part of the `apt` or the `apt-server` RPM packages. These scripts are as follows:

- ☞ `genbasedir` was described earlier in this chapter; it allows you to create a database suitable for an apt repository.
- ☞ `genpkglist` is run via `genbasedir` to create package list archives.
- ☞ `gensrclist` is also run via `genbasedir` to create source package archives.

5.5 SUMMARY

In this chapter, you learned to extend your knowledge of `apt` to RPM-based distributions. It is an alternative to the "dependency hell" often associated with installing RPM packages. The work of the Brazilian developers of the former Conectiva Linux have made this possible. You can now use `apt` to keep distributions, such as SUSE, Fedora, and even some Red Hat Enterprise Linux rebuilds, up to date.

The developers behind several distributions have configured their own apt repositories and have made them available online. Independent developers have configured additional apt repositories you can use and mirror locally on your network.

If an `apt` repository is not available for your distribution, you can create your own. You can still create a mirror of a standard repository on your network. With the `genbasedir` command and a little work organizing packages into local directories, you can create the databases which can make your local mirror useful as an `apt` repository.

In the next two chapters, we'll explore the major alternative to `apt`, known as `yum`.

## CHAPTER 6

Configuring a yum Client

Many experienced Linux users, historically, have not been satisfied with the patch management tools of the two Linux market leaders, Red Hat and SUSE. Their problems are, in part, related to their reliance on distribution-specific patch management tools. As we've seen in Chapters 1-3, SUSE's YaST Online Update and the Red Hat Update Agent are both excellent tools. Unfortunately, these tools are not easily used on other distributions, and they create bureaucratic filters on the contributions of the Linux community. In addition, they do not have the broad level of community support available for the `apt` or even the Smart Program Manager commands.

This lack of satisfaction began to change with the first release of Fedora Linux in the fall of 2003. As Red Hat moved toward a subscription support model for its Enterprise Linux distribution, Red Hat simultaneously moved toward the community with the Fedora Linux project. To enhance community support for Fedora, Red Hat incorporated the work of the Yellow Dog distribution on patch management. Their tool is known as `yum`, short for Yellowdog Updater, Modified. With the Fedora `apt` repositories described in Chapter 5, "Configuring apt for RPM Distributions," along with the Red Hat Update Agent described in Chapter 2, "Consolidating Patches on a Red Hat/Fedora Network," Fedora now incorporates a variety of tools for patch management.

The changes continued with the acquisition of SUSE by Novell in early 2004. As you've seen in Chapter 3, "SUSE's Update Systems and rsync Mirrors," SUSE has already incorporated its Online Update server in YaST. Novell has also incorporated Linux in its Zenworks system for patch management (formerly known as Red Carpet). As of this writing, it is too early to assess the response of the Linux community to the Zenworks Linux Management patch update tool.

In other words, if you want to manage patches on RPM-based distributions with tools familiar to the Linux community, you can use either `yum` or `apt`. Some developers prefer `yum` because it is customized for RPM-based distributions, especially those released by Red Hat. Others prefer `apt` because of the associated levels of community support. The `yum` commands are also supported by Fedora, AspLinux of Russia, and Yellow Dog Linux.

In this chapter, we will extend our discussion of yum for various Linux clients to show you how it can help you manage patches on a variety of RPM-based distributions. But first, we explore the history and workings of yum as an RPM-based system.

6.1   THE BASIC YUM PROCESS

Structurally, yum is built for RPM-based distributions. As noted in the yum HOWTO, available online from www.phy.duke.edu/~rgb/General/yum_ HOWTO.php, yum uses "the same tools and python bindings" associated with Red Hat and other RPM distributions to install packages and automatically resolve dependencies.

Both yum and apt rely on package headers. The header for each package includes forward and reverse dependency information. With this information in a complete database, yum (as well as apt) can help you install the packages of your choice along with any packages required to satisfy dependencies. As suggested by the acronym, yum is a modified version of the original update command developed for Yellow Dog Linux.

Modifications are continuing as the Fedora Linux community focuses on yum to meet its update needs. New packages and commands have been developed to keep yum systems and repositories up to date.

6.1.1   Yellow Dog and yum

The original version of yum is known as yup, the Yellowdog Updater. While Yellow Dog Linux was developed for various versions of the Apple Macintosh (www.yellowdoglinux.com), it is based on the same code that you can find in Linux for all architectures. Yellow Dog Linux also organizes its packages in RPMs.

6.1.2   yup and yum

The yup command has weaknesses. It's slow because it downloads complete RPMs before it can read header information for dependencies. In its original form, it could not be configured to download packages from more than one repository. It is now essentially obsolete. Today, even Yellow Dog Linux uses yum for its own updates.

Several developers at Duke University wanted to create an open source update manager that would work with Red Hat. Many at Duke were already familiar with this distribution, as they're practically neighbors with the Red Hat developers in the Raleigh-Durham area of North Carolina. According to the yum home page at linux.duke.edu/projects/yum/, they wanted a tool that did not require custom servers for their networks. Out of this came the first tools and repositories associated with yum.

6.1.3 Repositories and Headers

One advantage of `yum` is that you can use it to configure repositories on standard FTP or HTTP servers. To maximize compatibility with Red Hat, the `yum` developers wrote their packages in the Python language, which Red Hat happens to use for its Anaconda as well as its `up2date` systems.

The other advantage is how the `yum` command relies on RPM headers. You'll learn the commands required to copy just the headers from a directory of RPMs in Chapter 7, "Setting Up a yum Repository." To make sure your repository supports `yum`, look for the `headers/` or `repodata/` subdirectories.

6.1.4 Required yum Packages

The `yum` system is compact. The binary `yum` RPM package is less than 200KB. It includes everything you need to manage patches and create a repository on your system: the `yum` and `yum-arch` commands. As you'll see in Chapter 7, Fedora Core 3/4 and later distributions substitute the `createrepo` RPM instead of the `yum-arch` command to help you configure a `yum` repository on your own network.

If you're running Red Hat or Fedora Linux and want to continue to use `up2date` as an update tool, you can modify the associated configuration files to acquire updates from `yum` repositories. Alternatively, if you're willing to learn the yum client commands, you'll never have to use `up2date` ever again.

Note

It's unclear as of this writing, but SUSE may move toward yum-based repositories as well, possibly as soon as SUSE 10.1. Whether they use apt or yum repositories, they will likely use the Smart package manager (http://smartpm.org).

6.2 SAMPLE YUM CLIENTS

This book is focused on Red Hat/Fedora, SUSE, and Debian. The only distribution from this list that natively supports yum is Fedora Linux. However, a variety of yum repositories is also available for Red Hat Enterprise Linux. And several of the Red Hat Enterprise Linux rebuild distributions use yum as their primary means for patch management.

Note

Before adding a yum repository to your configuration files, make sure the cited URL exists. As you'll see in Chapter 7, yum repository URLs should include either a `headers/` or `repodata/` subdirectory, which includes the headers from all of the enclosed RPM packages.

6.2.1   Fedora

We examined how you can configure Fedora as a yum client briefly in Chapter 1, "Patch Management Systems." In this section, we'll examine the configuration process in more detail. There are two parts to this process. You've already configured your Fedora computer as a `yum` client. In this section, you'll direct Fedora's version of the Red Hat Update Agent to the same `yum` repositories.

Note

Starting with Fedora Core 5, Red Hat has replaced the Update Agent with the Package Updater, also known as Pup. If you prefer the Update Agent, you can still install the up2date and up2date-gnome packages from the Fedora Core 5 repository. Unfortunately, I could not include Fedora Core 5 in this chapter, as the first test (beta) release was made available as this book was being sent to the printer.

Fedora's Red Hat Update Agent and yum

By default, Fedora's version of the Red Hat Update Agent is configured to use `yum`. The key configuration file associated with the Update Agent is the `sources` file in the `/etc/sysconfig/rhn` directory. For Fedora Core 3, default repositories were directly cited in this file. Starting with Fedora Core 4, the following command searches through repositories as specified in the `/etc/yum.repos.d` directory:

```
repomd fedora http://fedora.redhat.com/
```

In this section, I'll examine configuration files from Fedora Core 3 and 4. While this may be confusing at first, I believe you can learn a lot about configuring yum for updates, based on the contrasts. In addition, if you use Red Hat Enterprise Linux 4 (or one of the related "rebuild" distributions), you'll see later in the chapter why it helps to know how to configure yum on Fedora Core 3.

As suggested in Chapter 1, there are four repositories associated with Fedora Linux releases (and two more of interest):

☞ `os` is associated with the basic release files and includes those packages that you would find on the Fedora installation CDs.

☞ `updates` includes stable packages that are updated or otherwise revised to address security problems or introduce new features.

☞ `updates-testing` adds candidate files for `updates` that are not considered to be production-ready (but what you might consider if you're desperate for an update).

☞ `development` includes those unstable packages that may be revised as often as every day.

☞ `extras` is a fifth super-category; there are actually several additional developmental and testing repositories available in the `extras` category. If you're interested in this level of detail, search the `extras` subdirectory of your favorite Fedora mirror.

☞ `extras-development` is a sixth category, similar to the regular `development` repository.

The default configuration for Fedora Core 3 includes the following four command lines, which configure connections to the yum installation (`os`) and `updates` repositories:

```
yum fedora-core-3
http://download.fedora.redhat.com/pub/fedora/linux/core/3/$ARCH/os/
yum updates-released-fc3
http://download.fedora.redhat.com/pub/fedora/linux/core/updates/3/
$ARCH/
yum-mirror fedora-core-3 http://fedora.redhat.com/download/up2date-
mirrors/fedora-core-3
yum-mirror updates-released-fc3
http://fedora.redhat.com/download/up2date-mirrors/updates-released-fc3
```

In contrast, the default configuration for Fedora Core 4 points to default repositories in files in the `/etc/yum.repos.d` directory. The files associated with the installation (`os`) and `updates` repositories are `fedora.repo` and `fedora-updates.repo`. The key commands from these files include the following:

```
mirrorlist=http://fedora.redhat.com/download/mirrors/fedora-core-
$releasever
mirrorlist=http://fedora.redhat.com/download/mirrors/updates-released-
fc$releasever
```

These files (and any others in the `/etc/yum.repos.d` directory) are active if you see the following directive in the configuration file:

```
enabled=0
```

For both Fedora Core 3 and Fedora Core 4, these commands connect your computer to the `os` and `updates` repositories on two different servers: download.fedora.redhat.com and a random mirror as specified in the `fedora-core-3` and `updates-released-fc3` files (as well as `fedora-core-4` and `updates-released-fc4` files) at http://fedora.redhat.com/download/up2date-mirrors/.

It's best to change these command lines to point to a different mirror. A list of mirrors is available from http://fedora.redhat.com/download/mirrors.html. Before making any change to the URL, check the associated directory. You may need to change that as well.

For example, as of this writing, if you were to use the mirror server at the University of Southern California, the server URL is http://mirrors.usc.edu. However, because the subdirectories with the `os` and `updates` repositories are different; the resulting command lines would be

```
yum fedora-core-3
http://mirrors.usc.edu/pub/linux/distributions/fedora/3/$ARCH/os/
yum updates-released-fc3
http://mirrors.usc.edu/pub/linux/distributions/fedora/updates/3/$ARCH/
```

In Fedora Core 3, you'll find two sets of command lines in /etc/sysconfig/rhn/sources. The second two command lines are an attempt to select a second repository. The defaults actually select a random repository from the list available from the following files:

```
http://fedora.redhat.com/download/up2date-mirrors/fedora-core-3
http://fedora.redhat.com/download/up2date-mirrors/updates-released-fc3
```

Take a look at these files. You'll find URLs pointing to servers all over the world. In principle, listing alternate servers for the `os` and `updates` repositories is an excellent idea. But be careful. If you're in Korea and you get connected to a repository in Austria, patch management performance may suffer.

> **Note**
> When you test the Red Hat Update Agent with aforementioned mirrors files, run `up2date -u` at the command line interface. The first lines of output tell you which mirrors are used. Remember, the actual mirror varies at random among those mirrors listed in the aforementioned files linked via `/etc/sysconfig/rhn/sources`.

On the other hand, there are country-based mirror lists available at http://fedora.redhat.com/download/mirrors/ and http://fedora.redhat.com/download/up2date-mirrors/. These directories includes a list of files with country name extensions, in ICANN top-level domain format. For more information, see http://www.iana.org/cctld/cctld-whois.htm.

For example, if you're located in Germany, you might consider the `fedora-core-4.de` file, which includes URLs for several different servers. If these servers are acceptably close to you, they are excellent options that can ensure you're able to connect to appropriate yum repositories even when there are connection problems.

Don't accept these files blindly; it's possible that someone may include a server from a different continent in a file by mistake. Some of these files may be empty. And some files may not be suitable. For example, if you're located in eastern Canada, the fedora-core-3.ca file may not be right for you, because it currently lists only one server, which happens to be in western Canada (Calgary, Alberta). While the corresponding file for Fedora Core 4 includes a wider variety of Canadian mirrors, it's possible that mirrors in the U.S. may be closer than any of the four listed in the fedora-core-4.ca file. (However, I certainly understand that some prefer to keep their international Internet traffic to a minimum.)

I'm located on the West coast of the U.S. Because the list of mirrors in the fedora-core-3.us.west file suits my location well, I've included that URL in the /etc/sysconfig/rhn/sources file on my Fedora Core 3 computer:

```
yum-mirror fedora-core-3 http://fedora.redhat.com/download/up2date-
mirrors/fedora-core-3.us.west
yum-mirror updates-released-fc3
http://fedora.redhat.com/download/up2date-mirrors/updates-released-
fc3.us.west
```

As for my Fedora Core 4 computer, I've revised my /etc/yum.repos.d/fedora-updates.repo file to point to the file with the list of U.S. West Coast mirrors:

```
http://fedora.redhat.com/download/up2date-mirrors/updates-released-
fc4.us.west
```

Using the same tools, you can also connect your computer to updates-testing, development and even the extras repositories. Unfortunately, in several cases, the list of repositories in a mirrors file is too short. If it includes only one repository, or if there is no geographically appropriate file, you may want to create your own list using several baseurl directives. For example, a user in Switzerland might not be satisfied with the one server listed in the fedora-core-4.ch mirror list file (ch is the standard two-letter code associated with Switzerland). If I were in Switzerland, I'd include the following in my /etc/yum.repos.d/fedora.repo configuration file, which includes the Swiss mirror, along with a mirror in southern Germany:

```
[base]
name=Fedora Core $releasever - $basearch - Base
baseurl=http://mirror.switch.ch/ftp/mirror/fedora/linux/core/4/$ARCH/
os/
baseurl=http://ftp-stud.fht-
esslingen.de/pub/Mirrors/fedora.redhat.com/linux/core/4/$ARCH/os/
enabled=1
gpgcheck=1
gpgkey=file:///etc/pki/rpm-gpg/RPM-GPG-KEY-fedora
```

If you're running Fedora Core 4, you'll have to update the appropriate files in the /etc/yum.repos.d directory. For example, if you're interested in the latest package builds and want to activate the development repository, take the following steps:

1. Open the `fedora-devel.repo` file, from the `/etc/yum.repos.d` directory, in the text editor of your choice.

2. Change the `mirrorlist` directive to point to the most appropriate geographically based mirror file. For example, if you're on the East Coast of the U.S., you might replace the `mirrorlist` directive with the following:

```
mirrorlist=http://fedora.redhat.com/download/mirrors/fedora-core-
rawhide.us.east
```

3. Make sure the `enabled` directive is active, or set to 1. By default, it is inactive, or set to 0:

```
enabled=1
```

4. Make sure the `gpgcheck` directive is active, or set to 1. By default, it is inactive, or set to 0:

```
gpgcheck=1
```

5. Cite the appropriate GPG file, in this case with the following directive:

```
gpgkey=file:///etc/pki/rpm-gpg/RPM-GPG-KEY-fedora-rawhide
```

6. Save the file. The next time you run `up2date`, you should find the `development` repository in the channel list.

Note

Don't activate the `development` repository on production computers. This repository includes nightly builds of the latest packages, designed for testing. By definition, they may still have bugs.

Note

Be careful. For all versions of Fedora Linux released as of this writing, there is one command in the `sources` file that would try to connect your Fedora Linux computer to the Red Hat Network. If you have a subscription to Red Hat Enterprise Linux, activating the following command would cause the Red Hat Update Agent to prompt you to register this computer on the Red Hat Network, which could use up a valuable subscription to this service. *Do not activate this command!*

```
#up2date default
```

Before running the Red Hat Update Agent, you should make sure that the key components are themselves up to date. You can do so with two simple commands:

```
up2date up2date
up2date yum
```

Updates don't happen often to either of these two packages. However, if you configure a script to automate updates, you should make these commands part of that script.

When properly configured, you can proceed in two ways. If you want to update all but kernel packages from the command line interface, run the following command, which downloads and installs all available updates by default.

```
up2date -u
```

Gosh, isn't that simple? But be warned, the first time you run this command with Fedora Linux, it could take some time. In my case, this command downloaded around 2,000 headers to `/var/spool/up2date`; the process took nearly a full hour.

But you may not want to update all packages. For example, as of this writing, updates to the Firefox Web browser can break any plugins that you've installed. In that case, you may want to keep Firefox off the update list. You can find the list of available updates with the following command:

```
up2date -l
```

If the list is long, you may want to pipe the output. For example, if you want to see if there's an upgrade to Firefox in the update list, you could run the following command:

```
up2date -l | grep firefox
```

If Firefox is on the list, you can make the Update Agent exclude it. Sure, you could configure it with `up2date --configure`, but this is only a temporary measure. I'm assuming that you eventually do want the security updates associated with new versions of the Firefox browser.

With Fedora Linux, the Update Agent is configured to use yum by default. That means you can take advantage of the switches and options associated with the `yum` command. You can use `yum` command switches, such as `--exclude`. In this case, you can exclude Firefox from the update list with the following command:

```
up2date -u --exclude=firefox
```

You can use the `--exclude` switch for as many packages as you want to exclude from the update list. Now, isn't that easy?

Even with the versatility of the command line version of the Update Agent, there are administrators who prefer the interactive mode available when you run the Update Agent in the GUI. If this is what you want to do, take the following steps:

1. Run the `up2date` command from a command line interface.

2. Unless you've logged in as the root user, you're prompted for the root administrative password.

3. When you see the Welcome to Red Hat Update Agent window, select Forward.

4. You'll see the channels associated with your repository configuration file (`/etc/sysconfig/rhn/sources` for Fedora Core 3; the files with the `enabled=1` directive in the `/etc/yum.repos.d` directory for Fedora Core 4), along with the mirror selected, as shown in Figure 6-1. Unselect any channels that you do not desire to use in this update, and select Forward to continue.

Fedora systems are not part of the Red Hat Network described in Chapter 2, "Consolidating Patches on a Red Hat/Fedora Network," so ignore the message about subscribing to channels in Figure 6-1.

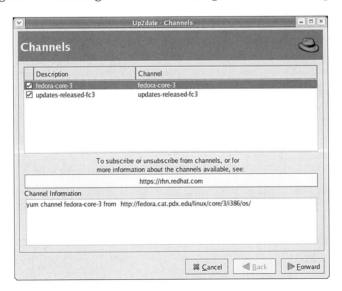

Figure 6-1   Fedora updates with a random mirror

5. You're taken to the Packages Flagged to be Skipped window. As with most updates, it's generally not desirable to download or install a new kernel unless you know your system is ready. Unless you're ready to install a new kernel, do not select the kernel related packages; click Forward to continue.

6. You're taken to a long list of available package updates, such as those shown in Figure 6-2. Select those packages that you want updated, and select Forward to continue.

7. The Update Agent begins to test dependencies, using yum. Any dependent packages are added to the update list. The Update Agent then proceeds with retrieving packages. When the process is complete, click Forward to continue.

8. The Update Agent proceeds with installing the downloaded packages. When the process is complete, click Forward to continue.

9. The Update Agent lists the packages that it installed or upgraded on your system. Click Finish when you've reviewed these packages.

Figure 6-2   List of available package updates

Troubleshooting

With thousands of packages, the first rule when running the Red Hat Update Agent is patience. You may be downloading hundreds of MB of headers. Only after the headers are installed can yum check your requested updates for dependencies. Only then does the Update Agent download the actual packages. Then the packages are installed. By default, they are then deleted from the /var/spool/up2date directory. Each of these steps takes time. My first update for Fedora Core 3 took over two hours on a high-speed cable modem connection. Naturally, this should focus your mind on how much you need patch management, along with a local repository.

There can be problems even after `yum` resolves dependencies. If you run into a problem, you could rerun the Update Agent in verbose mode with the `-v` switch:

```
up2date -v -u
```

Alternatively, you could watch the messages as they appear with the following command:

```
tail -f /var/log/up2date
```

There are occasional errors, such as `IOError: Not a gzipped file`. In that case, try a different mirror. Updates may not be as consistent on the mirror that you've selected.

One other error I've encountered relates to an unresolvable dependency. You might think this is not possible with `yum`, because it automatically resolves dependencies. However, by default, the Update Agent does not download or install a newer version of the Linux kernel. The related error I encountered is

```
Unresolvable chain of dependencies:
hal-0.4.7-1.FC3                         requires kernel >= 2.6.10
```

While we discuss `yum` in detail later in this chapter, we already know that the `--exclude` switch is useful; for example, the following command excludes the `hal` RPM from that list:

```
up2date -u --exclude=hal
```

I can also exclude the Firefox browser (and similarly named packages, courtesy of the wildcard) from the update list:

```
up2date -u --exclude=hal --exclude=firefox*
```

6.2.2   Red Hat Enterprise Linux

In Chapter 2, we explored how you can configure Red Hat Enterprise Linux (RHEL) on the Red Hat Network. You can also configure `yum` on RHEL. While this package isn't available as of this writing through normal Red Hat Network channels, it is available from third parties.

Note

Before looking to third parties, check all available RHEL channels. Red Hat provides a number of additional packages for its Enterprise Linux distributions in alternative channels. These include packages such as Java, Macromedia Flash, and Real Player. Run a search. You might be pleasantly surprised. My educated guess is that Red Hat will add yum to one of these channels sometime in the future.

You can get yum from a Fedora or Red Hat mirror or from one of the rebuilds of RHEL that uses yum repositories. If you're running RHEL 3, you can get a compatible version of yum from a RHEL 3 rebuild or Red Hat Linux 9. If you're running RHEL 4, you can get a compatible yum from a RHEL 4 rebuild or Fedora Core 3. As described earlier, Fedora mirrors are listed at fedora.redhat.com/download/mirrors.html. Red Hat Linux 9 is often available from the same mirrors; you may need to do some searching up or down the directory tree to find those files. As of this writing, useful RHEL repositories are available from the following sources:

☞ ATrpms includes four levels of repositories. The `stable` repository is straightforward. The `good` repository includes `stable` packages along with a few others that have not undergone sufficient testing to be considered stable. The `testing` repository includes `good` packages along with a few that are equivalent to betas on many systems. The `bleeding` repository includes all current ATrpms packages, including many which are currently in development. For more information, see http://atrpms.net.

☞ The Dag Wieers repositories are excellent sources for packages such as the pine email reader. While pine is still popular (www.washington.edu/pine/), it is not included in distributions, such as RHEL 4, for licensing reasons. For more information on connecting to these repositories, see http://dag.wieers.com/home-made/apt/.

☞ The Macromedia repository is available for the Flash plugin associated with many Web sites. While available as part of the Extras channel for RHEL 4, the Extras channel is not available for RHEL 3.

Note

Many of the developers behind these disparate repositories are combining their efforts. You may be able to find RHEL 4 repositories at www.rpmforge.net.

With the following steps, we'll download yum from a mirror for Fedora Core 3 and install the pine email reader on RHEL 4. Then we'll connect RHEL 4 to two different yum repositories. You can use the same basic steps to connect to other yum repositories of your choice, even those that you've configured locally. If you don't qualify for support, you can connect to the repositories of one of the RHEL rebuilds, as described in the next section.

Note

Any package that you install on RHEL that is not part of one of your subscription channels on the Red Hat Network will not be supported by Red Hat. If you install a third-party RPM, you may put the Red Hat support for your system at risk.

---

1. From your RHEL 4 computer, navigate to http://fedora.redhat.com/download/mirrors.html. Select the mirror appropriate for your location.
2. Navigate to the directory with Fedora Core 3 operating system files. The actual directory may vary by mirror. In my case, I've navigated to http://fedora.cat.pdx.edu/linux/core/3/i386/os/Fedora/RPMS/.
3. Download and install the `yum` RPM. For Fedora Core 3, it's `yum-2.1.11-3.noarch.rpm`.
4. Review the installed `/etc/yum.conf`. As you can see from the comments, you can specify `yum` repositories in the `/etc/yum.repos.d` directory.
5. Now, add an `atrpms.repo` file in the `/etc/yum.repos.d` directory. Open this file in a text editor. Per http://atrpms.net/install.html, add the following commands to that file (If there is a mirror closer to you, substitute it for the URL shown below):

```
[at-stable]
name=ATrpms for Fedora Core $releasever stable
baseurl=http://apt.atrpms.net/rhel/4/en/$basearch/at-stable
```

Before implementing this change, make sure the cited URL still exists and includes the desired `yum` repository. Save the file.
6. Test the result. Run the `yum list` command. You should be able to watch as your system connects to the repository and lists the available packages.
7. Next, add a `dag.repo` file in the `/etc/yum.repos.d` directory. Open this file in a text editor. Per the installation instructions available from http://dag.wieers.com/home-made/apt/, add the following commands to that file (if there is a mirror closer to you, substitute it for the following URL):

```
[dag]
name=Dag RPM Repository for Red Hat Enterprise Linux
baseurl=http://apt.sw.be/redhat/el4/en/$basearch/dag
gpgcheck=1
enabled=1
```

8. Test the result. Run the `yum list` command. You should be able to watch as your system connects to the repository and lists the available packages.

9. Import the associated RPM GPG (GNU Privacy Guard) key, available from http://dag.wieers.com/home-made/apt/FAQ.php#B5. You can do so with the following command:

```
rpm --import http://dag.wieers.com/packages/RPM-GPG-KEY.dag.txt
```

10. Make sure the pine email reader is available from your configured repositories with the following command:

```
yum list | grep pine
```

The output should include a line similar to the following, which cites the package, architecture, version, and repository:

```
pine.i386      4.62-1.2.el4.rf      dag
```

11. Install the pine email reader with the following command:

```
yum install pine
```

12. Confirm installation with the `rpm -q pine` command.

13. Configure pine for your users.

Note

There are reports of Fedora users who connect to multiple third-party repositories who experience unresolvable dependencies. Take care when using non-Fedora or non-Red Hat repositories.

6.2.3 Red Hat Enterprise Linux Rebuilds

Several rebuilds of RHEL use `yum` for updates, with techniques and configuration files similar to those described earlier for Fedora Linux.

In Chapter 2, we reconfigured a CentOS-4 system to point toward more local mirrors. The key file is `CentOS-Base.repo`, in the `/etc/yum.repos.d` directory. If you want to activate all the repository directories listed, be careful. The names and locations of each repository directory may vary by mirror. Check each repository directory URL yourself. For example, the CentOS-4 `testing` repository may not be available on many mirrors.

You can add the same files described previously for `yum` on RHEL 4. In fact, I've copied the files that I created from the previous section directly and installed the pine email reader on my CentOS-4 system from the Dag Wieers repository.

However, CentOS-4, like RHEL, Fedora, and other RHEL rebuilds, relies on the Red Hat Update Agent to keep its systems up to date. As discussed earlier in this chapter, the Update Agent relies on how you configure the `sources` file in the `/etc/sysconfig/rhn` directory. By default, the CentOS-4 version of this file points to the following repositories:

```
yum centos4-Base http://mirror.centos.org/centos/4/os/$ARCH/
yum centos4-Updates http://mirror.centos.org/centos/4/updates/$ARCH/
yum centos4-extras http://mirror.centos.org/centos/4/extras/$ARCH/
yum centos4-contrib http://mirror.centos.org/centos/4/contrib/$ARCH/
yum centos4-addons http://mirror.centos.org/centos/4/addons/$ARCH/
```

As discussed earlier in this book, CentOS-4 is built by volunteers. If you connect to a mirror, as opposed to directly to their servers, you can help keep their costs down. To do so, revise these URLs to point to a CentOS mirror closer to your location. For a full list, navigate to www.centos.org/modules/tinycontent/index.php?id=13. For example, if you're located in California, you might use the mirror located at the University of California, Riverside. The base URL cites a different base directory:

```
http://centos.cs.ucr.edu/centos/centos/4.0/
```

You would substitute this URL for http://mirror.centos.org/centos/4/ in the command lines shown previously. To make sure things worked, you can check available channels with the following command:

```
up2date --show-channels
```

But this command does not check the URLs. You should see the available channels as you check the list of available updates. If there's a problem with one of your URLs, you should see a connect error. For example, when I made a mistake typing in an HTTP URL, I got a 404 (file not found) error. Problems should be saved in the Update Agent log file, `/var/log/up2date`.

The first time I ran `up2date -1`, I found two critical packages in the list: `centos-yumconf` and `up2date`. The `centos-yumconf` package provides the rebuild specific yum configuration file, `/etc/yum.repos.d/CentOS-Base.repo`. If you're using a different rebuild, it will have a different, equally important package. Naturally, these packages affect how other packages are updated. I wanted to download and install these packages first before downloading others. I could do so with the following command:

```
up2date up2date centos-yumconf
```

Updates don't happen often to either of these two packages. However, if you configure a script to automate updates, you should make these commands part of that script. You never know when a package will be updated.

If you've already revised associated configuration files, such as `/etc/sysconfig/rhn/sources` and `/etc/yum.repos.d/CentOS-Base.repo`, they are not changed when new versions of the `up2date` and `centos-yumconf` RPMs are installed. The proposed updated files are stored in the same directories, with `.rpmnew` extensions.

After updating the Update Agent, it's appropriate to run `up2date -l` again. In my case, I wanted to keep the current versions of the `ipsec-tools` and `firefox` RPMs and install all other non-kernel updates. I performed this task with the following command:

```
up2date -u --exclude=firefox --exclude=ipsec-tools
```

Of course, you can run the Update Agent from the GUI. Run the `up2date` command in a GUI console. As you can see in Figure 6-3, the Update Agent shows available channels as you configured in `/etc/sysconfig/rhn/sources`.

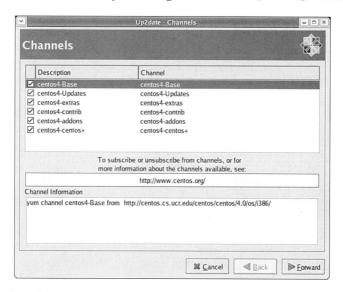

Figure 6-3   CentOS-4 updates with a random mirror

As with other yum enabled Red Hat-style systems, headers are downloaded and stored in `/var/spool/up2date` during this process. In Chapter 7, you'll learn to use this directory of headers to help create a general repository for your network.

6.3   SPECIAL yum COMMANDS

The yum command is rich and diverse. Run yum from the command line interface, by itself, and you'll get a hint of what it can do for you. Naturally, more information is available from the associated man page. As shown in Figure 6-4, there is a wide variety of switches and options, many of which we'll explore in the following sections.

```
root@centos4a:/var/log                          _ □ ✕
[root@centos4a log]# yum

  Usage:  yum [options] < update | install | info | remove | list |
          clean | provides | search | check-update | groupinstall |
          groupupdate | grouplist | groupinfo | groupremove | generate-rss |
          makecache | localinstall >

      Options:
      -c [config file] - specify the config file to use
      -e [error level] - set the error logging level
      -d [debug level] - set the debugging level
      -y - answer yes to all questions
      -R [time in minutes] - set the max amount of time to randomly run in
      -C run from cache only - do not update the cache
      --installroot=[path] - set the install root (default '/')
      --version - output the version of yum
      --rss-filename=[path/filename] - set the filename to generate rss to
      --exclude=package to exclude
      --disablerepo=repository id to disable (overrides config file)
      --enablerepo=repository id to enable (overrides config file)

      -h, --help  - this screen

[root@centos4a log]#
```

Figure 6-4   A variety of yum commands

As you go through the yum command options and measure its effects on your system, you'll note that as with apt for RPM-based systems, dependent packages that were installed are not always removed. In addition, the first time you use yum, updates to the local header database in /var/spool/up2date take some time. Subsequent updates are faster because they use the headers stored locally to identify any dependencies that need to be installed.

6.3.1   Caching Available Packages by yum

If you insist on using a remote repository, one way to keep your patch management time to a minimum is to use the following command:

```
yum makecache
```

Functionally similar to apt-get update, this command downloads all xml-based file and package data from your repositories, keeping search time to a minimum.

On a patch management server, it may be appropriate to keep a local cache of updates from an online mirror. If you do choose to run the `yum make-cache` command to cache updates, you should make sure this command is run on a daily (or perhaps nightly) basis to ensure that your local cache matches those associated with the remote repositories to which you connect.

By default, packages and headers downloaded from `yum` repositories are stored in the `/var/cache/yum` directory. You can change these settings in the `/etc/yum.conf` file. If you want to see what's downloaded on your system, look around in that directory. You'll see subdirectories associated with each repository specified in `/etc/yum.conf` or different files in the `/etc/yum.repos.d` directory. For example, downloads from the standard CentOS-4 repository are stored in the `base/` subdirectory.

In each repository subdirectory, there are `packages` and `headers` subdirectories. Any downloaded packages and headers are stored in these directories. Naturally, you can reinstall from those directories. As you'll see shortly, all you need is the `-c` option. However, caches aren't always up to date. It may be appropriate to run one of the `yum clean` commands described later in this chapter on a periodic basis.

6.3.2 Checking Available Updates by yum

After you've configured repositories in files in the `/etc/yum.repos.d` directory, you might want to know which of the available packages are upgrades to what is installed on your system. You can identify those packages with later revision numbers with the following command:

```
yum check-update
```

If you've configured some of the third-party repositories described earlier, the resulting list may be misleading. By definition, third parties build packages using their own tools and often use different build numbers and conventions. This is equivalent to the following command:

```
yum list updates
```

As described later, these are the packages that would be installed (along with any dependencies) if you run the `yum update` command.

6.3.3 Finding a Needed File

Sometimes, you just need a particular file. Perhaps you want to install that special wireless card. You may have noticed online that wireless cards with the Atheros chipset require the `ath_pci` driver module. You can find the package(s) associated with this module by running the following command:

```
yum provides ath_pci
```

You can substitute the `whatprovides` switch for `provides`. When I ran this command on my CentOS-4 system, the following is an excerpt from the result, which is in package name, version number, repository format, followed by the full location of the file:

```
madwifi-kmdl-2.6.9-5.0.3.EL.i686      0.9.4.12-15.el3.999.at at-stable
Matched from:
/lib/modules/2.6.9-5.0.3.EL/updates/net/ath_pci.ko
```

6.3.4   Identifying a Needed Package

If you want to identify a package associated with a specific search term, the `yum search` command can help. For example, if I wanted to identify those packages associated with the Atheros chipset, I would run the following command:

```
yum search atheros
```

This command is roughly equivalent to the `apt-cache search atheros` command described earlier in this book. However, as you can see from the output, this particular `yum` command may be more useful:

```
madwifi.i386      0.9.4.12-15.el3.999.at    at-stable
Matched from:
A linux device driver for Atheros chipsets (ar5210, ar5211, ar5212).
This package contains the Multiband Atheros Driver for WiFi, A linux
device driver for 802.11a/b/g universal NIC cards - either Cardbus,
PCI or MiniPCI - that use Atheros chipsets (ar5210, ar5211, ar5212).
```

6.3.5   Listing Available Packages

If you want to create a package database, the `yum list` command can help. You can limit the scope of any of the commands in this section by adding a package name to the end of the command. In any case, the following command creates a list of all installed and available packages:

```
yum list
```

This is equivalent to `yum list all`. If you want to limit the search to those packages that correspond to a certain name, you can specify it. For example, the following command lists the installed version of `yum`, plus an alternative from the `at-stable` repository:

```
yum list yum
```

The command yields output similar to this:

```
Installed Packages
yum.noarch      2.2.0-1.centos4.2      installed
Available Packages
yum.i386      2.2.1-55.el3.999.at      at-stable
```

There are several additional options associated with the `yum list` command. You can limit the search to installed packages with the following command:

```
yum list installed
```

Alternatively, you can limit the search to those packages that you can install from configured repositories with the following command:

```
yum list available
```

As suggested earlier, the following command, equivalent to `yum check-updates`, lists those packages that may serve as upgrades to those you have installed.

```
yum list updates
```

If you've installed packages from other than your configured `yum` repositories, your RPM database could be affected. You might need to configure a different repository. You can find a list of installed packages from other sources with the following command:

```
yum list extras
```

If you have a package that might be made obsolete by one you can install from a configured repository, you can identify them with the following command:

```
yum list obsoletes
```

6.3.6 Getting More Information

You can get more information on any available or installed package from your repositories. By itself, the `yum info` command is useless, except possibly as a database of package information. However, if you want information on an uninstalled package, you can get more with the `yum info` *packagename* command. For example, if you want more information on the `madwifi` package, and it's available from a configured repository, try the following command:

```
yum info madwifi
```

As you can see from the output in Figure 6-5, this is almost equivalent to a `rpm -qi madwifi` command. But the package does not have to be installed for `yum info` to work. Thus, you can get more information about a package you might want to install before actually putting it on your system.

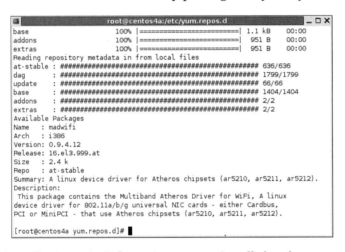

Figure 6-5   Getting more information on an uninstalled package

6.3.7 Updates or Installations by yum

Before you start any substantial update from a `yum` repository, you should confirm that you have the latest version of the `yum` RPM package. The most straightforward way to confirm is with the following command, which checks your repositories for an update to `yum`:

```
yum update yum
```

Naturally, you should consider adding this command to any automated update script that you configure for your computer.

If you want to download and install upgrades for every package listed by `yum check-update` or the `yum list updates` commands, the following command is for you:

```
yum update
```

It's quite possible that this might upgrade packages before you're ready. As suggested earlier, an upgrade to the Firefox Web browser may cause problems with plugins. If you've configured third-party repositories, it's possible that the list of packages that you don't want upgraded may increase. You can specify the packages you want to update. For example, if you're ready to upgrade the Firefox Web browser, you could run the following command:

```
yum update firefox
```

Alternatively, you could just use the install option. If the Firefox browser is already installed, the `yum` command looks for a later version and, if available, the package is downloaded and used to upgrade your system:

```
yum install firefox
```

Alternatively, if you want to upgrade every package in your `yum check-updates` list except Firefox, the `--exclude` switch can help.

However, if you haven't yet installed the Firefox Web browser, the `update` switch will not work. You'll have to install Firefox.

6.3.8 Deletions by yum

If you want to remove a package, the `yum` command can also take care of dependencies. For example, if you remove the OpenOffice.org suite, yum can help you remove associated dependent libraries. The following command causes the `yum` system to check dependencies and remove other associated packages, as shown in Figure 6-6:

```
yum remove
```

```
root@centos4a:/etc/yum.repos.d                          _ □ ✕
--> Processing Dependency: openoffice.org = 1.1.2-18.6.EL4 for package: openoffi
ce.org-i18n
--> Processing Dependency: openoffice.org = 1.1.2-18.6.EL4 for package: openoffi
ce.org-libs
--> Restarting Dependency Resolution with new changes.
--> Populating transaction set with selected packages. Please wait.
---> Package openoffice.org-libs.i386 0:1.1.2-18.6.EL4 set to be erased
---> Package openoffice.org-i18n.i386 0:1.1.2-18.6.EL4 set to be erased
--> Running transaction check

Dependencies Resolved
Transaction Listing:
  Remove: openoffice.org.i386 0:1.1.2-18.6.EL4
  Remove: openoffice.org-i18n.i386 0:1.1.2-18.6.EL4
  Remove: openoffice.org-libs.i386 0:1.1.2-18.6.EL4
Total download size: 0
Is this ok [y/N]: y
Downloading Packages:
Running Transaction Test
Finished Transaction Test
Transaction Test Succeeded
Running Transaction
Erasing: openoffice.org 1/3
[]
```

Figure 6-6   Getting more information on an uninstalled package

6.3.9   Cleaning yum Caches

As described earlier, the `yum` system stores downloads in the `/var/cache/yum` directory by default. With yum, unlike the Red Hat Update Agent, downloaded RPMs are not deleted by default. If your disk or partition space has limits, you may want to clean these caches on occasion.

If you want to clean the RPMs from each of the `/var/cache/yum` subdirectories, you can run the following command:

```
yum clean packages
```

If you want to clean the headers from the `/var/cache/yum` subdirectories, you can run the following command:

```
yum clean headers
```

If you see compressed XML files in each repository subdirectory, that is the metadata associated with the `yum` cache, which can be used to configure the cache as a `yum` repository. Metadata can become corrupt or perhaps just too large for available disk space. You can remove the metadata with the following command:

```
yum clean metadata
```

One thing that keeps `yum` startup times to a minimum is something known as the "pickle cache," which you can find in various `/var/cache/yum` sub-directories as compressed XML files with the `.pickle` extension. If these files become corrupt, the benefit is lost until you can clean up this cache with the following command:

```
yum clean cache
```

Naturally, if you just want to start your cache from scratch, run the following command:

```
yum clean all
```

You can restore the caches. Assuming your configured repositories are up to date, all you need to do is run the following command, as described earlier:

```
yum makecache
```

In fact, this is an excellent idea because it can reduce the wait time often associated with yum-based updates.

6.3.10   Group Management by yum

Many RPM-based distributions organize their packages in groups, such as Graphics, GNOME, Kernel Development, and so on. As you may have seen in Chapter 5, you can use the `apt` commands to manage these groups. You can also use `yum` to manage RPM package groups.

Finding Available Groups

Before you can manage the groups you have available, you need to know their names. You can list them with the following command:

```
yum grouplist | more
```

I pipe the output to the `more` command because the list for most RPM-based distributions is fairly long. The following excerpt from the CentOS-4 distribution lists installed groups, along with those available for installation. We illustrate one example in Figure 6-7.

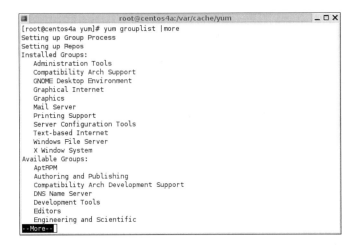

Figure 6-7   Getting more information on an available group

Note

Not all packages are necessarily part of groups. For example, if you include an Extras repository, you may get an error message related to an inability to read a `repomd.xml` file. In that case, you would have to disable that repository.

What's in a Group?

You can find the packages associated with each group. You can use the group names defined in the output from the `yum grouplist` command. Because many of these groups have multi-word names, you may need to use quotes to define the group name. For example, if you want to find the packages in the Administration Tools list, you'd run the following command:

```
yum groupinfo "Administration Tools"
```

The quotes are required; otherwise `yum` searches for two different groups, named Administration and Tools. You may also note that the group name is case sensitive.

Naturally, you can install individual packages from this group, with the following command, as defined in Figure 6-8. As with the `apt` commands discussed in Chapter 5, if you install a group, you'll install just the default and mandatory packages associated with that group.

```
yum groupinstall "Administration Tools"
```

```
                root@centos4a:/var/cache/yum                    _ □ ✕
dag              100% |========================| 1.1 kB   00:00
contribs         100% |========================|  951 B   00:00
update           100% |========================|  951 B   00:00
extras           100% |========================| 1.1 kB   00:00
base             100% |========================| 1.1 kB   00:00
centosplus       100% |========================|  951 B   00:00
addons           100% |========================|  951 B   00:00

Group: Administration Tools
 Default Packages:
   authconfig-gtk
   system-config-lvm
   system-config-packages
   system-config-soundcard
   system-config-network
   system-config-keyboard
   system-logviewer
   system-config-users
   system-config-language
   system-config-date
   system-config-rootpassword
 Optional Packages
   system-config-kickstart
[root@centos4a yum]# yum groupinfo "Administration Tools"▯
```

Figure 6-8 Installing default/mandatory packages from an available group

6.3.11 The yum Command Options

There is more that you can do with yum. As described earlier, you're free to modify the repositories listed in the /etc/yum.repos.d directory. You can also test a set of defaults other than what is configured in /etc/yum.conf. For example, if you want to test a muy.conf file currently in your home directory, you could run the yum command of your choice with the -c switch:

```
yum -c ~/muy.conf <yum actions>
```

Typically, yum requests confirmation before installing or removing specific packages. If you're comfortable with what you're doing, you can automate the process. With the -y switch, the yum command automatically answers prompts with a y to confirm changes:

```
yum -y <yum actions>
```

If you have problems, you may want to do some debugging. By default in /etc/yum.conf, the debuglevel is set to 2. If you need more information about what happens during a specific command, you can increase this variable with the -d switch. For example, the following command sets a much higher debug level for installing the packages associated with the Administration Tools group:

```
yum -d 5 groupinstall "Administration Tools"
```

You can also revise the level at which errors are reported. The following command sets a minimal level of error reporting:

```
yum -e 2 groupinstall "Administration Tools"
```

In both cases, a debug or error level of 0 disables reporting. A debug or error level of 1 tells yum to report all debugging messages or errors. A debug level of 2 provides a minimum level of debugging, which goes numerically up to 10.

There's one more switch to cover, the -R. It sets a maximum wait time before this particular yum command is run. The actual wait time is random. For example, the following command could be started anytime in the next two minutes:

```
yum -R 2 groupinstall "Administration Tools"
```

If you're configuring a cron job, you should disable error and debug reporting. If you're confident enough to configure a cron job, you should be sufficiently confident that there will be no problems during the update process. If there are problems, you can still analyze output in the /var/log/yum.log file.

If you've already downloaded the packages you need in the yum cache, you can reinstall from that cache. For this book, I've installed and removed the Administration Tools package group several times. After I've downloaded locally, I can reinstall with the following command:

```
yum -C groupinstall "Administration Tools"
```

As described earlier, you can use the --exclude switch to avoid updates of the packages of your choice. Naturally, many administrators will want to avoid updating the kernel; you can add the following switch to the yum command of your choice to avoid updating or downloading all kernel packages:

```
--exclude=kernel*
```

You can also disable the repositories of your choice. For example, if you've configured the ATrpms repositories on your system, you can disable it with the following command:

```
--disablerepo=at-stable
```

The name you use for the repository comes from the label in its stanza; in this case, the atrpms.repo file in the /etc/yum.repos.d directory starts with

```
[at-stable]
```

6.4 CONFIGURING AUTOMATIC UPDATES

If you're comfortable with your repositories, you may want to automate your updates by using what you now know about the `yum` command. In this section, I'll show the variety of available update commands available for yum and how automated updates are configured for various distributions, such as CentOS-4 and Fedora Core 4.

6.4.1 Finding the Right Update Command

As described earlier, the following command looks for packages that can be updated in all configured repositories. You can do so with the following command:

```
yum update
```

Unfortunately, this command requires confirmation, which is not something you want to leave to ordinary users. If you're comfortable with the way updates are maintained, you can run the command to automatically confirm downloads:

```
yum -y update
```

However, many administrators will want to avoid updates of several different types of packages. Most common on this list is related to the Linux kernel; for example, updates of the Linux kernel can require updates of other software that you may have compiled. So to avoid kernel updates (until you're ready), you can add the `--exclude` switch described earlier. Such an update might look like this:

```
yum --exclude=kernel* -y update
```

Naturally, this might not be enough. As suggested earlier, updates of the Firefox Web browser can be troublesome. Therefore, if you want to avoid updating Firefox packages, you can expand this command a bit further:

```
yum --exclude=*firefox* --exclude=kernel* -y update
```

If you've connected to a specialty repository, you may not want to take updates from that server. You can avoid updates from a repository with the `--disablerepo` switch. For example, if you've configured the Dag Wieers repositories described earlier in the `/etc/yum.repos.d`, you can avoid any updates from that repository with the following command:

```
yum --disablerepo=dag --exclude=*firefox* --exclude=kernel* -y update
```

6.4.2   Automating the Process

There are two ways to automate the update process. If you have confidence in the way your distribution keeps packages up to date, you could configure the previous command in a cron job. For example, you could set up a nightly cron job with an appropriate file in the /etc/cron.daily directory. You might even include a weekly cron job in the /etc/cron.weekly directory.

In fact, the yum RPM often includes a cron job in these directories. The script is straightforward. It starts with the standard #!/bin/sh, which invokes the bash shell. The default versions of this script vary by distribution and release.

The Original yum cron Job

The following is what you see for the /etc/cron.daily/yum.cron update script if you're running Fedora Core 3 or the Red Hat Enterprise Linux 4 rebuilds that use yum for updates, such as CentOS-4.

```
#!/bin/sh
if [ -f /var/lock/subsys/yum ]; then
        /usr/bin/yum -R 10 -e 0 -d 0 -y update yum
        /usr/bin/yum -R 120 -e 0 -d 0 -y update
fi
```

This job is active if there's a /var/lock/subsys/yum file, which is created if the yum daemon is active in your runlevel. If this file exists, this cron job runs two commands, within 10 and then 120 minutes after the scheduled start of this job. The first yum command makes sure that your system has the most up to date version of yum, and then the second command runs the yum update command to update all the RPMs to the latest versions as defined in the updates repositories.

The Newer yum cron Jobs

Red Hat has revised the cron jobs for Fedora Core 4. There are now two jobs: a daily job for updates and a weekly job to clean packages which accumulate in the caches. As you can see, the following is the new default /etc/cron.daily/yum.cron script:

```
#!/bin/sh
if [ -f /var/lock/subsys/yum ]; then
        /usr/bin/yum -R 120 -e 0 -d 0 -y update yum
        /usr/bin/yum -R 10 -e 0 -d 0 -y shell /etc/yum/yum-daily.yum
fi
```

The first yum command makes sure that your system has the most up-to-date version of yum, and then the second command drops into the yum shell, which has its own commands. The yum shell works only in Fedora Core 4 or later. It calls the /etc/yum/yum-daily.yum file, which contributes three commands to the script:

☞ `update` runs the yum update command, which, in this case, downloads the updated RPMs from the repositories as configured.

☞ `ts run` executes the transaction, which uses the downloaded RPMs to upgrade your system.

☞ `exit` leaves the yum shell.

Then there is the weekly cron job, also named `yum.cron`, available in the `/etc/cron.weekly` directory. The script is straightforward:

```
#!/bin/sh
if [ -f /var/lock/subsys/yum ]; then
        /usr/bin/yum -e 0 -d 0 clean packages
fi
```

Based on the same conditions as previous `yum` scripts, where the `if` command makes sure that yum isn't currently running, this script cleans all packages in the default yum cache directory, as defined by the `cachedir` directive in the `/etc/yum.conf` configuration file.

Activating the yum cron Jobs

The simplest way to make sure the `yum` cron job(s) are active is with the following command:

```
/etc/init.d/yum start
```

This creates the `yum` file in the `/var/lock/subsys` directory. And the following command can help you make sure `yum` is active the next time you reboot this computer:

```
chkconfig yum on
```

This particular command activates `yum` in runlevels 2 through 5.

6.4.3 Other Automated Updates

If you're working with just a few computers, you may want more detailed control over updates. You can configure updates on a different schedule. If you're familiar with cron jobs, you should already know that you can also configure regular updates on an hourly, weekly, or monthly basis. The file described earlier should be fine; all you would need to do is move it to the appropriate directory, such as `/etc/cron.hourly`, `/etc/cron.weekly`, or `/etc/cron.monthly`.

Alternatively, you could set up the job using the `at` daemon. When configured, the job runs once, at a time of your choosing. You can run the job again at any time. For example, you could move the `yum.cron` job to your home directory and then run it as an `at` job. If you no longer want that job to be run as a cron job, make sure the file no longer exists in a cron directory.

After you've created a script, such as `yum.cron`, in your home directory, it's easy to configure as an `at` job. For example, my home directory is `/home/michael`, and I can schedule that script to run at 2 a.m. tomorrow morning with the following sequence of commands:

```
at 2:00 tomorrow
at> /home/michael/yum.cron
at> Ctrl-D
```

When you run the `at` command, it opens the `at` command line prompt. When you see the prompt, you can enter the commands of your choice, which the `at` daemon will run at the time specified. Naturally, there is much more that you can do with this daemon; for more information, the associated man page can guide you through how you can find pending jobs with the `atq` command, how you can remove pending jobs with the `atrm` command, and how you can run `batch` jobs only when the system is not busy.

6.5   A yum GUI Tool

There are some administrators who need the GUI. Visual aids do help some become better administrators. Graphical `yum`-based tools are currently under development. The only one I've found being actively developed as of this writing is the Yum Extender. For more information, see http://linux.rasmil.dk/yumex/ or http://sourceforge.net/projects/yumex/. The Yum Extender is available from the Fedora Extras repository, as the yumex RPM. A brief examination of the Yum Extender has helped me understand more of what's available from various `yum` repositories.

Note

As of this writing, Red Hat developers are working on the Package Updater, also known as Pup, to replace the Red Hat Update Agent. It may also replace the current `system-config-packages` tool. I cover the Yum Extender because it is already a useful yum GUI tool. And the Fedora selection of a yum GUI tool is subject to change.

Because the Yum Extender is still under development, I suspect that a number of the options in this section will change, especially if it is formally adapted as a Fedora package. Therefore, we'll limit the discussion to a brief view of the capabilities of Yum Extender. If you've read the chapter up to this point, everything you see here should be familiar.

When installed, you can only run the Yum Extender from the GUI. You can start it with the Applications -> System Tools -> Yum Extender command or with the `yumex` command in a GUI console. You're prompted for the root password, after which you see the Yum Extender, with currently configured repositories, as shown in Figure 6-9.

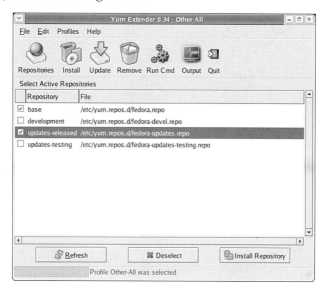

Figure 6-9   The Yum Extender

Similar to Synaptic for apt, the Yum Extender is a genuine front-end to the yum command. You can watch the output messages as they occur. After you run a command in the Yum Extender, click the Output button. Watch as the messages associated with installing, upgrading, or removing your packages scroll across the screen.

6.5.1   Basic Configuration

Before you run the Yum Extender, it's important to make sure that you've configured some basic parameters:

☞ If you need to configure a Proxy Server between your network and the remote repositories, click Edit -> Preferences. Place a check mark in the box associated with Use Proxy. A http_proxy text box will appear, where you can enter the URL information for your proxy server.

☞ If you want to avoid installation or updates to certain packages, you can place them on the exclude list. Click Edit -> Exclude List. This opens the Exclude List window where you can specify the packages that you do not want updated.

The list is straightforward; for example, if you want to exclude all `kernel*` and `firefox*` packages from updates, just include those terms (wildcards are allowed) in the Exclude List text box.

6.5.2   Adding More Repositories

The available menus are straightforward. You can add as many repositories as
you need. Any changes that you make are reflected in files in the
/etc/yum.repos.d directory. If you want to add new repositories, use the
following steps:

1. Click Install Repository to start the Repository Installer shown in
   Figure 6-10.

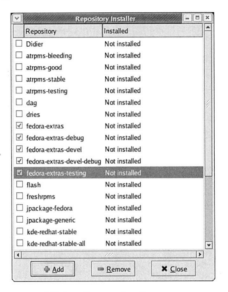

Figure 6-10   Selecting additional repositories

As you can see, there is a wide variety of pre-configured repositories
which you can add to your system.

2. Select the repositories of your choice, click Add, and click OK to confirm.
3. Close the Repository Installer window to return to the main Yum
   Extender menu.
4. Select the repositories of your choice and click Refresh to download associated metadata.

Alternatively, if there's a repository not in the Repository Installer list,
you can add it through a different menu, following these steps:

1. Click Edit -> Repositories. This opens the Edit Repository menu.
2. In the Edit Repository menu, click File -> New. This opens the New
   Repository window. Enter the name of your choice in the associated text
   box. This opens a new Edit Repository menu.

3. You'll need to enter several parameters, as shown in Table 6-1.

Table 6-1   Editing in a new repository

Item	Description
Title	Title of repository; used with yum to define contents.
Name	Name of repository; often includes parameters such as `$releasever` (Release Version), as defined through the `/etc/yum.conf distroverpkg` file; and `$basearch` (Base Architecture), as defined by the `archwork.py` script in the `/usr/lib/python-2.3/site-packages/yum` directory.
URL Type	There are two options; `baseurl` means that the URL that you specify points directly to the repository; Mirrorlist means that the URL points to a file with a list of mirrors, as described earlier.
URLs	You can add URLs for the repositories or mirror lists of your choice directly in this text box.
gpgkey	If there's a GPG key associated with your selected repository, you can add it here; naturally, you'll need to enable GPG checks.
Flags—Enabled	If the flag is active (1), your system will access this repository.
Flags—gpgcheck	If the flag is active (1), your system will confirm GPG (GNU Privacy Guard) signatures for each package downloaded from this repository.

4. Select OK when you're finished. You'll still need to confirm configuration as was done previously.

6.5.3   Installing Packages

While you can install packages from your repositories more quickly from the command line interface, the GUI can help you browse what is available. Now that you've selected the active repositories for your system, click the Install button. Browse through the packages available for installation. If you highlight one, you can see some information about that package, including the identified repository, as shown in Figure 6-11.

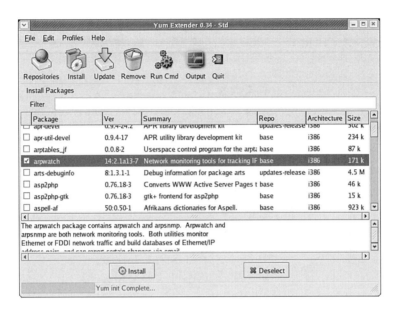

Figure 6-11   Selecting packages to install

The installation process is straightforward. Select the packages you want to install, and then click the Install button. After the yum database is processed, you're shown a list of packages to be installed, along with dependencies. Click OK to confirm. When the process is complete, you'll see a message such as "Install completed OK."

Tip

If you see a dependency error during the update process, the most common cause is your settings associated with updating the Linux kernel. In other words, if the package you want to install requires a later version of the kernel, you have to decide whether to accept a kernel update, with all the associated risks.

6.5.4   Updating Packages

The update process is straightforward. Click the Update button. Browse through the packages available for installation. If you highlight one, you can see some information about that package, including the associated repository.

The update process is straightforward. Select the packages you want to install, and then click the Install button. After the yum database is processed, you're shown a list of packages to be installed, along with dependencies. Click OK to confirm. When the process is complete, you'll see a message such as "Install completed OK."

6.5.5   Removing Packages

The package removal process is also straightforward. Click the Remove button. Browse through the packages already installed on your computer. If you highlight one, you can see some information about that package, including the associated repository.

For example, I used the Yum Extender to remove the Apache Web Server from my system. As you can see in Figure 6-12, there are a lot of packages that depend on Apache, the httpd RPM package. I clicked OK to confirm, and all the packages noted in the Dependencies list were also uninstalled. When the process is complete, you'll see a message such as "Remove completed OK."

Figure 6-12   Confirming packages to remove

6.5.6   Using Your Own Commands

There will be times where the GUI tool won't be enough. If that is your situation, you do not need to exit. If you know how yum works from the command line, the Yum Extender allows you to enter the commands of your choice. Click the Run Cmd button.

Now you can configure the yum commands of your choice. The drop-down command text box includes all the yum command options listed earlier in this chapter. You can enter the data you need in the Yum parameters text box, as shown in Figure 6-13.

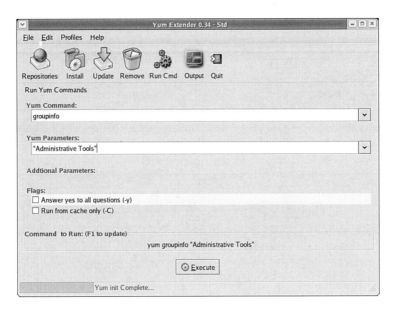

Figure 6-13   Running a yum command in the GUI

You're not limited to the `-y` and `-c` flags shown in the figure. If you need to enter a different flag, you can include it in the Yum Command text box. For example, you might want to run the following command:

```
yum -R 2 groupinfo "Administrative Tools"
```

If so, type in `-R 2 groupinfo` in the Yum Command text box. Click the Execute button when you're ready. When you do, the Yum Extender takes you to the Output window to give you the output information that you asked for.

6.6 SUMMARY

In this chapter, you learned all about using `yum` as a patch management tool. The original version of this tool was developed for the Yellow Dog Linux distribution, to help manage patches on that RPM-based distribution. It was enhanced into `yum` by developers at Duke University and eventually adapted by the Fedora and several RHEL rebuild distributions.

In Chapter 5, you read about `apt` as a viable alternative for RPM-based distributions. One advantage of `yum` is that it is built using Python, which is a critical building block for RPM-based distributions.

The `yum` commands rely on headers, the key information from each RPM package, which cites any packages that may depend on that RPM. With this information, `yum` can help you avoid the "dependency hell" often associated with RPMs.

Fedora and the RHEL rebuilds already have various `yum` repositories that you can configure. Third parties also have `yum` repositories which may be useful. Starting with Fedora Core 4, they are configured in the `/etc/yum.repos.d` directory.

The `yum` commands rely on caches, which can take time to download. They can help you manage individual packages or package groups. The `yum` package includes a script which you can use to automate the update process.

The Yum Extender is a GUI front-end to the `yum` command, which you can use to manage individual systems. If you're fairly new to `yum` and prefer GUI tools, it can help you learn how to use `yum` to manage patches.

In the final chapter, we'll describe how you can create your own local repository of RPMs for `yum` clients on RPM-based distributions.

CHAPTER 7

Setting Up a yum Repository

As discussed in Chapter 6, "Configuring a yum Client," yum is built on the Python programming language, which is a building block for the Red Hat/Fedora distributions. While current support is limited to the Red Hat/Fedora/Yellow Dog/Mandriva/Asp distributions, per the latest available Netcraft survey (http://news.netcraft.com/archives/2005/03/index.html), that's over half the Linux market. If you want to learn patch management for Linux, you need to know how to use yum and configure, or "yummify," associated repositories.

The simplest way to configure a yum repository is to mirror one that already exists. Most Fedora repositories already support yum. But you do not have to mirror the entire repository, because much of it is built from installation CDs. In addition, as packages change, or if you combine packages from different mirrors, you may prefer to create yum headers on your own system rather than download them from a remote mirror.

We've divided this chapter into several major sections. You can take most of the packages for a repository from the installation CDs. You'll need to manage headers for those repositories. You'll need to configure sharing of that repository with other computers on your network. You'll need to download other repositories associated with updates, developmental packages, and those created by third parties. Finally, you'll need to keep these repositories up to date.

When configured, you'll be able to update your computers from local repositories, minimizing the loads on your Internet connections, giving you more control over what is installed on your systems. You can focus on making sure that critical packages, including those related to security, are up to date. That is the essence of good patch management.

At the end of this chapter, we'll show you how you can create a yum repository for Red Hat Enterprise Linux (RHEL) 4 clients with an authorized subscription to the Red Hat Network. If you have valid subscriptions, this is a viable alternative to the Red Hat Network Proxy Server described in Chapter 2, "Consolidating Patches on a Red Hat/Fedora Network."

7.1 GETTING THE PACKAGES

You already have many of the packages that you'll want in a yum repository: the same RPMs that are already included with the installation CDs/DVDs for your distribution. With those RPMs, you can use yum to populate the base repository and add the headers needed for easy access from the other computers on your network.

In this part of the chapter, we'll show you how to start your repository, install yum, create an appropriate yum directory tree, add headers to the appropriate directory, and test the base repository on your local system. We'll start with the Fedora Core 4 Updates repository. When you see how it's done, you can use the same techniques to create other repositories on your system.

While you could use the rsync command described in earlier chapters to mirror an entire repository, each version of Fedora requires well over 10GB of space. You do not need to mirror the directory with the 6GB+ of ISO files. As described earlier in this book, there are ways to cut that down with appropriate --exclude switches to the rsync command. But if the loads on your Internet connection are not a problem, you might not need a local patch management repository in the first place.

Note

SUSE supports two different patch management tools described in Chapter 3, "SUSE's Update Systems and rsync Mirrors": YaST Online Update and Zenworks Linux Management. As noted in Chapters 5 and 6, they now support apt, and plan to support yum in the future.

7.1.1 Strategy

Before you create your repository, decide what you want to store locally. Viable options vary. If you have only two or three workstations, a local repository might not be so important. However, it can become profitable to configure a local repository if you have a substantial number of workstations. What you configure locally depends on your patch management strategy. Consider the following:

☞ To keep a substantial number of computers up to date, it can help to configure a local repository for updates. Alternatively, if your Internet bandwidth is unlimited, and the people behind your remote mirror do not object to the load, you may prefer to use remote mirrors, as they may be more up to date.

☞ If you frequently change the base software on your systems, you should load the installation RPMs on your repository.

☞ If you need packages outside the standards available on the installation CDs, look for other directories of RPMs on your favorite mirror. For example, Fedora includes the Extras repository with many useful packages.

☞ If you need packages simply unavailable from mirrors associated with your distribution, there are also third-party repositories described throughout this book.

☞ If your users test updates before they're moved to the stable update repository, consider mirroring such repositories. You may even have reason to mirror a development repository. However, be warned that these packages are generally not stable or suitable for a production environment.

Note

The Fedora development repositories, formerly known as "Rawhide," are collections of RPMs that may change on a day-to-day basis. They are, by definition, not stable. They are not suitable for production use. However, they may be of considerable interest to developers and others looking for the latest available solutions.

After you decide what you're going to mirror, you can set up a yum directory tree for your local repository. In the following sections, we'll focus on creating an Updates repository. If you have the installation CD available, you can use the same steps to create an Installation repository.

In my case, I've created a Fedora Core 4 repository on a system running RHEL 4, as it is a fairly stable distribution. You'll want to leave room for future releases of Fedora Core. It might even make sense to add a new hard drive for that purpose so that the packages won't overwhelm other files on your system. In any case, it's an excellent idea to at least configure a separate partition for your repository.

7.1.2 Creating a yum Directory Tree

We're assuming that you're ready to create your own yum repository directory tree for your own network and that the tree does not have to be identical to the one on your favorite mirror. For example, assume that you've created the /var/ftp/pub/yum directory in a separate partition. Assume that for now, all you need to provide for are standard 32-bit systems. If you wanted to create a yum directory tree for Fedora Core 4, you might end up with the following directories:

```
/var/ftp/pub/yum/4/i386/os
/var/ftp/pub/yum/4/i386/updates
/var/ftp/pub/yum/4/i386/extras
/var/ftp/pub/yum/4/i386/dag
```

The `/var/ftp/pub` directory is the default directory associated with the vsFTP server. It happens to be the default FTP server for Fedora and Red Hat distributions. With the right settings, you can link to this directory from an Apache Web server. You can also share this directory on the local network using NFS. In fact, NFS is generally preferred on a network of Linux computers because shared NFS directories can be treated as if they were on the local computer.

Note

To promote security, the vsFTP server does not allow symbolic links (also known as symlinks). Therefore, you can't use the vsFTP server for packages downloaded to directories, such as `/var/spool/up2date`.

As the noted directories are several levels below `/var/ftp/pub`, you might feel like you'll have to run the `mkdir` command a thousand times. There is one minor trick that can speed the process. The following command creates all needed subdirectories in one shot:

```
mkdir -p /var/ftp/pub/yum/4/i386/os
```

Note that the structure of these directories does not correspond to those you see in current Fedora Core mirrors. The directory structure of different Fedora Core mirrors varies. Unless you're creating a mirror for public use, there is no need to create a directory structure similar to any existing Fedora Core mirror.

7.1.3   Start with a Distribution

For the purpose of this chapter, I've downloaded the Fedora Core 4 installation DVD, to create repositories for Fedora Core 4 systems. As noted earlier, it'll be on a RHEL 4 computer so that I can add repositories for future releases of Fedora Core. As RHEL 4 was developed in large part from Fedora Core 3, I'll be using Fedora-based yum packages. Naturally, the following instructions will also work for a repository configured on Fedora Core 3.

Note

For Fedora Core 3, this section works in the same way. Just substitute appropriate file names. I could not test these settings on Fedora Core 5, as Red Hat was just starting its test (beta) releases for this distribution as this book was going to print.

For example, if you've download the Fedora Core DVD, you can mount the ISO file almost as if it were a DVD/CD with the following command:

```
mount -o loop FC4-i386-DVD.iso /media/cdrecorder
```

Of course, you can "burn" the DVD `.iso` file (or associated CD `.iso` files) to appropriate media. It may be handy to have a DVD available. But, in my opinion, because you can mount the ISO directly, you don't need a physical DVD.

Note

If you can't work with DVD-sized files, you can still create a local repository. For example, if you've downloaded the four Fedora Core 4 binary CDs, all you need to do is mount the CDs one at a time, and copy their contents (including the `.discinfo` file from the first CD) to the directory of your choice. For example, you could run the following commands:

```
mount -o loop FC4-i386-disc1.iso /media/cdrecorder
cp -ar /media/cdrecorder/* \
/var/ftp/pub/yum/4/i386/os/
```

If it's the first CD, don't forget to copy the `.discinfo` file to the noted directory. Change CDs:

```
mount -o loop FC4-i386-disc2.iso /media/cdrecorder
cp -ar /media/cdrecorder/* \
/var/ftp/pub/yum/4/i386/os/
```

Repeat the process until you've reached the fourth CD.

A quick look at other mirrors confirms that the contents of the Fedora Core DVD are part of the `os/` repository directory. You can make it part of your own local repository, by copying the contents of the DVD to the corresponding directory described earlier:

```
cp -ar /media/cdrecorder/* /var/ftp/pub/yum/4/i386/os/
```

7.1.4 Installing yum

For Fedora Core 3 and above, you'll need at least the `yum` and `createrepo` RPMs, along with the packages associated with the way you plan to share your repository on your network (FTP, Apache, or NFS server). Earlier versions of Fedora Core did not include a `createrepo` RPM; if you want to create a repository from Fedora Core 1 or 2, use the `yum-arch` command, which is part of the `yum` RPM and is functionally similar to `createrepo`.

When the appropriate CD or DVD is mounted, you can then install the Fedora Core 3 `yum` and `createrepo` RPMs with the following commands:

```
rpm -Uvh /media/cdrecorder/Fedora/RPMS/yum*
rpm -Uvh /media/cdrecorder/Fedora/RPMS/createrepo*
```

Note

Because RHEL 4 is built on Fedora Core 3, it generally works when you use Fedora Core 3 RPMs on RHEL 4. However, Fedora Core 4 RPMs sometimes require more advanced dependent packages. If you install those dependencies, that might cause problems for other RHEL 4 applications.

If you're working with a RHEL 4 rebuild distribution, such as CentOS-4, the appropriate yum packages may already be installed on your system. The actual directory with these packages may vary; for example, the CentOS-4 version of the `createrepo` RPM is part of the CentOS-4 `addons/` repository directory.

Note

If you are also using this server for installations, copy the `.iso` files associated with the DVD or CDs to the `/var/ftp/pub` directory. The Red Hat installation program, Anaconda, can automatically mount and read appropriate `.iso` files. When shared, you can use this directory as a network installation source, which can help you automate the installation of additional PCs.

If you're working with RHEL 4, you can install the yum and `createrepo` RPMs from Fedora Core 3. If you don't have the associated installation media, you can download the RPMs directly from your favorite mirror from among those listed at http://fedora.redhat.com/download/mirrors.html.

7.1.5 Synchronizing Updates

More important than the installation RPMs are the updates. While you can use tools, such as `system-config-packages`, to install and remove Fedora packages from the installation files, you need access to the updates to manage patches on your system. Based on the directories described earlier, we're planning to store RPMs from the Fedora Core 4 Updates repository on the following directory:

```
/var/ftp/pub/yum/4/i386/updates
```

Based on the `rsync` commands described in Chapter 2, you should find an Updates repository in the `rsync` mirror of your choice. Fedora `rsync` mirrors are listed at http://fedora.redhat.com/download/mirrors.html. One `rsync` mirror that I use is rsync://mirrors.kernel.org/fedora/core.

You can list the directories and files on a remote `rsync` server. Just make sure to include the last forward slash in your command. For example, the following command lists the directories available in the Kernel.org Fedora Core repository:

```
rsync rsync://mirrors.kernel.org/fedora/core/
```

You'll see `updates/` in the directory tree. As you continue this process, you'll find the actual `updates/` RPMs in the `updates/4/i386/` subdirectory.

Search through the subdirectory. You'll find `debug/` and `repodata/` subdirectories. While you may be able to use the data in the `repodata/` subdirectory in your own `yum` repository, you don't need to download the hundreds of megabytes of files in the `debug/` subdirectory. To avoid downloading files from that directory, you'll need to apply the `--exclude` switch. For example, the following `rsync` command synchronizes the packages from the remote `updates/` repository, without `debug/` packages:

Note

Through Fedora Core 3, the noted repository included a `headers/` subdirectory, as created with the `yum-arch` command.

```
rsync -av --exclude debug \
rsync://mirrors.kernel.org/fedora/core/updates/4/i386/* \
/var/ftp/pub/yum/4/i386/updates/
```

As noted in Chapter 3, this synchronizes the noted remote and local directories in (`-a`) archive mode, with (`-v`) verbose output. Contents from the debug directory are (`--exclude`) excluded.

Note

Note the backslashes (\) at the end of the first two parts of the command line. It's an escape character, which cancels out the carriage return; in other words, all three lines are run as a single command.

7.2 MANAGING HEADERS

One key skill in maintaining a repository is header management. Headers, stripped from RPM packages, allow yum to determine dependent packages. Unless the packages you download are identical to those on your selected mirror, you won't be able to use the headers created on the mirror. You will have to learn to create your own headers. There are two major header creation commands, which we'll review in this section and then use on a Fedora Core 4 repository.

7.2.1 Header Creation Commands

As noted earlier, there are two different commands associated with creating headers for a `yum` repository. Before Fedora Core 3, the key command was `yum-arch`. It may still be the primary command for the distribution for which you're managing patches. The alternative, starting with Fedora Core 3, is `createrepo`.

yum-arch

The `yum-arch` command comes with the `yum` RPM and is the first method to strip headers from associated RPM packages and organize them in a headers subdirectory. When the headers are available, various `yum` commands described in Chapter 6 can use them to identify packages and package groups, along with any dependencies for the purposes of installation, upgrades, and removals.

There are several different options associated with the `yum-arch` command. While none are absolutely necessary, they can help you in various special cases. They do not always work. For more information on the options associated with the `yum-arch` command, see Table 7-1.

Table 7-1   The yum-arch command options

Option	Description
-d	Checks for dependencies and conflicts from listed RPM packages
-n	Creates the database without headers; may be appropriate if you've already download headers
-s	Creates headers from source packages
-c	Checks package integrity against available checksums
-l	Follows any noted symlinks
-z	Compresses headers

createrepo

The `createrepo` command now creates metadata from the headers in XML format. If you're familiar with the Red Hat `comps.xml` file (available from the first installation CD's `RedHat/base` or `Fedora/base` subdirectory), you understand how these distributions use XML to organize packages and their associated package groups for installation. As Fedora (and perhaps other Linux distributions) evolves, they might move toward XML as a Linux standard to organize packages and their associated package groups.

There are several different options associated with the `createrepo` command. While none are absolutely necessary, they can help you in various special cases. For more information on `createrepo` options, see Table 7-2.

Table 7-2 The createrepo command options

Option	Description
-g	Supports commands associated with Red Hat/Fedora groups from the `comps.xml` file
-p	Supports output in XML format
-s	Selects the type of checksum to use, such as `md5`
-c	Checks package integrity against available checksums
-u	Creates headers from a list of files at a specified URL
-x	Excludes specified files; wildcards are allowed

If you want to see how the `createrepo` command works, you can analyze its code in the `/usr/bin/createrepo` script. As with `yum`, this command is written in Python.

7.2.2 Adding the Headers

As suggested earlier, there are two commands you can use to create the headers needed for a `yum` repository: `yum-arch` and `createrepo`. If you use `yum-arch` in Fedora Core 3 or above, you'll see the following message:

```
THIS PROGRAM IS DEPRECATED!
You should be generating xml metadata instead.
Please see http://linux.duke.edu/metadata
```

If you're running RHEL 4 or the associated rebuild distributions, you should use the `createrepo` command, because these distributions are based on Fedora Core 3. However, several other distributions still use `yum-arch`. If you don't see the "deprecated" message, use the `yum-arch` command, which is a part of the `yum` RPM.

yum-arch

The yum-arch command is fairly straightforward. All you have to do is navigate to the directory with the RPMs and you can create the headers in the local directory with the following command (don't forget the dot, which specifies the files in the current directory):

```
yum-arch .
```

As you can see in Figure 7-1, headers are generated and "digested." You'll find the headers in the local headers/ subdirectory.

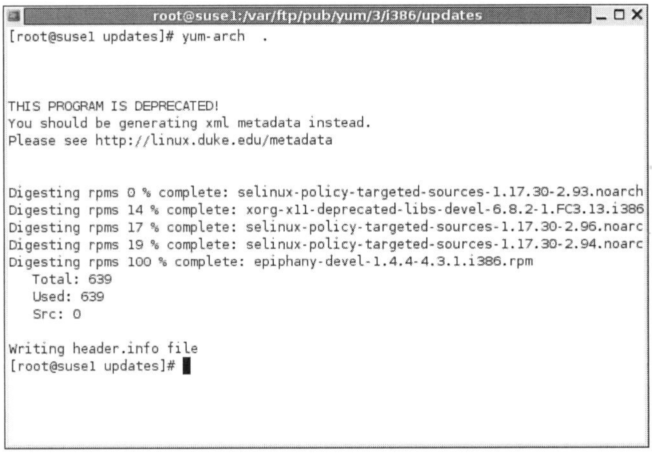

Figure 7-1   The yum-arch command digests RPMs and exhales headers

If you're successful, the numbers associated with Total and Used in the output should match. In other words, Figure 7-1 tells me that there are 639 RPMs in this repository, and all were used to create headers.

If there are problems, there may be older RPMs in the repository. Updates to an update repository where older RPMs conflict with others could be the cause. Therefore, if you use the rsync command to synchronize your repository, you should take care to delete older RPMs. Alternatively, you can wipe the repository directories before downloading updates.

This repository is now ready. You'll still need to share the directory with an FTP, Apache, or an NFS server.

createrepo

While the yum-arch command was developed for RPMs, Red Hat's move to organize packages in XML files is fairly recent. The createrepo command consolidates headers in compressed XML files. It creates the headers that the yum command needs to specify dependencies.

As you can see in Figure 7-2, the `createrepo -v <PATH>` command creates metadata. You'll find the headers in compressed XML files in the local `repodata/` subdirectory.

```
root@suse1:/var/ftp/pub/yum/3/i386/os                    _ □ ✕
1627/1645 - dvgrab-1.6-1.i386.rpm
1628/1645 - info-4.7-5.i386.rpm
1629/1645 - GConf-1.0.9-15.i386.rpm
1630/1645 - automake-1.9.2-3.noarch.rpm
1631/1645 - xfdesktop-4.0.6-2.i386.rpm
1632/1645 - bluez-utils-2.10-2.i386.rpm
1633/1645 - ttfonts-ta-1.6-1.noarch.rpm
1634/1645 - epic-1.0.1-18.i386.rpm
1635/1645 - fonts-KOI8-R-100dpi-1.0-7.noarch.rpm
1636/1645 - gd-2.0.28-1.i386.rpm
1637/1645 - bluez-libs-devel-2.10-2.i386.rpm
1638/1645 - file-roller-2.8.1-1.i386.rpm
1639/1645 - arpwatch-2.1a13-7.i386.rpm
1640/1645 - webalizer-2.01_10-25.i386.rpm
1641/1645 - synaptics-0.13.5-5.i386.rpm
1642/1645 - dbh-devel-1.0.18-5.i386.rpm
1643/1645 - automake16-1.6.3-5.noarch.rpm
1644/1645 - pkgconfig-0.15.0-3.i386.rpm
1645/1645 - e2fsprogs-1.35-11.2.i386.rpm

Saving Primary metadata
Saving file lists metadata
Saving other metadata
[root@suse1 os]#
```

Figure 7-2   The createrepo command

This repository is now ready. You'll still need to share the directory with an FTP, Apache, or an NFS server.

7.3   Configuring a Local yum Server

The skills you need to configure a local yum server are not related to yum. They require knowledge of the FTP, Apache, or NFS services. While this section is not designed to provide a complete guide to any of these services, it provides a description of how you can configure a yum repository server based on the settings described earlier for Fedora Core 4 updates.

Because I personally prefer the efficiency of the FTP and NFS services for sharing files, I've covered the configuration steps required only for those services. For completeness, I've described how you can configure an Apache server to share files on a RHEL 4 yum repository near the end of this chapter. If you're configuring a yum server, what you do will vary based on the following factors:

☞ Distribution and version

☞ Preferred version of a server (configuration steps vary for different FTP and HTTP servers and, to some extent, the way different distributions implement NFS servers)

☞ Availability of yum for the distribution (i.e., if it isn't available, be prepared to compile yum from a source RPM)

As with other network services, `yum` servers may be sensitive to any firewalls that you may configure. If you have a firewall between the `yum` server computer and associated clients, you'll need to make sure traffic can travel through appropriate TCP/IP ports; for example, Apache services require access through TCP/IP port 80. Sure, there are ways to "tunnel" data through other services, such as SSH, but that should not be necessary for updates limited to your internal network. In any case, that level of detail is beyond the scope of this book.

7.3.1   Configuring an FTP yum Server

On current Red Hat/Fedora distributions, the default FTP server is vsFTP. According to its home page at http://vsftpd.beasts.org/, it's the default FTP server used to share a number of Linux distributions, including Red Hat and Debian. It's even used to share kernels through ftp.kernel.org.

The default version of vsFTP is configured in the `vsftpd` RPM. The default installation works well in most cases. The vsFTP configuration file is stored in `/etc/vsftpd/vsftpd.conf` for Red Hat/Fedora distributions (`/etc/vsftpd.conf` for SUSE and Debian distributions). In this case, we're working from the RHEL 4 version of vsFTP.

By default, vsFTP files are stored in the `/var/ftp` directory. By convention, files that you copy for downloads are stored in the `pub/` subdirectory. Therefore, the repository that you create should be in the `/var/ftp/pub` directory. For the example described earlier, update RPMs are stored in the following directory:

```
/var/ftp/pub/yum/4/i386/updates
```

If you've used the commands described earlier for Fedora Core 4, you'll find the update header database in the `repodata/` subdirectory.

There is a substantial number of options for vsFTP, most of which you can configure in the `vsftpd.conf` configuration file. The following is a review of active options in the RHEL 4 version of this file. If you want to check the current defaults for these and other options, read the `vsftpd.conf` man page associated with your vsFTP RPM.

```
anonymous_enable=yes
```

You absolutely want to enable anonymous access for a FTP-based `yum` server. Anonymous access is normally enabled by default on a vsFTP server.

```
local_enable=yes
```

It's normally best to disable access by regular users to a FTP-based yum server. As it is disabled by default, all you need to do is comment out this option.

```
write_enable=yes
```

Naturally, because you do not want anyone (unless authorized) to over-write (or even add) to a yum-repository, you should disable write access.

```
local_umask=022
```

If you do authorize write access (I believe you should not do so on an FTP-based yum server), this option sets the umask for any files created by users who are logged into your FTP server.

```
dirmessage_enable=yes
```

If active, this option looks for and reads any .message file that exists in the local directory. This can be useful if you want to send messages to other administrators.

```
xferlog_enable=yes
```

If active, this option logs downloads (and uploads) on the vsFTP server in the /var/log/xferlog file. For example, when I downloaded an updated version of yum, the vsFTP server placed the following entry in that file:

```
Mon Sep 2 17:18:25 2005 1 192.168.0.20 390363
/pub/yum/4/i386/updates/yum-2.4.0-0.fc4.noarch.rpm b _ o a anonymous@
ftp 0 * c
```

As you can see, this lists the date and time of the transfer, the client IP address, as well as the size and location of the file. This is a standard format shared with the WU-FTP server and can be mined as a database for more information on client computers that connect to your server.

```
connect_from_port_20=yes
```

Some FTP clients require this option, which uses TCP/IP port 20 for data transfers.

```
xferlog_std_format=yes
```

If you've activated the `xferlog_enable` option noted earlier, this option supports a standard format shared with the WU-FTP server.

```
pam_service_name=vsftpd
```

The `pam_service_name` option defers to Pluggable Authentication Modules to help secure the vsFTP service. This particular option sets rules in `/etc/pam.d/vsftpd`. One of the key options in this file prohibits users listed in `/etc/vsftpd.ftpusers` from logging into this vsFTP server.

```
userlist_enable=YES
```

As configured, this is redundant with the previous command. When enabled, it makes the vsFTP server read the `/etc/vsftpd.user_list` file and deny access to all who attempt to connect as one of the users listed in this file. By default, this file contains the same list of users as shown in `/etc/vsftpd.users`.

```
listen=YES
```

By default, Red Hat / Fedora configures the vsFTP server as a stand-alone service, with a `vsftpd` activation script in the `/etc/rc.d/init.d` directory. In contrast, SUSE does not configure vsFTP as a stand-alone service and configures `listen=NO` by default.

```
tcp_wrappers=YES
```

As configured, Red Hat / Fedora configures the vsFTP server for one more level of security, through TCP Wrappers support, which allows you to configure more security related commands in the `/etc/hosts.allow` and `/etc/hosts.deny` files. When you're satisfied with the configuration, you should activate the vsFTP server with the following command (which is not required if you've set `listen=NO`):

```
/etc/init.d/vsftpd start
```

Finally, you can make sure that vsFTP is active the next time you reboot Linux with the following command:

```
chkconfig vsftpd on
```

This command activates the vsFTP server whenever you're in run levels 2, 3, 4, or 5. (If you configure vsFTP in xinetd, it activates it in the /etc/xinetd.d directory.) For the purpose of this chapter, assume the name of this server is yum.example.com.

7.3.2 Configuring a yum Client for an FTP-Based yum Repository

After you've configured this FTP yum server, configuring the associated yum client is a straightforward process. As you've seen in Chapter 6, yum configuration files that point to yum servers are normally configured in the `/etc/yum.repos.d` directory. For Fedora Core 4, we will examine the client file that points to the yum Update server: `fedora-updates.repo`.

For the yum FTP server as configured, all you need to include in the `fedora-updates.repo` file is the following:

```
[updates-released]
name=Fedora Core $releasever - $basearch - Released Updates
baseurl=ftp://yum.example.com/pub/yum/4/i386/updates
enabled=1
gpgcheck=1
```

As described earlier, for a vsFTP server, this means that update RPMs as well as the associated `repodata/` subdirectory are stored on the yum.example.com computer in the `/var/ftp/pub/yum/4/i386/updates` directory.

7.3.3 Configuring an NFS yum Server

On current Red Hat/Fedora distributions, an NFS server is installed by default, courtesy of the `nfs-utils` RPM. The default installation works well in most cases. You can specify shared NFS directories in the `/etc/exports` configuration file. In this case, we're working from the RHEL 4 version of NFS.

You can share directories as configured on an NFS server. For the example described earlier, update RPMs are stored in the following directory:

```
/var/ftp/pub/yum/4/i386/updates
```

Therefore, you can share this directory at any level, as long as the mount point on the NFS client is consistent. For example, I've added the following line to my `/etc/exports` configuration file:

```
/var/ftp/pub    192.168.1.0/24(ro,sync)
```

This particular configuration command shares the `/var/ftp/pub` directory. It limits access to clients in the noted IP address range. Clients are allowed read-only (`ro`) access. Changes are committed to disk before any new requests are made (`sync`).

Note

The notation shown in `/etc/exports` is associated with Classless Inter-Domain Routing (CIDR). The 192.168.1.0/24 address corresponds to a range of client IP addresses from 192.168.1.1 and 192.168.1.254 (the range excludes network and broadcast addresses).

For more information, see the exports man page *Linux Administration Handbook* by Evi Nemeth, Garth Snyder, and Trent Hein (Upper Saddle River, NJ: Prentice Hall, 2002). After you're satisfied with the configuration in `/etc/exports`, deactivate the NFS server with the following command:

```
/etc/init.d/nfs stop
```

Note

Remember, this chapter is focused on Fedora/Red Hat. The NFS server script goes by different names on other Linux distributions.

By default, this should stop any NFS services, quotas, the NFS daemon, as well as the `mountd` daemon. Next, export the changes to `/etc/exports` with the following command:

```
exportfs -a
```

Now restart the NFS services with the following command:

```
/etc/init.d/nfs start
```

Confirm the exports in from the local list with the following command:

```
showmount -e
```

If you're on another system, you can find the shared NFS directories. For example, you can list those on a server named yum.example.com with the following command:

```
showmount -e yum.example.com
```

Finally, you can make sure that NFS is active the next time you reboot Linux with the following command:

```
chkconfig nfs on
```

This command activates the NFS server whenever you're in run levels 2, 3, 4, or 5.

7.3.4 Configuring an NFS yum Client

You'll need to mount the NFS share on an appropriate local directory, and then configure the associated file in /etc/yum.repos.d to point to that share. Because we're configuring a share for Fedora updates, we'll modify the fedora-updates.repo file.

First, on the NFS client, you should confirm your ability to connect to a shared NFS directory. The following command connects to the yum.example.com NFS server to find what shares are available on that server:

```
showmount -e yum.example.com
```

You'll see the shared directories that you configured earlier, including /var/ftp/pub. I've mounted it on the local /var/yum directory with the following command:

```
mount yum.example.com:/var/ftp/pub /var/yum
```

If the /var/yum directory does not yet exist, you'll get an error message. Now you can configure your fedora-updates.repo file in your /etc/yum.repos.d directory. For the yum NFS server as configured, all you need in fedora-updates.repo is the following:

```
[updates-released]
name=Fedora Core $releasever - $basearch - Released Updates
baseurl=file:///var/yum/yum/4/i386/updates
enabled=1
gpgcheck=1
```

As described earlier, for a vsFTP server, this means that update RPMs as well as the associated repodata/ subdirectory are stored in the yum/4/i386/updates subdirectory, mounted on the /var/yum directory.

Note the syntax associated with the baseurl command. The file: command works in place of ftp: or http:. The triple forward slash (////) is the standard syntax required for mounted directories.

If you've configured a Fedora Updates repository on a Fedora Core server, this command may be slightly different. Based on the directory specified earlier, you would substitute the following baseurl command:

```
baseurl=file:///var/ftp/pub/yum/4/i386/updates
```

Naturally, you may want to configure this shared directory as part of the boot process for each NFS client. It's possible to configure it in the default `/etc/fstab` configuration file, as well as through the Automounter daemon. I recommend the latter, which avoids hangups when there are network problems. The Automounter daemon is easy to configure; it requires the `autofs` RPM. After that RPM is installed, here's how you can configure a NFS client for Fedora updates as configured in this chapter:

1. Install the `autofs` RPM; if you've configured `yum`, the simplest way is with the following command. Even if you're not sure if `autofs` is installed, this command makes sure that you have the latest version of the Automounter:

   ```
   yum install autofs
   ```

2. Configure the Automounter master file to read from `/etc/auto.misc`. Open the `/etc/auto.master` configuration file. You'll see sample commands; activate the following to read from the noted file. The timeout prevents your system from hanging if there's a problem with your network or the NFS server.

   ```
   /misc   /etc/auto.misc --timeout=60
   ```

   Automounter shares configured in `/etc/auto.misc` are configured as subdirectories of `/misc`.

3. Configure the Automounter `/etc/auto.misc` file to read from the shared NFS directory. Based on the shared directory and NFS server name described earlier, add the following line to that file:

   ```
   yum     -ro,soft,intr     yum.example.com:/var/ftp/pub
   ```

4. Start the Automounter service with the following command:

   ```
   /etc/init.d/autofs start
   ```

Note

Yes, it is possible to use the `/etc/auto.net` script to find and connect to shared NFS directories. But it might not be compatible with SE Linux. For more information, see bug 174156 on bugzilla.redhat.com.

---

5. Test the result. If your network is connected and the NFS server is running, you should be able to see the shared NFS directory with the following command:

   ```
   ls /misc/yum
   ```

   Occasionally, you may need to run this command more than once to establish the connection.

6. Configure the `/etc/yum.repos.d/fedora-updates.repo` file to point to this directory as shared. Based on the previously shared NFS directory, the `baseurl` command would be

   ```
   baseurl=file:///var/ftp/pub/yum/4/i386/updates
   ```

7. Test the result with the `yum update` command. You should see messages similar to a regular `yum update` from other local or remote servers.

7.4 ADDING OTHER REPOSITORIES

You might want to maintain other repositories on a local server. Based on the chapter so far, you should have the tools you need to create the server and configure your clients to read from that server.

As suggested earlier, there are several different repositories available for Fedora, such as Extras, Development, and Testing repositories. In many cases, you might want to add repositories from allied distributions. For example, Fedora Core 3 repositories may be suitable for RHEL 4 and related rebuild distributions. There are also third-party repositories available; many of the same third-party `apt` repositories described in Chapter 5, "Configuring apt for RPM Distributions," also include "yummified" RPM repositories of possible interest.

7.4.1 Using Distribution Installation Files

If you've followed the steps described earlier, you've copied the files from the Fedora Core 4 installation CDs to a directory in your yum repository. You should have a copy of the installation DVD (or CDs) in the following directory:

```
/var/ftp/pub/yum/4/i386/os/
```

You can now yummify this repository with one of the following commands. Naturally, if you're using Fedora Core 3 or later, you should install the `createrepo` RPM and then yummify the repository with the second command:

```
yum-arch /var/ftp/pub/yum/4/i386/os/*
createrepo /var/ftp/pub/yum/4/i386/os/*
```

If you're running Fedora Core 4 on your clients, you can now point the `fedora.repo` configuration file in the `/etc/yum.repos.d` directory to the installation repository. If you've configured the FTP server described earlier, you should use the following `baseurl` command in that file:

```
baseurl=ftp://yum.example.com/pub/yum/4/i386/os/
```

7.4.2 Keeping Extras with yum

One useful Fedora repository is known as Extras. It includes a number of packages not integral to the smooth running of the distribution. However, the Fedora Core 4 Extras repository includes a number of packages of interest, including Tripwire, the WindowMaker GUI, the BitTorrent download manager, and even the `apt` tools described in Chapter 5.

Depending on how frequently you or your users need Extras packages, you might want a local copy of that repository. It might not be easy to find this repository in the `rsync` mirrors. For example, the mirror listed for the University of Southern California (USC) is rsync://mirrors.usc.edu/fedora/. Sometimes, you'll find seemingly duplicate copies of the same repository in different directories. For example, the following two commands return the same list of packages from the Fedora Core 3 Extras repository:

```
rsync rsync://mirrors.usc.edu/fedora/fedora/fedora/3/i386/RPMS.extras/
rsync rsync://mirrors.usc.edu/fedora-core/extras/3/i386/
```

In this case, the packages from the first repository are newer than those I found in the second. Naturally, I want the newest version of all packages, so I synchronize with that repository.

You can copy this repository to your own system. Based on the directories and `rsync` commands described earlier, the following command would synchronize your system with the `rsync` repository from USC:

```
rsync -av --exclude debug \
rsync://mirrors.usc.edu/fedora/fedora/fedora/3/i386/RPMS.extras/* \
/var/ftp/pub/yum/3/i386/extras/
```

You can review the output in Figure 7-3. As you can see, the information includes the amount of data transmitted across the network. In this case, I downloaded over a gigabyte of data. You do not want to repeat this process often.

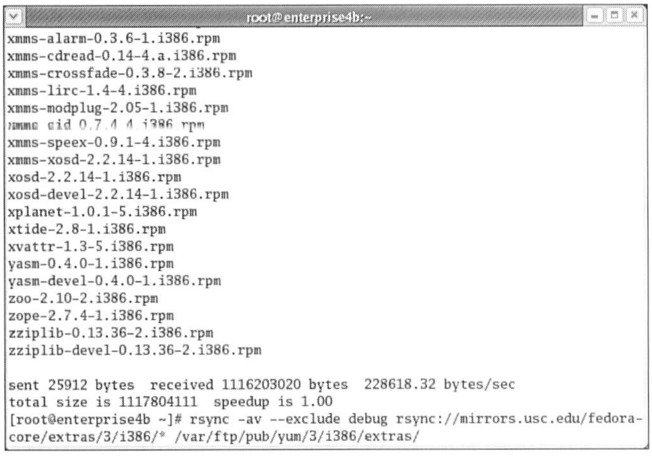

Figure 7-3   A lot of data is downloaded the first time you synchronize

7.4.3   Adding Development Repositories

Do not mirror a Development repository unless it is absolutely necessary. Development RPMs are, by definition, not stable. They are not suitable for production systems. Because the RPMs in this repository are updated frequently, sometimes daily, updates take up a lot of bandwidth.

You or your users might want access to development repositories for different reasons. For example, your users might be interested in helping with Linux development. You might need to test the latest version of a package that is adding new features that you may need. You might want to test Fedora Linux on an architecture other than standard PC 32- or 64-bit CPUs.

Development repositories are available through most of the same mirrors associated with Fedora Linux. Unless your users need access to such packages frequently, it's best to leave such repositories on remote mirrors.

Using the techniques described earlier, find the development/ repository associated with your favorite mirror. For example, as shown in Figure 7-4, the following command returns a substantial list of architectures available through this repository:

```
rsync rsync://mirrors.kernel.org/fedora/core/development/
```

```
                                        root@Fedora3:~                                    _ □ ×
MOTD:    This site includes publicly available encryption source code
MOTD:    which, together with object code resulting from the compiling of
MOTD:    publicly available source code, may be exported from the United
MOTD:    States under License Exception "TSU" pursuant to 15 C.F.R. Section
MOTD:    740.13(e).
MOTD:
MOTD:    This legal notice applies to cryptographic software only.
MOTD:    Please see the Bureau of Industry and Security,
MOTD:    http://www.bis.doc.gov/ for more information about current
MOTD:    U.S. regulations.
MOTD:

drwxr-sr-x          4096 2005/05/04 04:44:38 .
-rw-r--r--          3101 2003/11/04 09:23:24 README
drwxr-sr-x         65536 2005/05/04 02:06:06 SRPMS
drwxr-xr-x       1150976 2005/05/04 04:57:57 headers
drwxr-sr-x          4096 2005/05/04 04:38:23 i386
drwxr-sr-x          4096 2005/05/04 04:31:17 ia64
drwxr-sr-x          4096 2005/05/04 04:52:03 ppc
drwxr-sr-x          4096 2005/05/04 04:32:04 ppc64
drwxr-sr-x          4096 2005/05/04 04:50:20 s390
drwxr-sr-x          4096 2005/05/04 04:47:12 s390x
drwxr-sr-x          4096 2005/05/04 04:45:58 x86_64
[root@Fedora3 ~]# rsync rsync://mirrors.kernel.org/fedora/core/development/
```

Figure 7-4   Many architectures associated with the Fedora Development repository

> **Note**
>
> Use the Development repository at your own risk. As defined by the README file associated with the repository, "DO NOT USE THESE RELEASES FOR ANY WORK WHERE YOU CARE ABOUT YOUR APPLICATION RUNNING, THE ACCURACY OF YOUR DATA, THE INTEGRITY OF YOUR NETWORK, OR ANY OTHER PURPOSE FOR WHICH A RESPONSIBLE HUMAN WOULD USE A COMPUTER."

The available architectures are defined in Table 7-3.

Table 7-3   Fedora architectures

Label	Description
i386	Standard 32-bit PCs
ia64	Itanium 64-bit PCs
ppc	32-bit Power PC-based computers
ppc64	64-bit Power PC-based computers
s390	System 390 IBM computers; now known as zSeries
s390x	System 390 IBM computers; now known as zSeries
x86_64	AMD 64-bit PCs

7.4.4   Other Distribution Repositories

In some cases, you might want access to repositories available for other distributions. For example, if you're running RHEL 4, you might want access to Fedora Core 3 repositories for additional packages. As RHEL 4 is based on Fedora Core 3, many packages from this version of Fedora work fine without modifications.

While you can mirror the repositories from other distributions, you should not do so unless you use packages from those repositories frequently. Otherwise, you'll be using a lot of space with packages that might not work with your system. In fact, any Fedora Core 3 packages that you install on RHEL 4 are not supported by Red Hat.

If you've installed the yum and createrepo RPMs from Fedora Core 3 on RHEL 4, you can include the files of your choice in the /etc/yum.repos.d directory. However, you should not install the RPM that installs Fedora Core 3 repository files in this directory because it may change the version associated with your system and affect the way your RHEL 4 system communicates with the Red Hat Network.

If you do not have access to Fedora Core 3, you can get more information about the files in the /etc/yum.repos.d directory at http://fedoranews.org/tchung/yum-mirrorlist/. For details on how these files work (as well as those for Fedora Core 4), see Chapter 6.

7.4.5   Third-Party Repositories

In some cases, you might want access to repositories available from third parties. We've covered several of the third-party repositories in Chapter 6. As you've read, they're available for several different distributions, especially those related to Red Hat Enterprise Linux or Fedora.

Evaluation copies of RHEL are available as of this writing from www.redhat.com/software/rhel/eval/. The subscription is valid for 30 days, and it includes access and administration privileges on the Red Hat Network. You can read about some of the associated features in Chapter 2. After the subscription expires, you might be able to update your RHEL system using the repositories available from one of the RHEL rebuild distributions. Naturally, any packages that you download and install from a third-party are not supported by Red Hat and are done so at your own risk.

Unfortunately, many third-party repositories discussed in this book do not have `rsync` servers available. You'll have to use more conventional methods, such as FTP, to download the files associated with these repositories. Many of these mirrors are administered by small groups or even individuals. They might not be able to support enterprise-level package downloads. Therefore, if you use a third-party repository frequently, consider creating your own mirror of that repository.

7.5   MAINTAINING THE REPOSITORY

Patch management means that you have to maintain updates for all the computers on your network. For the repositories that you've created, that means you need to keep them up to date. Generally, that means configuring updates as a cron job, not only for clients, but between your local repository and the mirror of your choice. You've seen samples of the cron jobs you can use for clients in Chapter 6. In this section, we'll see how you can maintain a local repository.

As repositories are kept up to date, sometimes headers can be corrupted. In that case, you can delete the headers, whether from the `headers/` directory or from the compressed files in the `repodata/` directory.

7.5.1   Updating Packages

Generally, you'll want to update repositories on a daily (or nightly) basis. After a repository is created, the required downloads go down significantly. In most cases, you'll be able to create your own script in the `/etc/cron.daily` directory, which is automatically run on a daily basis, as determined by the schedule as defined in `/etc/crontab`.

As you saw earlier, the following command can synchronize files on the noted local directory with a remote server at mirrors.kernel.org:

```
rsync -av --exclude debug \
rsync://mirrors.kernel.org/fedora/core/updates/3/i386/* \
/var/ftp/pub/yum/3/i386/updates/
```

I've created the `repo` file in my `/etc/cron.daily` directory and added the following commands:

```
#!/bin/sh

rsync -av --exclude debug \
rsync://mirrors.kernel.org/fedora/core/updates/3/i386/* \
/var/ftp/pub/yum/3/i386/updates/
```

7.5.2   Cleaning Header Information

If there are problems with updates, check the applicable log file. It's available in the `yum.log` file in the `/var/log` directory. In many cases, it can help to regenerate headers. In other words, you would take the following steps:

1. Delete the `headers/` or `repodata/` subdirectory in your repository.
2. Navigate to the directory with the repository.
3. Regenerate the headers with the command that applies to your distribution: `yum-arch` or `createrepo`.

7.6   CREATING AN ENTERPRISE REPOSITORY

In Chapter 2, you learned about patch management on RHEL computers. The Red Hat Network Proxy Server is an effective way to cache RPMs for multiple RHEL systems. However, some administrators prefer standard tools, such as `apt` and `yum`.

In this section, we'll show you how you can configure a `yum`-based repository from packages downloaded using the Red Hat Update Agent. If you want to use update other RHEL clients from this repository, you may be required by contract to have valid subscription for each of these clients, even if the packages are covered by an open source license.

Note

Do not use this book to update RHEL systems unless they have a current, valid subscription.

A working RHEL repository requires a combination of the existing installation packages, as well as the updates available over the Red Hat Network. When combined, you'll have a set of packages that includes all the dependencies you might need.

The repository creation process on an RHEL system requires four basic steps:

1. Download the packages required to update your system; make sure they aren't deleted after they're installed. Add the packages associated with the RHEL installation CDs.

2. Apply the `yum-arch` or `createrepo` commands to "yummify" the repository.

3. Share the repository directory with an appropriate service, such as Apache, FTP, or NFS.

4. Configure your clients to update from the new repository.

Depending on the channels you want to mirror, this process may require 2GB or more of downloads. If you have only one or two RHEL systems, you may find this process not to be worth the trouble. However, if you have several dozen RHEL systems, this might save you time and bandwidth.

If you have a substantial number of RHEL systems, you should consider the Red Hat Network Proxy Server described in Chapter 2. However, if you prefer standard tools, such as `yum`, and have the authorized Red Hat subscriptions for the RHEL clients on your network, you the approach taken in the following sections is a viable alternative.

Note

If you're working with a RHEL rebuild distribution, it's best if you use the patch management tool (`yum` or `apt`) configured for that distribution. Then you can keep it up to date by synchronizing your repository with that available from the mirror of your choice.

7.6.1 Creating a RHEL Update Repository

In Chapter 2, you learned to use the Red Hat Update Agent to update RHEL systems. With the right configuration, you can save the updated RPMs as an RHEL update repository. There are several basic steps in this process:

1. First, log into the Red Hat Network and assign desired channels to the RHEL Update Repository system.

2. Next, configure the Update Agent to keep downloaded packages.

3. Configure the system where you'll store packages as needed.

4. Download desired RPMs into your repository.

5. Add RPMs from the installation CDs.

Assign Desired Channels from the Red Hat Network

First, log into the Red Hat Network. Make sure your system is subscribed to the channels from which you want to create your repository.

As shown in Figure 7-5, you can configure your system with available channels, assuming that you have allowed subscriptions to that channel. To find your currently allowed subscriptions, click Channels on the top bar, then click Channel Entitlements on the left pane. Assign the channels of your choice, and then click Change Subscriptions. If you see the following error message, you may need additional subscriptions:

```
The assignment would exceed your allowed subscriptions in one or more
channels
```

Figure 7-5   Assigning RHEL Channel Subscriptions

To confirm your channel assignments, log into the computer that you intend to use as the repository. The following command should return the channels that you've assigned:

```
up2date --showchannel
```

Based on Figure 7-5, the channels that you should see are as follows:

```
rhel-i386-as-4
rhel-i386-as-4-extras
rhel-i386-as-4-hwcert
rhel-i386-as-4-sdk
rhn-tools-rhel-4-as-i386
```

Configure the Update Agent to Keep Downloaded RPMs

Log into the computer that you intend to use as a repository. Updated RPMs are stored by default in the `/var/spool/up2date` directory. Make sure that updated RPMs are not deleted. To do so, run the `up2date-config` command. You'll see the screen shown in Figure 7-6.

Note

If you're in the GUI, you might need to run the `up2date-config --nox` command to access the options shown in Figure 7-6.

```
▣                              root@enterprise4a:~                      _ □ ✕
17. keepAfterInstall    Yes
18. useGPG              No
19. headerCacheSize     40
20. forceInstall        No
21. systemIdPath        /etc/sysconfig/rhn/systemid
22. retrieveSource      No
23. enableRollbacks     Yes
24. gpgKeyRing          /etc/sysconfig/rhn/up2date-keyring.gpg
25. adminAddress        ['root@localhost']
26. serverURL           https://xmlrpc.rhn.redhat.com/XMLRPC
27. fileSkipList        []
28. versionOverride
29. sslCACert           /usr/share/rhn/RHNS-CA-CERT
30. noReplaceConfig     Yes
31. enableProxyAuth     No
32. disallowConfChange  ['noReboot', 'sslCACert', 'useNoSSLForPackages', 'noSSLSe
33. headerFetchCount    10
34. proxyUser
35. removeSkipList      ['kernel*']
36. httpProxy
37. noReboot            No

Enter number of item to edit <return to exit, q to quit without saving>: []
```

Figure 7-6   Configuring the Update Agent to keep RPMs

Enter option 17 (the option number may vary). This is associated with the "`keepAfterInstall`" variable. If set to yes, packages which are downloaded remain available in `/var/spool/up2date` after they're installed. The next time you download packages from the Red Hat Network, packages will be stored in that directory, and they won't be deleted.

Note

You may also want to disable automatic updates to the `up2date` RPM, which is usually the option before `keepAfterInstall`. Any updates to up2date substitutes the default settings in `/etc/sysconfig/rhn/up2date`. If the `up2date` RPM is upgraded, you can restore your custom settings from the `up2date.rpmnew` file in the same directory. Just be aware, if you disable updates of `up2date`, updates will be disabled the next time there's a new version of `up2date` available.

Configure the Repository with Appropriate Partitions

As you've seen throughout this book, repositories require gigabytes of space. It often makes sense to configure repositories in separate partitions. For the purpose of this repository, I've configured `/var/spool/up2date` on a new partition or logical volume.

For details on how you can configure a new partition, refer to any good basic book on Linux administration, including *Linux Administration Handbook* by Evi Nemeth, Garth Snyder, and Trent Hein (Upper Saddle River, NJ: Prentice Hall, 2002) or *Mastering Red Hat Enterprise Linux 3* by Michael Jang (Alameda, CA: Sybex, 2004) . If you want more information on these commands or settings, refer to that book. If you have free space on an available partition, you can assign it to `/var/spool/up2date`. One method would use the following steps, which assume that you've added a new hard drive. The steps may vary widely depending on the hard drive and whether there are existing partitions on that drive.

1. Open the hard disk of your choice for editing. For example, assume you've added a new hard drive. If this drive is the first SCSI or SATA hard drive on your system, run the `fdisk /dev/sda` command.

2. Assign a new partition with the `n` command. You'll need to press `p` to assign a new primary partition. Assign partition number 1, start with the first cylinder, and assign the room you need. You can do so with a +10GB entry when prompted for the last cylinder. Press w to write the new partition table to the hard drive.

3. Format the drive. To format it with the default ext3 file system, run the following command:

```
mkfs -t ext3 /dev/sda1
```

4. Mount the `/var/spool/up2date` directory on that drive.

```
mount /dev/sda1 /var/spool/up2date
```

5. Make sure the drive is mounted the next time you reboot your computer. Add the following line to your `/etc/fstab` configuration file:

```
/dev/sda1 /var/spool/up2date ext3 defaults 1 2
```

Download Desired RPMs from the Repository

Now you can download the desired RPMs from the Red Hat Network. You can download just the updates, but because of dependencies, those might not be enough. Therefore, download all available RPMs from the Red Hat Network channels to which you subscribe. This is a multi-step process. With the following command (which specifies a RHEL 4 Workstation channel), you can download the RPMs from your desired channel not currently installed on your system. Shortly, you'll add RPMs from your installation CDs.

```
up2date -d --installall --channel=rhel-i386-ws-4
```

There is no separate updates repository on the Red Hat Network. New packages are incorporated into existing channels. Therefore, this command downloads all packages you do not have installed, including any updated RPMs.

Naturally, because there are around 2GB of data on RHEL installation RPMs, the download may be extensive. Depending on the speed of your connection, you may need to wait several hours for downloads. One example is shown in Figure 7-7.

```
root@enterprise4b:~                                            _ □ ✗
xorg-x11-doc-6.8.1-23.EL.i3 ######################### Done.
xorg-x11-sdk-6.8.1-23.EL.i3 ######################### Done.
xorg-x11-twm-6.8.1-23.EL.i3 ######################### Done.
xorg-x11-xdm-6.8.1-23.EL.i3 ######################### Done.
xpdf-3.00-11.5.i386.rpm:       ######################### Done.
xrestop-0.2-4.i386.rpm:        ######################### Done.
xsane-0.92-13.i386.rpm:        ######################### Done.
xsane-gimp-0.92-13.i386.rpm ######################### Done.
xterm-192-1.i386.rpm:          ######################### Done.
zisofs-tools-1.0.6-1.i386.r ######################### Done.
zsh-4.2.0-3.i386.rpm:          ######################### Done.
zsh-html-4.2.0-3.i386.rpm:  ######################### Done.
The following Packages were marked to be skipped by your configuration:

Name                          Version        Rel  Reason
- - - - - - - - - - - - - - - - - - - - - - - - - - - - - - - - - - - - - - - - - - - - - - - - - -
kernel                        2.6.9          5.0.5.ELPkg name/pattern
kernel-devel                  2.6.9          5.0.5.ELPkg name/pattern
kernel-doc                    2.6.9          5.0.5.ELPkg name/pattern
kernel-hugemem                2.6.9          5.0.5.ELPkg name/pattern
kernel-hugemem-devel          2.6.9          5.0.5.ELPkg name/pattern
kernel-smp                    2.6.9          5.0.5.ELPkg name/pattern
kernel-smp-devel              2.6.9          5.0.5.ELPkg name/pattern
```

Figure 7-7   Downloading updates

Add RPMs from the Installation CDs

Now you should add the RPMs from the RHEL installation CDs. If you have the physical CDs, the mount command is elementary. If you have the ISO files (as I do), the mount command requires a small trick. For example, when I've stored the ISOs on my /mnt/test partition, I can mount the first RHEL ISO with the following command:

```
mount -o loop /mnt/test/RHEL4-i386-AS-disc1.iso /media/cdrecorder
```

You can then copy the RPMs to the /var/spool/up2date directory with the following command:

```
cp -ar /media/cdrecorder/RedHat/RPMS/* /var/spool/up2date/
```

Naturally, when the process is complete with the first CD, you'll want to unmount and repeat the process with the other RHEL CDs until you've copied all available RPMs to the /var/spool/up2date directory.

7.6.2   Yummifying the RHEL Update Repository

After you've configured the files you need in the RHEL repository, you can set it up as a `yum` repository. As described earlier in this chapter, this requires the `yum-arch` or `createrepo` commands, depending on your distribution. The `createrepo` package was adapted for Fedora Core 3. Because RHEL 4 was built from Fedora Core 3, we'll use this package to "yummify" this repository.

If you haven't already done so, install the `yum` and `createrepo` RPMs. As discussed earlier in this chapter, they are not currently available from RHEL 4 channels. However, compatible versions are available from Fedora Core 3 repositories. Download guidelines are described earlier in this chapter.

Now you can yummify your repository with one of the following commands, whichever is appropriate to your distribution:

```
yum-arch /var/spool/up2date
createrepo /var/spool/up2date
```

If successful, you'll find `headers/` or `repodata/` subdirectories in the `/var/spool/up2date` directory. I've used the second command on my RHEL 4 system, with downloaded updates and installation RPMs that I've just described.

7.6.3   Sharing the RHEL Repository

Now you can share the RHEL 4 repository that you've just created. You can configure the Apache or NFS servers described earlier. Unfortunately, as described earlier, the vsFTP service does not follow symlinks, for the security reasons described earlier. In this case, we'll configure the server that we did not configure before, the Apache Web Server. We won't go into detail on how to configure Apache on your system; we'll just create a basic configuration that you can use for a RHEL repository.

If you want more information on how you can configure Apache on RHEL, there are many excellent books available, including *Apache Administrator's Handbook* by Rich Bowen (Indianapolis, IN: Sams Publishing, 2002).

In this case, I've just installed the `httpd` RPM package on RHEL 4. To make sure it works, start the daemon with the following command:

```
apachectl start
```

If you see a message related to "Could not determine the server's fully qualified domain name," do not be concerned. There is no URL specified in the default version of the Apache configuration file, `httpd.conf`, in the `/etc/httpd/conf` directory.

Test the result. If you're on the computer with the repository, open a browser and navigate to 127.0.0.1. If the service is working, you'll see the Red Hat Enterprise Linux Test Page. Test the result on a remote computer. I've configured the repository computer with an URL of yum.example.com, and therefore can navigate to that URL to see the same test Web page.

By default, Apache files on this distribution are stored in the `/var/www/html` directory. You already have a repository in the `/var/spool/up2date` directory. To allow apache to work with the repository, you need to link directories. One method is with the following command:

```
ln -s /var/spool/up2date /var/www/html/up2date
```

If everything goes right, you should be able to navigate to the `up2date/`directory on the Apache server. In my case, I've navigated to http://yum.example.com/up2date/. However, that doesn't work at first. I've started with the default RHEL 4 Apache configuration file. For more information, see the `error_log` in the `/var/log/httpd` directory. The key error message from this file is

```
Directory index forbidden by rule: /var/www/html/
```

To address this issue, I've modified the messages associated with the Apache root directory. The default configuration file includes the following stanza about 25 percent of the way into the file:

```
<Directory />
    Options FollowSymLinks
    AllowOverride None
</Directory>
```

The `Options` directive you need is `Indexes`, which leads me to substitute the following command line:

```
Options Indexes FollowSymLinks
```

Now, you can try the desired URL again. You should see a result similar to Figure 7-8, with a list of files linked from the `/var/spool/up2date` repository.

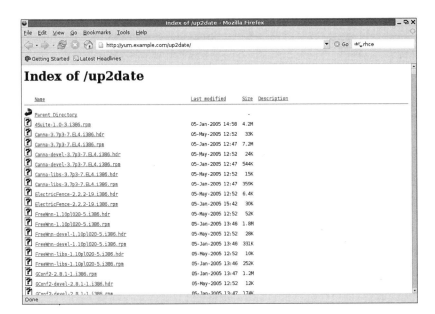

Figure 7-8   A RHEL 4 yum Repository

Naturally, you can also share /var/spool/up2date with an NFS server by using the techniques described earlier in this chapter.

7.6.4   Configuring Updates to the RHEL Repository

After you've added the packages you need to /var/spool/up2date, it is up to you to maintain that RHEL repository. While the Red Hat Network does not include a rsync server, the effect from updates is essentially the same. You can repeat the same commands described earlier, and only new packages are downloaded. However, obsolete packages are not removed from the local mirror.

However, if you've copied all of the installation files to the /var/spool/up2date directory, this is not necessary. You just need the updated RPMs, which are available with the following command:

```
up2date -u
```

If you want to keep using /var/spool/up2date, make sure that you never restore the defaults associated with the Red Hat Update Agent. Otherwise, the updated RPMs would be deleted after the next update. (You may also want to disable upgrades to the up2date RPM, as described in an earlier note.)

7.6.5 Configuring Clients to Use the RHEL Repository

Naturally, if you've created a repository on a RHEL computer, you may want to use it for that computer. You've already downloaded and installed the yum RPM package. You can now create a configuration file in the `/etc/yum.repos.d` directory similar to those you've created in Chapter 6. In this case, the repository is local; therefore, you can specify the `file:///` (that's three forward slashes) label described earlier to point to the `/var/spool/up2date` directory.

For example, I've entered the following in the `local.repo` file in the `/etc/yum.repos.d` directory:

```
[local]
name=Mike's local RHEL 4 repo
baseurl=file:///var/spool/up2date
gpgcheck=1
enabled=1
```

Now I can use the `yum` commands described in Chapter 6 to update the system with the repository. Naturally, you can configure other RHEL 4 clients to use the same repository. Based on the Apache server configured earlier, I've modified the aforementioned `local.repo` file accordingly:

```
[local]
name=Mike's local RHEL 4 repo
baseurl=http://yum.example.com/up2date
gpgcheck=1
enabled=1
```

7.7 SUMMARY

While there are many Linux users who prefer other tools for doing their patch management, yum is designed for RPM-based distributions. Its popularity has grown as Fedora Linux has adapted yum as its primary patch management tool. Because the Red Hat Network is not available unless you're a subscriber, many RHEL rebuild distributions have also adapted yum for updates and more.

The repository creation process can be time-consuming. If you use packages from installation CDs, you can save some time. With the rsync command, you can download the remaining packages that you need. The advantage of `rsync` is that you can keep your repositories up to date with the same commands that you've used to download the packages you need.

When created, you'll need to share your repositories. There are three major sharing services: NFS, Apache, and FTP. When shared, you can configure your clients to point to the repositories on your local network, minimizing the loads on your Internet connection, allowing you to focus on those packages critical to security and functionality on your network.

While you can use the Red Hat Network Proxy Server described in Chapter 2 to manage patches and updates on RHEL computers, you can also configure a yum repository based on an amalgamation of RHEL installation packages and updates.

We've covered a broad array of patch management tools that you can use on almost any Linux distribution. There are other excellent tools exclusive to specific distributions, such as uprmi for Mandriva and emerge for Gentoo. Our lack of coverage of these tools is not intended to denigrate these excellent tools but simply reflects the scope of this book.

Symbols

\ (backslashes), 225

/// (triple forward slash), 235

A

acquiring CDs for RHEL, 13-14

activating subscriptions for RHEL, 13

activations, ZLM, 110

adding

    clients to ZLM, 108-110

    headers, 227-229

    repositories, 237

        development repositories, 239-240

        distribution repositories, 240

        Extras, 237-238

        third-party repositories, 241

        using distribution installation files, 237

        Yum Extender, 212-213

    RPMs from installation CDs, 247

administrators, configuring in ZLM, 108

Advanced Package Tool. *See* apt

aggregating RHEL updates, 23-25

Anaconda, 224

application patches, testing, 8-9

apt (Advanced Package Tool), 115

    aptitude, 124-125

        configuring patch management, 128-129

        making changes, 131-132

        menu organization, 127

        patch management, 129-131

        running, 125-126

    commands. *See* commands, apt

    configuring, 156

        on your computer, 117-120

    configuring for Fedora Linux, 157-159

    configuring for Red Hat rebuilds, 165-166

        atrpms.list, 166-167

        dag.list, 167

        freshrpms.list, 167

        newrpms.list, 168

        os.list, 168

    configuring for RPM, 155-156

    configuring for SUSE Linux, 161-163, 165

    creating repositories, 170

        organizing customized repositories, 171

        organizing like mirrors, 170-171

        processing RPM-based repositories, 171-173

    history of apt for RPM, 152-153

    installing on

        Debian-based distribution, 115-117

        RPM-based distribution, 117

    overview of apt for RPM-based distributions, 154-155

    packages, 116

    remote repositories, mirroring, 168-170

    removing package groups, Fedora Linux, 158

    setting up local repositories, 168

    Synaptic Package Manager, 132-133

        configuring, 134-136

        keeping updated, 134

        making changes, 138-140

        selecting packages, 136-138

apt repositories, 140

    creating Debian mirrors, 144

        configuring apt-mirror, 147-150

        configuring debmirror, 145-147

        using local packages, 144-145

    Debian repositories, 140-144

apt system, Debian, 32-33

apt-build, 177

apt-cache depends/rdepends, 175

apt-cache pkgnames, 175

apt-cache show, 174

apt-cache showpkg, 173-174

apt-cache showsrc, 174

apt-cdrom, 122

apt-file, 122-123

apt-ftparchive, 123-124, 177

apt-get, 121-122, 175

BOOKS ONLINE
ENABLED

THIS BOOK IS SAFARI ENABLED

INCLUDES FREE 45-DAY ACCESS TO THE ONLINE EDITION

The Safari® Enabled icon on the cover of your favorite technology book means the book is available through Safari Bookshelf. When you buy this book, you get free access to the online edition for 45 days.

Safari Bookshelf is an electronic reference library that lets you easily search thousands of technical books, find code samples, download chapters, and access technical information whenever and wherever you need it.

TO GAIN 45-DAY SAFARI ENABLED ACCESS TO THIS BOOK:

● Go to **http://www.phptr.com/safarienabled**

● Complete the brief registration form

● Enter the coupon code found in the front of this book on the "Copyright" page

If you have difficulty registering on Safari Bookshelf or accessing the online edition, please e-mail customer-service@safaribooksonline.com.